IFP/WEST INDEPENDENT FILMMAKER'S MANUAL

IFP/WEST INDEPENDENT FILMMAKER'S MANUAL

Nicole Shay LaLoggia
Eden H. Wurmfeld

Focal
Press

Boston   Oxford   Auckland   Johannesburg   Melbourne   New Delhi

Recognizing the importance of preserving what has been written, Butterworth–Heinemann prints its books on acid
free paper whenever possible.

GLOBAL Butterworth–Heinemann supports the efforts of American Forests and the Global ReLeaf program in its cam-
RELEAF paign for the betterment of trees, forests, and our environment.
2000

Library of Congress Cataloging-in-Publication Data

LaLoggia, Nicole Shay.
    IFP/West independent filmmaker's manual / Nicole Shay LaLoggia and Eden H. Wurmfeld.
       p.   cm.
    Includes bibliographical references and index.
    ISBN 0-240-80389-2 (alk. paper)
    1. Motion pictures—Production and direction. 2. Low budget motion pictures. I. Wurmfeld, Eden H.
II. Title.
    PN1995.9.P7L26   1999
    791.43′0232′092—dc21
                                    99-19198
                                      CIP

British Library Cataloguing-in-Publication Data
A catalogue record for this book is available from the British Library.

The publisher offers special discounts on bulk orders of this book.
For information, please contact:

Manager of Special Sales
Butterworth–Heinemann
225 Wildwood Avenue
Woburn, MA 01801-2041
Tel: 781-904-2500
Fax: 781-904-2620

For information on all Focal Press publications available, contact our World Wide Web home page at:
http://www.focalpress.com

10 9 8 7 6 5 4 3 2 1

Printed in the United States of America

Book design by Justina Klimkevich.

The following figures are used with permission from Honthaner, Eve. *The Complete Film Production Handbook.* Boston: Butterworth–Heinemann, 1997.

Figure 7–4 (Call Sheet); Figure 7–9 (Mileage Log); Figure 7–12A (Raw Stock Inventory Form); Figure 7–12B (Daily Raw Stock Log); Figure 7–14 (Location Agreement); Figure 7–19 (Purchase Order); Figure 7–24 (Daily Cost Overview)

The following figures are used with permission from the Screen Actors Guild, Los Angeles, CA.

Figure 7–6 (Exhibit G Form); Figure 7–7 (SAG Taft-Hartley Report); Figure 7–8 (SAG Extra Taft-Hartley Report); Figure 7–28 (SAG Sign-in Sheet); Figure 7–29 (SAG Freelance Contract); Figure 7–30 (SAG Daily Contract)

The following figures are used with permission from Screenplay Systems (for Movie Magic Budgeting & Scheduling), Burbank, CA.

Figure 5–1 (*Swingers* Strip Board (Days 1–9)); Figure 5–2 (*Swingers* Shooting Schedule); Figure 5–3 (*Swingers* One-line Schedule (Days 1–9)); Figure 5–4 (*Swingers* Day-Out-of-Days Sheets (Cast, Extras, and Props)); Figure 6–1 (Sample Budget Form); Figure 6–2 (*Swingers* Budget ($279,577)); Figure 6–3 (*Swingers* Actualized Budget); Figure 6–4 (Sample Budget 1 ($741,040)); Figure 6–5 (Sample Budget 2 ($997,800)); Figure 6–6 (Sample Budget 3 ($1.5 million)); Figure 7–2 (*Swingers* Chart of Accounts)

Movie Magic is a registered trademark and Budgeting is a trademark of Screenplay Systems, Inc. All rights reserved.

I believe that there is an element of pixie dust involved in making films. Somebody smiles on your film, or they don't.
                    —*Kasi Lemmons, writer/director,* Eve's Bayou

ACKNOWLEDGMENTS

Writing this manual has been an inspiring, rewarding, and challenging experience. (It has also been a test of our patience, will, and discipline!) We are most grateful for the opportunities, experience, and newfound knowledge it has afforded us.

We'd like to express our sincere gratitude to Dawn Hudson and Michael Harrison of IFP/West for their confidence in us and for giving us the opportunity to share our experiences and our knowledge. We'd like to thank Mindy Pashkow, Michelle Bryant, and Claire Battersby of IFP/West for their help and support. Without all of them, we could not have done it. Their encouragement and enthusiasm were remarkable, and we thank them from the bottom of our hearts.

We would also like to express our gratitude and appreciation to all of the interviewees for their time and support: Tom Bernard, Peter Broderick, Michelle Byrd, Jon Favreau, Geoffrey Gilmore, Ted Hope, Marcus Hu, Ang Lee, Kasi Lemmons, Scott Mosier, Mark Pogachefsky, Kevin Smith, Billy Bob Thornton, and Christine Vachon. They have all been inspirational, and their experience and wisdom have helped to give this manual life.

We would like to thank Jack Ofield for tackling the enormous task of reviewing an early draft, and providing us with suggestions, advice, and revisions that were pivotal in helping us organize and focus this manual. His patience is commendable, and his help has been invaluable.

We'd like to thank Screenplay Systems (creator of the Movie Magic Scheduling and Budgeting programs) for allowing us the use of their products and forms and for their overall support. We are grateful to them for making film scheduling and budgeting easy and efficient and, therefore, making our lives easier and saving us on many occasions.

We are grateful for the legal advice of Michael Donaldson.

We are thankful for all of the wonderful resource guides and filmmaking handbooks to which we often referred both while working on films and writing this manual. (See the resource guide at the back of this book.) They have taught us much, and we are grateful to their authors.

We would like to express our utmost appreciation and gratitude to Kiersta Burke, Laura Gabbert, Charles Herman-Wurmfeld, Julianne Kelley, George LaVoo, Sheila Levine, Doug Liman, Sean Mahoney, and the faculty, staff, and students at the UCLA School of Film and Television. Their advice, generosity, knowledge, support, and encouragement have been invaluable.

To our parents: Y'all must have had a screw loose when you raised us to believe we could take on such feats! With some luck and your unconditional encouragement, we did it. Your support, advice, and belief in us kept us going. We love you.

1 BEFORE YOU BEGIN

Don't rush. Write a good script. Make sure it's something. . . . Let friends read it. . . . And get some other opinions.

—Marcus Hu, Strand Releasing

Before you begin official preproduction on your film, there are some serious considerations to take into account that too often get overlooked. Making a movie requires a tremendous amount of hard work and a lot of money. The script is the fundamental building block to a successful film. Make sure that the script represents the story you want to tell and that it is solid. One way to get some outside perspective is to select three trusted readers, who are not your relatives or friends and who are experienced at reading scripts, and ask them to give their *honest* opinion about your treatment or script. Are the characters interesting? Is the story engaging? Is there an audience for this film?

Do not start preproduction without a realistic budget. Run the budget numbers to ensure that you can get your film through production and out of postproduction. To give your script the best chance possible you must assess the true needs of your film. Can you make the movie with the resources you have access to? If the answer is no, put this project on the back burner and find a different script. In Chapters 4, 5, and 6, you'll find detailed cost considerations as they relate to the script, but in short, the fewer locations, stunts, special effects, and complexities needed to execute your story, the less it will cost you to make your film.

Give some serious thought to when you will shoot your film. Weather, for example, is an enormous factor that should be taken into consideration. Does the film in question require rain or shine, or both? Is it largely an exterior daytime shoot? Will it be too hot or too cold to shoot it in the summer or winter, depending on the city you're shooting in? In cold weather, productions tend to move more slowly. Equipment and film stock will be affected by extreme cold. Days are shorter in the winter, which means less light. For example, on *Swingers*, since one of the points of the story is that it's sunny in Los Angeles almost every day, to have shot in January might have been problematic since we didn't have the time or resources to rearrange our production schedule around the weather. We were much safer to shoot in the summer, when it usually is sunny day in and day out.

Finally, if one of your goals is to travel to specific festivals with your film, plan your shoot according to the festival submission deadlines. (Although there are festivals all year round, many people have their heart set on festivals such as Sundance, Telluride, Toronto, or Berlin.) Will the needs of your film—equipment, crew, locations, etc.—be available to you at the time of year you plan to shoot? Ask yourself if you can you afford to work for little money and dedicate all of your time to your film.

2 THE SCRIPT

The Swingers *script opened and closed with a helicopter shot. On low-budget films, those types of things get axed out fast. It's a compromise, but it's not a problem. It doesn't change the story. You just have to get creative.*

—*Jon Favreau, writer, actor, and coproducer,* Swingers

Although we come from a background of line producing, we never tell writers to think about the budget while they're writing. It causes too many creative roadblocks. During the first several passes, the writer should focus on making the script as rich as he or she dares. Then, reality must set in: You may not be able to secure the $10 million that you'd hoped for. You may only have $50,000 or $500,000. Remember, good films can be made for this amount of money. It is the line producer's job to read through the script with an eye toward the budget. It is the line producer's job to make the film as true to the script as possible for the money available. It is also the line producer's job to insist on changes if there is no way to achieve something with the available means. Adjustments may need to be made to the script. For example, in the original *Swingers* script, Jon Favreau opened the film with a helicopter montage shot of Hollywood. We decided that we could capture the essence of that opening scene by using photographs of Hollywood nightclubs shot with a 35mm still camera long after principal photography had wrapped. This was a compromise that everyone agreed could be made without sacrificing the feel or the essence of the story.

On *Swingers,* it was clear that the scripted Los Angeles bars were essential to the story. We felt we couldn't go outside L.A. or to a stage to shoot the bar scenes and expect the movie to look and feel the way it should. In addition, it would have been much more costly to have shot on a stage dressed to look like a bar. The only compromise we made was substituting a few *scripted* bars for other bars that would agree to our limited rental fees. For example, if you know L.A. well, you'll see that we shot the exterior of The Room and used the interior of the 3 of Clubs. We couldn't film at The Room for the money we had. On the other hand, the scripted Treasure Island Casino in Las Vegas was not essen-

tial to the overall feel of the film. We simply needed a casino, so we shot at one we could afford.

The *Swingers* script had a daunting number of extras for a low-budget film. They could not be eliminated because they were part of the look and feel of the movie. We decided to shoot in the bars while they were open to the public. This way, the bars didn't lose money, and willing barflies and members of the crew served as our extras. We were careful to secure personal releases from all of them. (See Figure 7–2 in Chapter 7.)

As a line producer, you must be creative when reading the script and making decisions with the writer and the producer about rewrites. Your job is to figure out how to best capture a scene for the money you have. It is ultimately your job to assess what is affordable and what is not. Some sacrifices usually need to be made to accommodate a low-budget shoot. Changes may or may not require rewriting. If rewrites prove necessary, be sensitive and tactful. The writer has invested a great deal of time, energy, and passion in the script and may be not be happy, willing, or agreeable when you ask for certain changes. Explain that your motivation is financial. Once all changes have been made to the script, you'll have what is called the "white copy," the initial shooting script.

OPTION/PURCHASE AGREEMENT

The *option/purchase agreement* has many purposes. Generally, you will use it first to option a script (or any literary property), not buy it outright. This gives you the right to develop the material, shop it around, and see if it is viable without spending the money it would cost to purchase the material. Typically, you option a property for 12 months with a renewal clause. When and if you secure financing for the work, you can exercise your option to buy the script in accordance with the terms of your option/purchase agreement.

Some key negotiation points are the length and cost of the option, the purchase price, the buyer's right to make changes to the material and own those changes, how many rewrites the initial option period includes, the credit granted to the writer, and the net profit participation of the writer. Figures 2–1 and 2–2 show sample option/purchase agreements from actual deals we've made. Note that these are not "standard" agreements. We have included them because they reflect the flexibility of the independent filmmaking world.

The terms of the option/purchase agreement are flexible and should reflect the needs and resources of the parties involved. Strange things can happen when money is lost or gained, so it's best to establish the terms up front. When you sign the option, agree on what the purchase price will be. Usually, the purchase price amounts to around 2.5% of the production budget. The purpose here is to agree beforehand

---

SAMPLE OPTION 1

DATE

Re: "Script"

Dear Owner/Writer:

The following is a proposed draft of the agreement reached between Producer and Producer (hereinafter referred to as "Producer") and Owner/Writer (hereinafter referred to as "Owner") with respect to the acquisition by Producer of an exclusive option to purchase (the "Option") motion picture, television, and allied rights in and to the screenplay written by Owner entitled "Script" (the "Work").

1.   Option: Owner hereby grants to Producer the Option for a period of twelve (12) months to commence upon the date of signature ("Initial Option Period"). In consideration of the grant of such Option, Producer shall pay to Owner the sum of _____ Dollars, payable upon execution of this agreement, which payment shall be applicable against the purchase price set forth herein.

2.   Setup Bonus (Second Option Period): If (but only if) prior to the expiration of the Initial Option Period, Producer enters into a written agreement with a third-party financial entity for the development of a motion picture based on the Work, Producer shall pay to Owner the sum of _____ Dollars. Such payment, which shall not be applicable against the purchase price set forth herein, shall be deemed to extend automatically the Initial Option Period for a period of twelve (12) additional months, commencing upon the expiration of the Initial Option Period (the "Second Option Period").

3 .   Purchase Price: If Producer elects to exercise the Option, it shall do so by written notice to Owner prior to the expiration of the applicable option period (it being understood, in any event, that commencement of principal photography of the initial version of the Work produced hereunder [the "Picture"] shall be deemed an exercise of the Option) and shall pay the Owner the following amounts:

    A.   Fixed Compensation. The fixed purchase price for exercising the option (the "Fixed Purchase Price") shall be an amount equal to two and one-half percent (2 1/2%) of the final approved cash production budget of the Picture, excluding any overhead charged by a principal financier, completion guaranty fees, deferred payments, finance costs, unspent portion of any contingency, and the fixed portion (i.e., the noncontingent portion) of the purchase price, it being further understood that the Fixed Purchase Price shall in no event be less than _____ Dollars nor more than _____ Dollars. The fixed purchase price shall be paid to Owner at a time and in a manner mutually agreed upon between Owner and Producer. Producer shall, in good faith, make every effort to make payment upon commencement of principal photography, however, the parties agree that such payment shall not be made if determined that it would forestall completion of the Picture.

    B.   Contingent Writer Compensation - Profit Participation. The contingent writer compensation for exercising the option shall be an amount equal to five percent (5%) of one hundred percent (100%) of the net profits of the Picture to Owner for sole "Screenplay by" credit in connection with such picture. For the purposes hereof, "net profits" shall be defined, computed, and payable in the same manner as for Producer.

Figure 2–1   Option/purchase agreement 1

The resource guide in the back of this book lists some guidebooks to legal issues and contracts in the entertainment industry. We recommend that you work with a reputable lawyer, but if you can't make that arrangement, it is possible to navigate through this on your own. Be thorough. Read as much as you can. Many of the standard legal contracts exist to protect all parties involved. It is advisable to let the system work for you and have the proper paperwork in place.

REGISTRATION WITH THE WRITERS GUILD OF AMERICA

Registration of your script (treatment, synopsis, outlines, and written ideas) with the *Writers Guild of America* (WGA) is available to members and nonmembers of the guild. Registering your script with the WGA serves as a record of the script's completion date and protects you. It's an easy process that can be done in person or by mail.

These are the submission requirements:

- An unbound copy of the script
- A cover sheet with the title and the writer's full legal name
- Your Social Security number, return address, and telephone number (if there is more than one writer, you must choose one)
- A check for $20 for nonmembers or $10 for members

When you receive your registration number, put it on the front page of your script. The term of registration is five years and can be renewed. Only the registrant has access to the registration information and will need to present a photo ID for access or renewal. On the West Coast, the WGA is located at:

7000 W. Third St.
Los Angeles, CA 90048
Phone: 323/782-4500
Fax: 323/782-4803

The WGA's New York address is:

555 W. 57th Street
New York, NY 10019
Phone: 212/767-7800
Fax: 212/582-1909

COPYRIGHT

Registration with the WGA does not take the place of copyright. Copyright protects "original works of authorship," and the copyright claimant can be the author or the owner of exclusive rights to the work. Registering your script with the copyright office in Washington, DC, is easy. These are the submission requirements:

- A completed and signed Form PA (Figures 2–3 and 2–4)
- A check for $20.00 payable to the Register of Copyrights
- One copy of the script

These three items should be submitted in one envelope to:

Register of Copyrights, Copyright Office
Library of Congress
Washington, DC 20559-6000

Registration is effective the day the Copyright Office receives your submission, but you may not receive paperwork back for up to 16 weeks. When you make a production deal, secure financing from a bank, or deliver your film to a distribution company, evidence of the *chain of title* will be required. At a minimum, you will have to provide a certificate of copyright, the option/purchase agreement, and the writer's agreement, if there is one. (See the resource guide for assistance with copyright law.)

✍Filling Out Application Form PA

Detach and read these instructions before completing this form.
Make sure all applicable spaces have been filled in before you return this form.

BASIC INFORMATION

When to Use This Form: Use Form PA for registration of published or unpublished works of the performing arts. This class includes works prepared for the purpose of being "performed" directly before an audience or indirectly "by means of any device or process." Works of the performing arts include: (1) musical works, including any accompanying words; (2) dramatic works, including any accompanying music; (3) pantomimes and choreographic works; and (4) motion pictures and other audiovisual works.

Deposit to Accompany Application: An application for copyright registration must be accompanied by a deposit consisting of copies or phonorecords representing the entire work for which registration is made. The following are the general deposit requirements as set forth in the statute:

Unpublished Work: Deposit one complete copy (or phonorecord).

Published Work: Deposit two complete copies (or one phonorecord) of the best edition.

Work First Published Outside the United States: Deposit one complete copy (or phonorecord) of the first foreign edition.

Contribution to a Collective Work: Deposit one complete copy (or phonorecord) of the best edition of the collective work.

Motion Pictures: Deposit *both* of the following: (1) a separate written description of the contents of the motion picture; and (2) for a published work, one complete copy of the best edition of the motion picture; or, for an unpublished work, one complete copy of the motion picture or identifying material. Identifying material may be either an audiorecording of the entire soundtrack or one frame enlargement or similar visual print from each 10-minute segment.

The Copyright Notice: For works first published on or after March 1, 1989, the law provides that a copyright notice in a specified form "may be placed on all publicly distributed copies from which the work can be visually perceived." Use of the copyright notice is the responsibility of the copyright owner and does not require advance permission from the Copyright Office. The required form of the notice for copies generally consists of three elements: (1) the symbol "©", or the word "Copyright," or the abbreviation "Copr."; (2) the year of first publication; and (3) the name of the owner of copyright. For example: "© 1995 Jane Cole." The notice is to be affixed to the copies "in such manner and location as to give reasonable notice of the claim of copyright." Works first published prior to March 1, 1989, **must** carry the notice or risk loss of copyright protection.

For information about requirements for works published before March 1, 1989, or other copyright information, write: Information Section, LM-401, Copyright Office, Library of Congress, Washington, D.C. 20559-6000.

LINE-BY-LINE INSTRUCTIONS
Please type or print using black ink.

1 SPACE 1: Title

Title of This Work: Every work submitted for copyright registration must be given a title to identify that particular work. If the copies or phonorecords of the work bear a title (or an identifying phrase that could serve as a title), transcribe that wording *completely* and *exactly* on the application. Indexing of the registration and future identification of the work will depend on the information you give here. If the work you are registering is an entire "collective work" (such as a collection of plays or songs), give the overall title of the collection. If you are registering one or more individual contributions to a collective work, give the title of each contribution, followed by the title of the collection. For an unpublished collection, you may give the titles of the individual works after the collection title.

Previous or Alternative Titles: Complete this space if there are any additional titles for the work under which someone searching for the registration might be likely to look, or under which a document pertaining to the work might be recorded.

Nature of This Work: Briefly describe the general nature or character of the work being registered for copyright. Examples: "Music"; "Song Lyrics"; "Words and Music"; "Drama"; "Musical Play"; "Choreography"; "Pantomime"; "Motion Picture"; "Audiovisual Work."

2 SPACE 2: Author(s)

General Instructions: After reading these instructions, decide who are the "authors" of this work for copyright purposes. Then, unless the work is a "collective work," give the requested information about every "author" who contributed any appreciable amount of copyrightable matter to this version of the work. If you need further space, request additional Continuation Sheets. In the case of a collective work, such as a songbook or a collection of plays, give the information about the author of the collective work as a whole.

Name of Author: The fullest form of the author's name should be given. Unless the work was "made for hire," the individual who actually created the work is its "author." In the case of a work made for hire, the statute provides that "the employer or other person for whom the work was prepared is considered the author."

What is a "Work Made for Hire"? A "work made for hire" is defined as: (1) "a work prepared by an employee within the scope of his or her employment"; or (2) "a work specially ordered or commissioned for use as a contribution to a collective work, as a part of a motion picture or other audiovisual work, as a translation, as a supplementary work, as a compilation, as an instructional text, as a test, as answer material for a test, or as an atlas, if the parties expressly agree in a written instrument signed by them that the work shall be considered a work made for hire." If you have checked "Yes" to indicate that the work was "made for hire," you must give the full legal name of the employer (or other person for whom the work was prepared). You may also include the name of the employee along with the name of the employer (for example: "Elster Music Co., employer for hire of John Ferguson").

"Anonymous" or "Pseudonymous" Work: An author's contribution to a work is "anonymous" if that author is not identified on the copies or phonorecords of the work. An author's contribution to a work is "pseudonymous" if that author is identified on the copies or phonorecords under a fictitious name. If the work is "anonymous" you may: (1) leave the line blank; or (2) state "anonymous" on the line; or (3) reveal the author's identity. If the work is "pseudonymous" you may: (1) leave the line blank; or (2) give the pseudonym and identify it as such (example: "Huntley Haverstock, pseudonym"); or (3) reveal the author's name, making clear which is the real name and which is the pseudonym (for example: "Judith Barton, whose pseudonym is Madeline Elster"). However, the citizenship or domicile of the author **must** be given in all cases.

Dates of Birth and Death: If the author is dead, the statute requires that the year of death be included in the application unless the work is anonymous or pseudonymous. The author's birth date is optional, but is useful as a form of identification. Leave this space blank if the author's contribution was a "work made for hire."

Author's Nationality or Domicile: Give the country of which the author is a citizen, or the country in which the author is domiciled. Nationality or domicile **must** be given in all cases.

Nature of Authorship: Give a brief general statement of the nature of this particular author's contribution to the work. Examples: "Words"; "Coauthor of Music"; "Words and Music"; "Arrangement"; "Coauthor of Book and Lyrics"; "Dramatization"; "Screen Play"; "Compilation and English Translation"; "Editorial Revisions."

Figure 2–3 Instructions for filling out Form PA

3 SPACE 3: Creation and Publication

General Instructions: Do not confuse "creation" with "publication." Every application for copyright registration must state "the year in which creation of the work was completed." Give the date and nation of first publication only if the work has been published.

Creation: Under the statute, a work is "created" when it is fixed in a copy or phonorecord for the first time. Where a work has been prepared over a period of time, the part of the work existing in fixed form on a particular date constitutes the created work on that date. The date you give here should be the year in which the author completed the particular version for which registration is now being sought, even if other versions exist or if further changes or additions are planned.

Publication: The statute defines "publication" as "the distribution of copies or phonorecords of a work to the public by sale or other transfer of ownership, or by rental, lease, or lending"; a work is also "published" if there has been an "offering to distribute copies or phonorecords to a group of persons for purposes of further distribution, public performance, or public display." Give the full date (month, day, year) when, and the country where, publication first occurred. If first publication took place simultaneously in the United States and other countries, it is sufficient to state "U.S.A."

4 SPACE 4: Claimant(s)

Name(s) and Address(es) of Copyright Claimant(s): Give the name(s) and address(es) of the copyright claimant(s) in this work even if the claimant is the same as the author. Copyright in a work belongs initially to the author of the work (including, in the case of a work made for hire, the employer or other person for whom the work was prepared). The copyright claimant is either the author of the work or a person or organization to whom the copyright initially belonging to the author has been transferred.

Transfer: The statute provides that, if the copyright claimant is not the author, the application for registration must contain "a brief statement of how the claimant obtained ownership of the copyright." If any copyright claimant named in space 4 is not an author named in space 2, give a brief statement explaining how the claimant(s) obtained ownership of the copyright. Examples: "By written contract"; "Transfer of all rights by author"; "Assignment"; "By will." Do not attach transfer documents or other attachments or riders.

5 SPACE 5: Previous Registration

General Instructions: The questions in space 5 are intended to show whether an earlier registration has been made for this work and, if so, whether there is any basis for a new registration. As a general rule, only one basic copyright registration can be made for the same version of a particular work.

Same Version: If this version is substantially the same as the work covered by a previous registration, a second registration is not generally possible unless: (1) the work has been registered in unpublished form and a second registration is now being sought to cover this first published edition; or (2) someone other than the author is identified as copyright claimant in the earlier registration, and the author is now seeking registration in his or her own name. If either of these two exceptions apply, check the appropriate box and give the earlier registration number and date. Otherwise, do not submit Form PA; instead, write the Copyright Office for information about supplementary registration or recordation of transfers of copyright ownership.

Changed Version: If the work has been changed, and you are now seeking registration to cover the additions or revisions, check the last box in space 5, give the earlier registration number and date, and complete both parts of space 6 in accordance with the instructions below.

Previous Registration Number and Date: If more than one previous registration has been made for the work, give the number and date of the latest registration.

6 SPACE 6: Derivative Work or Compilation

General Instructions: Complete space 6 if this work is a "changed version," "compilation," or "derivative work," and if it incorporates one or more earlier works that have already been published or registered for copyright or that have fallen into the public domain. A "compilation" is defined as "a work formed by the collection and assembling of preexisting materials or of data that are selected, coordinated, or arranged in such a way that the resulting work as a whole constitutes an original work of authorship." A "derivative work" is "a work based on one or more preexisting works." Examples of derivative works include musical arrangements, dramatizations, translations, abridgments, condensations, motion picture versions, or "any other form in which a work may be recast, transformed, or adapted." Derivative works also include works "consisting of editorial revisions, annotations, or other modifications" if these changes, as a whole, represent an original work of authorship.

Preexisting Material (space 6a): Complete this space **and** space 6b for derivative works. In this space identify the preexisting work that has been recast, transformed, or adapted. For example, the preexisting material might be: "French version of Hugo's 'Le Roi s'amuse'." Do not complete this space for compilations.

Material Added to This Work (space 6b): Give a brief, general statement of the **additional** new material covered by the copyright claim for which registration is sought. In the case of a derivative work, identify this new material. Examples: "Arrangement for piano and orchestra"; "Dramatization for television"; "New film version"; "Revisions throughout; Act III completely new." If the work is a compilation, give a brief, general statement describing both the material that has been compiled **and** the compilation itself. Example: "Compilation of 19th Century Military Songs."

7,8,9 SPACE 7, 8, 9: Fee, Correspondence, Certification, Return Address

Deposit Account: If you maintain a Deposit Account in the Copyright Office, identify it in space 7. Otherwise leave the space blank and send the fee of $20 with your application and deposit.

Correspondence (space 7): This space should contain the name, address, area code, and telephone number of the person to be consulted if correspondence about this application becomes necessary.

Certification (space 8): The application cannot be accepted unless it bears the date and the **handwritten signature** of the author or other copyright claimant, or of the owner of exclusive right(s), or of the duly authorized agent of the author, claimant, or owner of exclusive right(s).

Address for Return of Certificate (space 9): The address box must be completed legibly since the certificate will be returned in a window envelope.

MORE INFORMATION

How to Register a Recorded Work: If the musical or dramatic work that you are registering has been recorded (as a tape, disk, or cassette), you may choose either copyright application Form PA (Performing Arts) or Form SR (Sound Recordings), depending on the purpose of the registration.

Form PA should be used to register the underlying musical composition or dramatic work. Form SR has been developed specifically to register a "sound recording" as defined by the Copyright Act—a work resulting from the "fixation of a series of sounds," separate and distinct from the underlying musical or dramatic work. Form SR should be used when the copyright claim is limited to the sound recording itself. (In one instance, Form SR may also be used to file for a copyright registration for both kinds of works—see (4) below.) Therefore:

(1) File Form PA if you are seeking to register the musical or dramatic work, not the "sound recording," even though what you deposit for copyright purposes may be in the form of a phonorecord.

(2) File Form PA if you are seeking to register the audio portion of an audiovisual work, such as a motion picture soundtrack; these are considered integral parts of the audiovisual work.

(3) File Form SR if you are seeking to register the "sound recording" itself, that is, the work that results from the fixation of a series of musical, spoken, or other sounds, but not the underlying musical or dramatic work.

(4) File Form SR if you are the copyright claimant for both the underlying musical or dramatic work and the sound recording, *and* you prefer to register both on the same form.

(5) File both forms PA and SR if the copyright claimant for the underlying work and sound recording differ, or you prefer to have separate registration for them.

"Copies" and "Phonorecords": To register for copyright, you are required to deposit "copies" or "phonorecords." These are defined as follows:

Musical compositions may be embodied (fixed) in "copies," objects from which a work can be read or visually perceived, directly or with the aid of a machine or device, such as manuscripts, books, sheet music, film, and videotape. They may also be fixed in "phonorecords," objects embodying fixations of sounds, such as tapes and phonograph disks, commonly known as phonograph records. For example, a song (the work to be registered) can be reproduced in sheet music ("copies") or phonograph records ("phonorecords"), or both.

Figure 2–3   Instructions for filling out Form PA (continued)

FORM PA

For a Work of the Performing Arts
UNITED STATES COPYRIGHT OFFICE

REGISTRATION NUMBER

_____

PA   PAU

EFFECTIVE DATE OF REGISTRATION

_____

Month   Day   Year

DO NOT WRITE ABOVE THIS LINE. IF YOU NEED MORE SPACE, USE A SEPARATE CONTINUATION SHEET.

1

TITLE OF THIS WORK ▼

PREVIOUS OR ALTERNATIVE TITLES ▼

NATURE OF THIS WORK ▼ See instructions

2

a

NAME OF AUTHOR ▼

DATES OF BIRTH AND DEATH
Year Born ▼   Year Died ▼

Was this contribution to the work a "work made for hire"?
M Yes
M No

AUTHOR'S NATIONALITY OR DOMICILE
Name of Country
OR { Citizen of ▶
Domiciled in▶

WAS THIS AUTHOR'S CONTRIBUTION TO THE WORK
Anonymous? M Yes M No
Pseudonymous? M Yes M No

If the answer to either of these questions is "Yes," see detailed instructions.

NATURE OF AUTHORSHIP Briefly describe nature of material created by this author in which copyright is claimed. ▼

NOTE

Under the law, the "author" of a "work made for hire" is generally the employer, not the employee (see instructions). For any part of this work that was "made for hire" check "Yes" in the space provided, give the employer (or other person for whom the work was prepared) as "Author" of that part, and leave the space for dates of birth and death blank.

b

NAME OF AUTHOR ▼

DATES OF BIRTH AND DEATH
Year Born ▼   Year Died ▼

Was this contribution to the work a "work made for hire"?
M Yes
M No

AUTHOR'S NATIONALITY OR DOMICILE
Name of Country
OR { Citizen of ▶
Domiciled in▶

WAS THIS AUTHOR'S CONTRIBUTION TO THE WORK
Anonymous? M Yes M No
Pseudonymous? M Yes M No

If the answer to either of these questions is "Yes," see detailed instructions.

NATURE OF AUTHORSHIP Briefly describe nature of material created by this author in which copyright is claimed. ▼

c

NAME OF AUTHOR ▼

DATES OF BIRTH AND DEATH
Year Born ▼   Year Died ▼

Was this contribution to the work a "work made for hire"?
M Yes
M No

AUTHOR'S NATIONALITY OR DOMICILE
Name of Country
OR { Citizen of ▶
Domiciled in▶

WAS THIS AUTHOR'S CONTRIBUTION TO THE WORK
Anonymous? M Yes M No
Pseudonymous? M Yes M No

If the answer to either of these questions is "Yes," see detailed instructions.

NATURE OF AUTHORSHIP Briefly describe nature of material created by this author in which copyright is claimed. ▼

3

a YEAR IN WHICH CREATION OF THIS WORK WAS COMPLETED This information must be given ◀ Year in all cases.

b DATE AND NATION OF FIRST PUBLICATION OF THIS PARTICULAR WORK Complete this information ONLY if this work has been published. Month ▶ _____ Day▶ _____ Year▶ _____ ◀ Nation

4

See instructions before completing this space.

COPYRIGHT CLAIMANT(S) Name and address must be given even if the claimant is the same as the author given in space 2. ▼

TRANSFER If the claimant(s) named here in space 4 is (are) different from the author(s) named in space 2, give a brief statement of how the claimant(s) obtained ownership of the copyright. ▼

APPLICATION RECEIVED

ONE DEPOSIT RECEIVED

TWO DEPOSITS RECEIVED

FUNDS RECEIVED

DO NOT WRITE HERE OFFICE USE ONLY

MORE ON BACK ▶ • Complete all applicable spaces (numbers 5-9) on the reverse side of this page.
• See detailed instructions. • Sign the form at line 8.

DO NOT WRITE HERE

Page 1 of _____ pages

EXAMINED BY   FORM PA

CHECKED BY

☐ CORRESPONDENCE
Yes

FOR COPYRIGHT OFFICE USE ONLY

DO NOT WRITE ABOVE THIS LINE. IF YOU NEED MORE SPACE, USE A SEPARATE CONTINUATION SHEET.

5

PREVIOUS REGISTRATION Has registration for this work, or for an earlier version of this work, already been made in the Copyright Office?
M Yes M No If your answer is "Yes," why is another registration being sought? (Check appropriate box.) ▼
a. M This is the first published edition of a work previously registered in unpublished form.
b. M This is the first application submitted by this author as copyright claimant.
c. M This is a changed version of the work, as shown by space 6 on this application.
If your answer is "Yes," give: Previous Registration Number ▼   Year of Registration ▼

6

a   b

See instructions before completing this space.

DERIVATIVE WORK OR COMPILATION Complete both space 6a and 6b for a derivative work; complete only 6b for a compilation.
Preexisting Material Identify any preexisting work or works that this work is based on or incorporates. ▼

Material Added to This Work Give a brief, general statement of the material that has been added to this work and in which copyright is claimed. ▼

7

DEPOSIT ACCOUNT If the registration fee is to be charged to a Deposit Account established in the Copyright Office, give name and number of Account.
Name ▼   Account Number ▼

CORRESPONDENCE Give name and address to which correspondence about this application should be sent. Name/Address/Apt/City/State/ZIP ▼

Area code and daytime telephone number ▶ ( )
Email ▶

Fax number ▶ ( )

8

CERTIFICATION* I, the undersigned, hereby certify that I am the (check only one) ▼
M author
M other copyright claimant
M owner of exclusive right(s)
M authorized agent of _____
Name of author or other copyright claimant, or owner of exclusive right(s) ▲

of the work identified in this application and that the statements made by me in this application are correct to the best of my knowledge.

Typed or printed name and date ▼ If this application gives a date of publication in space 3, do not sign and submit it before that date.

Date ▶

Handwritten signature (X) ▼

x _____

9

MAIL CERTIFICATE TO

Name ▼

Number/Street/Apt ▼

City/State/ZIP ▼

Certificate will be mailed in window envelope

*17 U.S.C. § 506(e): Any person who knowingly makes a false representation of a material fact in the application for copyright registration provided for by section 409, or in any written statement filed in connection with the application, shall be fined not more than $2,500.

July 1998—250,000

☐ PRINTED ON RECYCLED PAPER

☆U.S. GOVERNMENT PRINTING OFFICE: 1998-432-381/80,013

Figure 2–4   Form PA

3 FINANCING

The point is, don't give up. Don't be the person who says, I wrote this, I want to make it, I want to be in it, this is the only way to do this, because the bottom line is, if I had not taken the opportunity to make the movie [Swingers] the way we did it, it would never have happened. I was able to enjoy probably more creative control as a coproducer on this film—being able to be in the editing room, picking the music, the people, the wardrobe—than if I were the director, much less a first-time director working with a studio or a mini studio. They would have never given me the amount of control that I had in this situation. So by not worrying about the credit or the money, I ended up getting the film that I wanted.

—*Jon Favreau*, Swingers

Getting your picture financed is not easy, and the process may cause you to reconsider many aspects of making a movie. We have found the financing process to be frustrating and difficult, but we also believe that the process itself is as important as the product and that there is much to be learned from it. The time you spend securing financing for your film can be one of the most trying and overwhelming periods of the filmmaking process. It's important to remain open to various options and to not cling to a specific idea of how you want to get your film made.

DANCING WITH A DOUBLE-EDGED SWORD

You can't secure financing without having talent attached, and you can't get commitments from talent unless you have financing. It's a catch-22. Ideally, you pursue both simultaneously and hope that you will find either the financier who loves the project and wants to be involved, or the actor who loves the piece and is willing to grant you permission to use his or her name to help finance the piece.

On *Swingers,* we had a difficult time for this very reason. We knew the cast we wanted, but unfortunately, few people knew of Vince Vaughn, Jon Favreau, Ron Livingston, Patrick Van Horn, or Alex Desert. In meeting after meeting, executives suggested that the movie might be viable if the role of Trent could be cast with a bankable star. We stuck to our guns, but none of those production companies ultimately wanted to finance the picture. The good news is that everyone is looking for a good role and a viable project, so it's

feasible—if you're prepared and persistent and if your material is good—that you will find financing for your film.

OPTIONS FOR FINANCING INDIE FILMS

Domestic Production-Distribution Deal

If you can make a domestic *production-distribution deal* (P-D deal) with a company, the money you receive for domestic rights should cover from 40% to 60% of your budget. The more money the company gives you, the more creative control it will want. Some of the key negotiating points on a P-D deal are the minimum prints-and-advertising (P&A) expenditure, the advance, above-the-line fees, and the release date. Increasingly, the role of the P&A expenditure figures largely in the success of any film. If you make a P-D deal, make sure that the company handles films like the one you intend to make and that they can get it out to the public in a way that makes sense. Remember, if you relinquish certain rights when you make your deal, you may have little control over whether and how the film is released.

Equity Financing

Equity financing is hard cash invested by a company or an individual—be it a family member, friend, or professional investor—in exchange for credit, profit points, or both. It's a high-risk, high-return-potential investment. People invest equity in films for myriad reasons, including experience in the film business, financial gain, and film credit. Companies that invest equity in pictures are constantly soliciting material in an attempt to find their next project.

Swingers was financed through straight equity by a few silent investors. This is, in many ways, a great way to finance a film because it typically allows for greater creative control than studio or mini-major financing. If you are raising equity to finance your film, you will need to form a *limited liability company* (LLC) or a *limited liability partnership* (LLP) to protect the investors. This structure literally limits the liability of the investors to the amount of money they have put into your film. For more information on how to establish an LLC or LLP, refer to the legal manuals cited in the resource guide at the back of this book, or consult an attorney.

Foreign Presales

With foreign presales, you sell the rights to your picture on a territory-by-territory basis before actually shooting the film. How much money you can presell your film for depends on the packaging of the film (that is, which elements are attached and the foreign value of those elements) and on the territory itself. To capitalize your picture through foreign presales, you should hire a foreign sales agent to assist you. Foreign sales agents run the gamut in terms of the types of films they handle. Find an agent who handles films along the lines of the one you're trying to make, both in terms of budget and genre. By attending film markets and exploiting his or her contacts, the agent will secure sales agreements with various foreign territories. He or she will take a percentage, usually 10% to 15% for straight presales and up to 25% if you want an advance from the agent. The agent will also charge you for the cost of attending a given market. You'll want to negotiate a cap on the expenses you're responsible for to ensure that you don't absorb too many of his or her costs, thereby negating the value of the sale. You can use these presale contracts as collateral on a bank loan, or if your film is extremely low-budget, you may be able to shoot it for the small advance you receive from your presales.

Gap Financing

When you have raised most of the capital needed to cover the full cost of your picture, the remaining amount is called the *gap*. Gap financing is a common but expensive way to finance a picture. Approach a bank that does gap financing. Be prepared to provide them with any presale contracts and guaranteed equity investment contracts as well as your budget, business plan, and proof of chain of title, to name a few. The bank will determine whether you are eligible for a gap loan and, depending on the assessed risk involved, will let you know how much it will cost you. You pay both interest on the loan (typically either LIBOR plus 2% or prime) and a flat fee to the bank. The killer on a gap deal is that you

continue to pay interest on the loan until it's paid back, and that duration is unknowable because it is contingent on further foreign sales or on performance of the picture at the box office.

Beg, Borrow, Steal

Depending on the budget of your film, it is conceivable to piece together money through personal savings, credit cards, and donations from family members and friends. Generally speaking, we can't say that it's a bad idea to invest your own money in your movie. If you believe in the project and you've got some cash, there's no reason not to, just be aware that you may not get it back.

As for credit cards, use them only as a last resort. Credit card money is expensive money; annual interest can be close to 20%, which adds up. Going into credit card debt is not a decision to be made without careful thought.

When asking loved ones, family members, and friends for money to make your movie, be up front about the risk of the investment. If you present it as a sure thing that they'll be paid back in full, you run the risk of burning bridges with people you care about. Establishing an LLC or an LLP is just as important when the money belongs to family and friends. This legal entity will protect any assets they own beyond the investment they've made in the film and will show them that you're serious.

ASKING PEOPLE TO WORK FOR FREE AND DEFERRALS

If your funds are short, you may want to consider going back through your budget to determine what changes and adjustments can be made. (See "When Your Budget Is Way Too High" in Chapter 6.) Although it is not ideal to ask people to work for little or no money, it may be the only way to make your movie. We have been involved with productions on which everyone worked for free. It is possible to find a committed crew willing to work for little or no money. The key is to find people who really want and need the experience. Find people who are eager to learn grip work, for example, and match them up with an affable, experienced key grip who can talk to them about the different aspects of the job. Figure out which shoot days will be the most complicated and would benefit from a more experienced crew. Ask more production-savvy crew people to donate one day of their time to cover these shoot days.

On *Swingers,* we paid all of the crew members $300 per week. We made no exceptions. We informed each potential

Swingers

14   INT. TREASURE ISLAND CASINO -- THE CLASSY SECTION -- NIGHT   14

Mike is at a blackjack table with Trent at his side. The
game has paused to observe the newcomers as Mike draws a
billfold out of his breast pocket. They're pulling it off
with only slightly noticeable effort.

                  MIKE
        I don't know. I guess I'll start
        with three hundred in, uh, blacks.

Mike tries to hand the DEALER a handful of twenties after
counting them twice.

                DEALER
        On the table.

                MIKE
        Sorry?

                DEALER
        You have to lay it on the table.   *8/8*

                MIKE
        Uh, I don't want to bet it all.

The other players grow impatient.

                DEALER
        You're not allowed to hand me money,
        sir. You'll have to lay it on the
        table if you want me to change it.

                MIKE
         (hastily laying down
         the bills)
        Oh...right.

The dealer lays out the bills such that the amount is visible
to the camera encased in the black glass globe overhead.

                DEALER
        Blacks?

                MIKE
        Huh?

                DEALER
        You want this in black chips.

                MIKE
        Sure, that'll be fine.

The dealer chirps out an unintelligible formality and the
PIT BOSS chirps the response.

                              (continued)

Figure 4–1 *Marked-up script pages for* Swingers *(continued)*

Swingers

14   CONTINUED: 14

Trent and Mike stare at the pit boss ten feet away.

The dealer plunks down the measly THREE CHIPS which represent
Mike's entire cash reserve. Not quite the effect he had
hoped for.

The swingers stare at the chips. The players stare at the
swingers. The dealer stares at the pit boss.

                    MIKE (CONT'D)
          Do you have anything smaller?

                    DEALER
          Yes, but I'm afraid this table has a
          hundred dollar minimum bet. Perhaps   8/8
          you'd be more comfortable at one of
          our lower stakes tables.

The dealer indicates a FIVE DOLLAR TABLE across the room
where a disheveled DEALER deals to a BLUEHAIR, a BIKER, and
a COUPLE in matching Siegfried & Roy tee shirts.

The swingers look back to the dealer who is now flanked by
the pit boss.

The tense silence is broken by...

                    CHRISTY
          Drinks?
               (then to Trent)
          How about you, Cap'n?

Trent looks over to see that it's the same WAITRESS who
flashed him a smile earlier.

                    MIKE
          Yes, I'll have a scotch on the rocks,
          please. Anything will do. As long
          as it's not a blend, of course. Any
          single malt. A Glenlivit or
          Glenfiddich, perhaps. Maybe a
          Glengowen. Any "Glen".

                    CHRISTY
               (under her breath)
          One scotch on the rocks.

She leaves.

2 pages total scene #14

Figure 4–1   Marked-up script pages for Swingers *(continued)*

52 <u>INT. MIKE'S APARTMENT -- LATER THAT NIGHT</u>   52

<u>Mike opens the door</u> and <u>flicks on</u> the <u>lights</u> in his <u>sparsely
furnished</u> single.

He drops his <u>keys</u> on the <u>table</u> and makes a bee line to the
<u>answering machine.</u>

He pushes the button.

                    ANSWERING MACHINE
                 (synthesized voice)
              She didn't call.

Mike <u>collapses</u> into his <u>futon</u> and <u>lights a smoke</u>.

Beat.

He pulls out the <u>COCKTAIL NAPKIN</u>. He stares at the number.

He looks at the <u>clock</u>. 2:20 AM.

He looks at the napkin.

He thinks better of it, and puts the napkin away.   *8/8*

Beat.

He takes out the napkin and picks up the <u>phone</u>.

                    ANSWERING MACHINE (CONT'D)
                 (synthesized voice)
              Don't do it, Mike.

                        MIKE
              Shut up.

He dials.

It rings twice, then...

                     NIKKI
                 (recorded)
              Hi. This is Nikki. Leave a message.
                 (beep)

                        MIKE
              Hi, Nikki. This is Mike. I met you
              tonight at the Dresden. I, uh, just
              called to say I, uh, I'm really glad
              we met and you should give me a call.
              So call me tomorrow, or, like, in
              two days, whatever. My number is
              213-555-4679.
                      (MORE)

                                                    (continued)

Figure 4–1 Marked-up script pages for Swingers *(continued)*

```
                                                            Swingers
   52   CONTINUED:                                                    52

                               MIKE (CONT'D)
                        (beep)

   Mike hangs up.

   Beat.

   He dials again.

                               NIKKI
                        (recorded)
                  Hi.  This is Nikki.  Leave a message.
                        (beep)


                               MIKE
                  Hi, Nikki.  This is Mike, again.  I
                  just called because it sounded like
                  your machine might've cut me off
                  before I gave you my number, and
                  also to say sorry for calling so
                  late, but you were still there when
                  I left the Dresden, so I knew I'd            8/8
                  get your machine.  Anyway, my number
                  is...
                        (beep)

   Mike calls back right away.

                               NIKKI
                        (recorded)
                  Hi.  This is Nikki.  Leave a message.
                        (beep)


                               MIKE
                  213.555.4679.  That's all.  I just
                  wanted to leave my number.  I don't
                  want you to think I'm weird, or
                  desperate or something
                        (he regrets saying
                         it immediately)
                  ...I mean, you  know, we should just
                  hang out.  That's it.  No
                  expectations.  Just, you know, hang
                  out.  Bye.
                        (beep)

   He hangs up.

   Beat.

   He dials.

                               NIKKI
                        (recorded)
                  Hi.  This is Nikki.  Leave a message.
                               (MORE)
```

Figure 4–1   Marked-up script pages for Swingers *(continued)*

Swingers

52   CONTINUED: (2)   52

                              NIKKI (CONT'D)
                         (beep)

                         MIKE
                    I just got out of a six year
                    relationship. Okay? That should
                    help explain why I'm acting so weird.
                    It's not you. It's me. I just wanted
                    to say that. Sorry.
                         (pause)
                    This is Mike.
                         (beep)

He dials again. There's no turning back.

                              NIKKI
                         (recorded)
                    Hi. This is Nikki. Leave a message.
                         (beep)

                         MIKE
                    Hi, Nikki. This is Mike again.
                    Could you just call me when you get
                    in? I'll be up for awhile, and I'd
                    just rather talk to you in person
                    instead of trying to squeeze it all...
                         (beep)   8/8

He dials yet again.

                              NIKKI
                         (recorded)
                    Hi. This is Nikki. Leave a message.
                         (beep)

                         MIKE
                    Hi, Nikki. Mike. I don't think
                    this is working out.
                    I think you're great, but maybe we
                    should just take some time off from
                    each other. It's not you, really.
                    It's me. It's only been six months...

                              NIKKI
                         (live, in person.
                          she picks up the
                          line)
                    Mike?

                         MIKE
                    Nikki! Great! Did you just walk
                    in, or were you listening all along?

(continued)

Figure 4–1   Marked-up script pages for Swingers *(continued)*

Swingers

52   CONTINUED: (3)   52

                              NIKKI
                        (calmly)
                  Don't call me ever again.

                              MIKE
                  Wow. I guess you were home...
                        (click)   3/8

She hung up on him.

He's frozen.

He hangs up.

Beat.

Beat.

Beat.

3 3/8 total
scene # 52

Figure 4–1   Marked-up script pages for Swingers *(continued)*

SWINGERS   Page 5

Breakdown Sheet

Sheet: **5**   I/E: **INT**   Set: **CASHIER'S WINDOW - CASINO**   D/N: **Night**

Scenes: **1 5**   Pages: **5 4/8**

Synopsis: **MIKE COLLECTS HIS MONEY; TRENT & MIKE TALK**

Location: **TREASURE ISLAND CASINO**

Sequence: _____   Script Day: **3** _____   Script Page: **18 - 24**

Cast Members
   1. MIKE
   2. TRENT
   8. CHRISTY

Extras
   1. BACKGROUND GAMBLERS
   2. TABLE DEALERS
   5. ATMOSPHERE EXTRAS
   6. CASHIER

Props
   9. CIGARETTES
   12. COCKTAIL NAPKIN
   13. COCKTAILS
   18. GAMBLING CHIPS
   24. MONEY

Costume
     CASINO WAITRESS OUTFITS

Music
     CASINO MUZAK IN BACKGROUND

Sound
     GAMBLING CHIPS
     LAUGHING, TALKING
     SLOT MACHINES

Security
     SECURITY IN CASINO

Figure 4–2   Breakdown sheets 1 to 5 for Swingers *(continued)*

	27	28
	2	2 6/8
	9	9
	INT - LIVING ROOM - PARTY - Night Scs. 42	INT - LIVING ROOM - PARTY - Night Scs. 43, 44, 45 ALL CONTINUOUS
	1	1
	2	2
	3	3
	4	4
		5
	10	10
TRENT & SUE PRETEND NOT TO LOOK AT GROUP OF GIRLS; TALK ABOUT GIRLS	E:1	
TRENT TALKING WITH GIRL WITH CIGAR; REST OF SWINGERS LOOKING ON		E:1

— End Of Day 9 – 9/15/95 — 7 5/8 pgs.

Figure 5–1 Swingers strip board (days 1–9) (continued)

SWINGERS

Shooting Schedule

SHOOT DAY #1 -- Tue, Sep 5, 1995

Scene #11   **EXT - CASINO DRIVEWAY - Night**   1/8 Pgs.

DETAIL INSERT OF TRENT'S CAR PULLING INTO CASINO DRIVEWAY

Props	**Vehicles**
15. DICE ON VALVE CAP	TRENT'S CAR

Scene #12   **EXT - CASINO DRIVEWAY - Night**   2/8 Pgs.

TRENT & MIKE EXIT CAR AT VALET STAND, TOSS VALET KEYS, ENTER CASINO

Cast Members
1. MIKE
2. TRENT
22. VALET

Extras
1. BACKGROUND GAMBLERS

Props
15. DICE ON VALVE CAP
20. KEYS

Vehicles
TRENT'S CAR

Costume
BUFFED SHOES
CUFF LINKS
POCKET CHAIN
VALET UNIFORM
ZOOT SUITS

Scene #13   **INT - CASINO HALLWAY - Night**   3/8 Pgs.

MIKE & TRENT WALK AND TALK DOWN THE CASINO HALLWAY

Cast Members
1. MIKE
2. TRENT

Extras
1. BACKGROUND GAMBLERS
2. TABLE DEALERS
3. TOURISTS
4. CASINO WAITRESSES

Security
SECURITY IN CASINO

Props
25. NAUTICAL DECOR

Music
CASINO MUZAK IN
BACKGROUND

Costume
CASINO WAITRESS OUTFITS
CUFF LINKS
POCKET CHAIN
ZOOT SUITS

Sound
GAMBLING CHIPS
SLOT MACHINES

Special Equipment
SLOT MACHINES

Figure 5–2 Swingers *shooting schedule (days 1–9)*

SWINGERS

Page 10

Shooting Schedule

Scene #42   **INT - LIVING ROOM - PARTY - Night**   2 Pgs.

TRENT & SUE PRETEND NOT TO LOOK AT GROUP OF GIRLS; TALK ABOUT
GIRLS

Cast Members   **Props**
  1. MIKE   5. BEER BOTTLES   **Costume**
  2. TRENT   9. CIGARETTES   TRENDY BACKPACKS
  3. ROB   10. CIGARS   **Sound**
  4. SUE   13. COCKTAILS   LAUGHING, TALKING
10. GIRL WITH CIGAR

Extras   **Music**
10. PARTY GUESTS   PARTY MUSIC

Security
  SECURITY AT PARTY

Scene #43, 44, 45   **INT - LIVING ROOM - PARTY - Night**   2 6/8 Pgs.
ALL CONTINUOUS   *TRENT TALKING WITH GIRL WITH CIGAR; REST OF SWINGERS LOOKING ON*

Cast Members   **Props**
  1. MIKE   5. BEER BOTTLES   **Costume**
  2. TRENT   9. CIGARETTES   TRENDY BACKPACKS
  3. ROB   10. CIGARS   **Sound**
  4. SUE   12. COCKTAIL NAPKIN   LAUGHING, TALKING
  5. CHARLES   13. COCKTAILS
10. GIRL WITH CIGAR   27. PEN

Extras
10. PARTY GUESTS   **Music**
    PARTY MUSIC

Security
  SECURITY AT PARTY

END OF DAY #9 – 7 5/8 Total Pages

Figure 5–2   Swingers *shooting schedule (days 1–9) (continued)*

SWINGERS

ONE-LINE SCHEDULE

Shoot Day #1 -- Tue, Sep 5, 1995

Scs. 11	EXT	CASINO DRIVEWAY	Night	1/8 pgs.

DETAIL INSERT OF TRENT'S CAR PULLING INTO CASINO DRIVEWAY
ID:

Scs. 12	EXT	CASINO DRIVEWAY	Night	2/8 pgs.

TRENT & MIKE EXIT CAR AT VALET STAND, TOSS VALET KEYS, ENTER CASINO
ID:1, 2, 22

Scs. 13	INT	CASINO HALLWAY	Night	3/8 pgs.

MIKE & TRENT WALK AND TALK DOWN THE CASINO HALLWAY
ID:1, 2

Scs. 15	INT	CASHIER'S WINDOW - CASINO	Night	5 4/8 pgs.

MIKE COLLECTS HIS MONEY; TRENT & MIKE TALK
ID:1, 2, 8

End Day #1 -- Total Pages: 6 2/8

Shoot Day #2 -- Wed, Sep 6, 1995

Scs. 14	INT	CASINO BLACKJACK TABLE	Night	4 pgs.

MIKE & TRENT AT THE BLACKJACK TABLE
ID:1, 2, 7, 12, 14, 15, 16, 19, 23

Scs. 16	INT	COFFEE SHOP - CASINO	Night	2 5/8 pgs.

TRENT & MIKE ORDER FOOD; TALK ABOUT GIRLS; ARRANGE TO MEET GIRLS
ID:1, 2, 7, 13

End Day #2 -- Total Pages: 6 5/8

Shoot Day #3 -- Thu, Sep 7, 1995

Scs. 33	EXT	ALLEYWAY BEHIND BAR	Night	1 1/8 pgs.

MIKE & ROB WALK DOWN ALLEY TO BAR ENTRANCE
ID:1, 3

Scs. 34	INT	HOLLYWOOD CLUB - BAR	Night	3 3/8 pgs.

MIKE & ROB ORDER DRINKS AND MEET UP WITH CHARLES AT HOLLYWOOD
CLUB
ID:1, 3, 5, 6

Scs. 17	INT	LANDLUBBER LOUNGE - TREASURE ISLAND	Night	2 6/8 pgs.

MIKE & TRENT MEET CHRISTY & HER FRIEND LISA AT LOUNGE
ID:1, 2, 6, 8, 18

End Day #3 -- Total Pages: 7 2/8

Shoot Day #4 -- Fri, Sep 8, 1995

Scs. 3	INT	MIKE'S APARTMENT LIVING ROOM	Night	4 1/8 pgs.

MIKE PLAYING MESSAGES FOR EX'S CALL; TRENT TELLS MIKE IT'S VEGAS
ID:1

Scs. 52	INT	MIKE'S APARTMENT LIVING ROOM	Night	3 3/8 pgs.

MIKE CALLING NIKKI, LEAVING PATHETIC MESSAGES
ID:1

Figure 5–3   Swingers one-line schedule (days 1–9)

September	Day of Month:	5	6	7	8	9	10	11	12	13	14	15	Rehearse	Travel	Work	Hold
	Day Of Week:	Tu	W	Th	F	Sa	Su	M	Tu	W	Th	F				
	Shooting Days:	1	2	3	4			5	6	7	8	9				
1.	BACKGROUND GAMBLER	SW	WF												2	
2.	TABLE DEALERS	SWF													1	
3.	TOURISTS	SWF													1	
4.	CASINO WAITRESSES	SW	W	H	H			H	H	W	WF				4	4
5.	ATMOSPHERE EXTRAS	SW	W	WF											3	
6.	CASHIER	SWF													1	
7.	DOORMAN			SWF											1	
8.	BAR PATRONS			SWF											1	
9.	DINER PATRONS									SW	WF				2	
10.	PARTY GUESTS											SWF			1	

	Day of Month:	Holiday	Loop	Start	Finish	TOTAL
	Day Of Week:					
	Shooting Days:					
1.	BACKGROUND GAMBLER			9/5	9/6	2
2.	TABLE DEALERS			9/5	9/5	1
3.	TOURISTS			9/5	9/5	1
4.	CASINO WAITRESSES			9/5	9/14	8
5.	ATMOSPHERE EXTRAS			9/5	9/7	3
6.	CASHIER			9/5	9/5	1
7.	DOORMAN			9/7	9/7	1
8.	BAR PATRONS			9/7	9/7	1
9.	DINER PATRONS			9/13	9/14	2
10.	PARTY GUESTS			9/15	9/15	1

September	Day of Month:	5	6	7	8	9	10	11	12	13	14	15	Rehearse	Travel	Work	Hold
	Day Of Week:	Tu	W	Th	F	Sa	Su	M	Tu	W	Th	F				
	Shooting Days:	1	2	3	4			5	6	7	8	9				
1.	12-PACK OF BEER								SWF						1	
2.	ANSWERING MACHINE				SW			WF							2	
3.	ASHTRAYS		SW	W	H			H	WF						3	2
4.	BEER BOTTLE			SW	H			H	H	H	H	WF			2	5
5.	BEER BOTTLES			SW	H			H	W	H	H	WF			3	4
6.	BILLFOLD		SWF												1	
7.	BREAKFAST FOOD										SWF				1	
8.	BROWN BAG							SWF							1	
9.	CIGARETTES	SW	W	W	H			W	W	W	H	WF			7	2
10.	CIGARS		SW	W	H			H	H	H	H	WF			3	5
11.	CLOCK				SW			WF							2	
12.	COCKTAIL NAPKIN	SW	H	H	W			H	H	H	H	WF			3	6
13.	COCKTAILS	SW	W	W	H			H	H	H	WF				4	5
14.	COFFEE CUPS		SW	H	H			H	H	W	WF				3	4
15.	DICE ON VALVE CAP	SWF													1	
16.	DINER FOOD		SW	H	H			H	H	W	WF				3	4
17.	ENCASED CAMERA		SWF												1	
18.	GAMBLING CHIPS	SW	WF												2	
19.	GREETING CARDS							SWF							1	
20.	KEYS	SW	H	H	WF										2	2
21.	LIQUOR BOTTLES										SWF				1	
22.	LORRAINE'S CARD							SWF							1	
23.	MENUS		SW	H	H			H	H	H	WF				2	5
24.	MONEY		SW	W	H	H		H	W	WF					4	3
25.	NAUTICAL DECOR	SWF													1	
26.	ORANGE JUICE							SWF							1	
27.	PEN							SW	H	H	H	WF			2	3
28.	PEPPERONI							SWF							1	
29.	PHONE			SW				W	WF						3	
30.	PIZZA BOXES								SWF						1	
31.	SEGA HOCKEY GAME								SWF						1	
32.	SEMOLINA							SWF							1	
33.	SWISS ARMY KNIFE							SWF							1	
34.	TABLE															
35.	WALL CALENDAR				SW			WF							2	

(continued)

Figure 5–4   Swingers *day-out-of-days sheets (cast, extras, and props) (continued)*

		Day of Month:	Holiday	Loop	Start	Finish	TOTAL
		Day Of Week:					
		Shooting Days:					
1.	12-PACK OF BEER				9/12	9/12	1
2.	ANSWERING MACHINE				9/8	9/11	2
3.	ASHTRAYS				9/6	9/12	5
4.	BEER BOTTLE				9/7	9/15	7
5.	BEER BOTTLES				9/7	9/15	7
6.	BILLFOLD				9/6	9/6	1
7.	BREAKFAST FOOD				9/14	9/14	1
8.	BROWN BAG				9/11	9/11	1
9.	CIGARETTES				9/5	9/15	9
10.	CIGARS				9/6	9/15	8
11.	CLOCK				9/8	9/11	2
12.	COCKTAIL NAPKIN				9/5	9/15	9
13.	COCKTAILS				9/5	9/15	9
14.	COFFEE CUPS				9/6	9/14	7
15.	DICE ON VALVE CAP				9/5	9/5	1
16.	DINER FOOD				9/6	9/14	7
17.	ENCASED CAMERA				9/6	9/6	1
18.	GAMBLING CHIPS				9/5	9/6	2
19.	GREETING CARDS				9/11	9/11	1
20.	KEYS				9/5	9/8	4
21.	LIQUOR BOTTLES				9/15	9/15	1
22.	LORRAINE'S CARD				9/11	9/11	1
23.	MENUS				9/6	9/14	7
24.	MONEY				9/5	9/13	7
25.	NAUTICAL DECOR				9/5	9/5	1
26.	ORANGE JUICE				9/11	9/11	1
27.	PEN				9/11	9/15	5
28.	PEPPERONI				9/11	9/11	1
29.	PHONE				9/8	9/12	3
30.	PIZZA BOXES				9/12	9/12	1
31.	SEGA HOCKEY GAME				9/12	9/12	1
32.	SEMOLINA				9/11	9/11	1
33.	SWISS ARMY KNIFE				9/11	9/11	1
34.	TABLE						
35.	WALL CALENDAR				9/8	9/11	2

Figure 5–4 Swingers *day-out-of-days sheets (cast, extras, and props) (continued)*

The following information can be derived from the day-out-of-days sheet for the *Swingers* cast:

- Mike started work on Tuesday, September 5, shoot day 1, and worked every day until the production was off on Saturday, September 9, and Sunday, September 10. Mike finished work on Friday, September 15, shoot day 9. He had no hold or travel days during this period.
- Trent started work on Tuesday, September 5, shoot day 1. He was on hold on Friday, September 8, Monday, September 11, and Thursday, September 14. He finished work the next day, shoot day 9.
- Lisa started work and finished work on Thursday, September 7, shoot day 3.

The day-out-of-days includes a summary page that reflects the total number of workdays, hold days, holidays, and looping days for each actor. According to Figure 5–4, Mike worked a total of nine days. He had no hold days. Trent worked six days and was on hold for three days, totaling nine days of pay. Rob worked five days and was on hold for two days, giving a total of seven days. None of these characters had rehearsal days or travel days during this period.

Refer to the day-out-of-days summary page when budgeting to determine how to pay each actor (that is, as a weekly player, a daily player, or a drop-pickup), and to determine which dates to secure locations, certain equipment, vehicles, extras, and so on. (See Chapter 6 for further detail.)

6 BUDGETING

You start with the script and the script becomes a movie and the movie obviously has a relationship to the script. But the script is sort of the skeleton and, in a way, that's what a budget is like, too. And your cost report, then, is really this living, breathing document that, as you're working, starts telling you the truth. Say you've budgeted for 4,500 feet of film a day, and you're consistently shooting 6,500 feet of film a day. You can hold onto that budget until the cows come home, but the fact is you are not doing what it said. Your cost report is a tool to find other places to work that cost in because that becomes the reality. And shooting film is always the hardest thing; it's the one place where you just can't say, "Stop shooting. Just don't shoot. We're overbudget here. Let's just have a day of not shooting, and we'll be back on track."

—Christine Vachon, producer, Killer Films

INTRODUCTION TO BUDGETING

Once you have completed the breakdown and preliminary schedule, you have to run the numbers to ensure that you can make the film you want for the money you have. The budget will tell you how much it will cost to make your film. It will help you keep track of all of the film's needs, and by actualizing the budget, you will track money spent and money available. Be certain that you have enough money to get the film both in and out of the can.

Be as precise as possible when budgeting a film. Contact potential vendors to verify any deals you think you may be able to make. Contact the locations you want to secure and the permit office of the city in which you are shooting to ascertain all fees involved. If the production will need to travel, get actual quotes from airlines and hotels. Compare quotes from several catering companies, or figure out a creative way to cater the shoot for less money. If the show is nonunion, determine the most cost-effective way to structure crew rates, keeping in mind that you need to be fair to everyone. Call the Screen Actors Guild if the show is a SAG show, for the rates and any financial assurances that you will have to pay. The bottom line is that your numbers must be real.

After an initial pass at the budget, go through it again and double-check your numbers. Budget extra money for some of the categories and line items, especially those areas in which you are still uncertain about what the actual costs will be. Padding the budget in this way ensures that you'll be covered. Have a budget wizard, or someone who has made a low-budget film before and is familiar with the costs you'll need to budget for, check and challenge your numbers.

The Budget Is Malleable

The budget is the best assessment of the costs involved in making a movie based on preliminary quotes. The budget is a blueprint. It is *not* set in stone. Most likely, the money actually spent on each line item will deviate from the original number allocated in the budget. Your budget must be flexible enough to support any unexpected costs. Each category need not conform to its initial allocation. You can use the money saved in one category to cover overages in another. (Try to avoid this, but it is an option.) This, in part, is why budgets are padded. You will never be able to anticipate everything that might come up, and the needs of the film might change during filming. Almost all independent films could use more money, but the budget is a tool that tells you whether the little you do have will allow you to make the film.

What You'll Need

Before you begin to compile your budget, gather the script, preliminary shooting schedule, day-out-of-days sheets, strip board, calculator, scratch paper, and a pencil. The schedule and day-out-of-days will dictate how long each actor, crew member, piece of equipment, vehicle, location, prop, and so on, is needed and will help you budget properly for all of the film's needs.

Using This Manual

As you use this manual for current and future productions, keep in mind that you may have to adjust the budget numbers upward by 10% to 15% to accommodate price increases, new union rates, and other market changes. Generally speaking, the budget formats and the sample figures included in this chapter will provide a helpful yardstick for planning and accounting for a film's costs and needs.

In this chapter, you will find the *Swingers* budget, three sample budgets prepared using the Movie Magic Budgeting software, and a $62,000 budget prepared without any budget software. Movie Magic Budgeting offers different blank budget forms that you can use when compiling a budget (Paramount, Universal, Sony, and HBO, for example). Depending on which budget form you choose, the budget categories and account codes will vary. You might also choose to create your own categories and account codes. The blank "Paramount" budget form reproduced in Figure 6–1 is the form that we used when compiling the three sample budgets. (See the end of Chapter 6, starting on page 90, to review all sample budgets mentioned in this chapter.)

This chapter includes definitions, examples, comparisons, and tips on budgeting the line items found within the sample budgets. It will be most helpful if you read through it once and then refer back to the budgets and line item definitions as you are budgeting, using this manual to help you determine the costs for which you will need to budget. Note that the *Swingers* budget and the sample budgets included here are not final shooting budgets.

A Note about Budgets and Line Items

Every film has different needs, and many of the budget categories and line items included in the forms provided by Movie Magic Budgeting and other budgeting programs may not represent items you'll need to account for when budgeting your film. The three sample budgets in this chapter don't always reflect the categories or line items of the blank budget form; each was compiled according to the individual film's needs. In some instances we created new line items and put them in the category that made most sense to us. We assigned them account codes accordingly.

Feel free to create and delete categories and line items as necessary. Don't worry if you need to create a line item that you've never seen before. It is important only that you budget for everything required to make the film and that you account for each item in the most appropriate category. This way, the costs will be included within the most appropriate section of the budget (Above-the-Line Costs, Production, Postproduction, Other). When examining the three sample budgets, you may notice that certain line items are accounted for in different categories or with different account codes. This will happen, and there will be crossovers. Read the explanations of the line items carefully. The definitions provided will help you determine your film's needs and budget properly for its costs.

Budget Structure

Layers

A budget is made up of three layers. The top sheet, the first of the layers, lists the totals for each category and section, as well as the grand total. The second layer is the account level, which lists all of the line items within each category by account code. The third layer is the detail level of the budget, which is where you will enter any information and equations and break out your rates and costs. A computer program will automatically do the math for you. The detail level is a subaccount of the account category it relates to.

Sections, Categories, and Line Items

Budgets are broken into four sections. In Figure 6–1, the sections are Above-the-Line Costs, Production, Postproduction, and Other. Each section includes categories specific to the section and account codes specific to each category. For example, the Story category is part of the Above-the-Line-Costs section and is assigned the account code 600 in Figure 6–1. The categories are further broken down into line items. Each line item is assigned the same three-digit account code as the category to which it belongs, plus a two-digit number specific to it. For example, the subaccount code for the Rights Purchase line item is 600-01. The line items in each category are added together to arrive at the total cost of a given category.

Account Codes

All of the sample budgets included in this chapter start with account code 600. Categories 600 through 650 include all of the above-the-line costs. Above-the-line costs cover the creative components of a film. The story, producer, director, and cast categories are the large ones, and these categories are broken down into related line items. Categories 700 through 798 include all of the below-the-line costs. Below-the-line costs cover the manual labor or technical aspects of a film: the crew, equipment, locations, props, wardrobe, sound, transportation, and so on. The total cost of the below-the-line section is the total for the shooting period. Categories 800 through 870 include all of the postproduction costs, such as editing and music. The postproduction section reflects the total for the completion period of the film.

Categories 910 through 950 include administrative and publicity costs. Below this fourth section is where you will find the budget grand total, and the combined total of the above- and below-the-line sections. You will also see totals for contractual charges and other costs. These other costs, figured as percentages of the overall budget, include the completion bond, contingency, overhead, and insurance. (See "Budget Terms" later in this chapter.) Except for the insurance, these contractual charges are not always amounts that will be spent. Movie Magic Budgeting allows you to set contractual charges that will automatically be applied to the budget once they are selected.

Using Movie Magic Budgeting

If you will be using Movie Magic Budgeting, refer to the instruction manual. It will save you time by introducing you to all of the features of the program. Keep in mind that account codes, categories, and line items can be created or deleted in any of the budget forms included in the program. Be sure to set all contractual charges so that they will be applied automatically to the budget. You will also need to apply fringes to the budget when appropriate. (See "Budget Terms" later in this chapter.) Apply fringes to selected line items by calling up the fringes box and choosing the fringes you want to apply to the selected line items. (The user's manual will tell you how.)

A global is any variable that will be used consistently throughout the budget and can be preset. Prep time is already preset in the global set up box. Adjust the number of weeks to reflect the amount of prep time you'll need. For example, if the prep time on the film is five weeks, enter the word *prep* into the column of the global set up box in which it belongs, and account for it as five weeks in the weeks column of the set up box. When you type the word *prep* into the detail level of a line item in which you are budgeting for prep time, the program will automatically account for prep time in the units field as five weeks and will perform the equation for you. Do the same for shoot and wrap time and other variables. You may change contractual charges, fringes, and globals at any time while you are budgeting.

About the Sample Budgets

The Swingers Budget

A preliminary budget for *Swingers* is reproduced in Figure 6–2, and the top sheet of the actualized budget appears in Figure 6–3. *Swingers* is a dialogue-driven script that was shot primarily in Los Angeles. The cast and crew were local to Los Angeles and therefore paid as nonunion locals with no per diem. Crew rates were budgeted on flat weekly rates,

and no overtime was paid. Because the actors were friends and the script was shopped for some time before financing was secured, the principal cast had rehearsed and performed readings of the script a number of times before preproduction; therefore, rehearsal time was not imperative. (In addition, it was an expense the budget could not absorb.) We knew we could shoot multiple scenes in a day because the actors were well rehearsed and the majority of the scenes required few principal actors.

Swingers required numerous extras, a problem that we solved by shooting in certain locations while they were open to the public. We posted filming notices and secured personal releases from patrons who appeared in the shot. (See Chapter 8.) No action sequences or stunts were required, and there was no need for any special equipment. We wanted the film to look as real as possible, so we shot in as many actual scripted locations as we could. As a result, the sets required little dressing and fewer props than would have been necessary had we shot on a stage. We used natural light whenever possible and kept our lighting package to a minimum. Using few lights kept the size of the crew and electrical costs down. The small crew also accommodated the size of the spaces we were filming in and enabled us to move quickly and complete the film in three weeks.

We were able to make deals on our equipment, processing, film stock, picture vehicles, and locations that kept the budget down. The difficult part was securing the casino in Las Vegas and transporting the crew, cast, vehicles, and equipment there inexpensively. We needed to provide hotel rooms and per diem to the cast and crew while filming in Las Vegas. (We will tell you how we dealt with these things more specifically when we address the line items below and in Chapter 8.) The bulk of the money was spent in cast, editing, locations, production staff, and production dailies. By running the initial numbers and considering the deals we were able to make, we knew that we could make the film for the money we had.

Sample Budget 1

Sample budget 1, shown in Figure 6–4, is for a character-driven piece that requires mostly interior daytime filming. The budget is based on a local, nonunion crew with flat weekly rates budgeted on a favored-nations basis. Preproduction will be five weeks, and production will be three six-day weeks. (Shooting three six-day weeks rather than four five-day weeks will save money on crew and equipment rentals.) Because of the nonunion status of the crew, six-day weeks do not necessarily have to be paid at time and a half or at a premium rate, as they would on a union show. No overtime has been applied to crew members, though a flat weekly kit rental will be paid to department heads who rent their own supplies to the production. The crew for this show is slightly larger than the crew for *Swingers*. Additions include a production accountant, a second second assistant director for two weeks of the shoot to keep the show moving on schedule and to avoid overtime, a lead man, a swing gang member, an extra grip and electrician, and both a makeup artist and a hairstylist.

The cast was budgeted based on SAG's low-budget agreement (under $2 million), and overtime was applied to the SAG cast. The film will be shot entirely in Los Angeles (no travel or lodging costs need to be allocated) in preexisting locations, many of which will be open to the public during the shoot, allowing the film to feel real and to save money on having to hire the extras needed in many of the locations. The two most expensive locations will be a bar and a club. Using preexisting locations will also save money on construction costs; stage fees; set, art, and prop rentals and purchases; and strike and rig fees.

Because this picture will be financed through a combination of personal savings and independent investors, only contingency was applied to the budget at 10%, and a bond company will not have to be engaged.

Sample Budget 2

Sample budget 2, shown in Figure 6–5, is for a local, nonunion crew paid on a daily rate. Overtime compensation for the crew is budgeted at 15% and cast overtime at 20%. It is a dialogue-driven piece that has more principal characters than *Swingers* as well as a greater number of locations (16 scripted locales, as opposed to *Swingers'* 15). With the exception of the Brighton Beach boardwalk and a casino in Atlantic City, it takes place in remote rural and suburban areas, in private homes, and in other relatively inexpensive locations.

Because of the nature of the financing for this picture (a combination of equity, foreign sales, and a bank loan), it was necessary to apply all contractual costs to the budget and to engage a bond company. The bond company set parameters for how the budget had to be structured. (See "Dealing with a Bond Company" later in this chapter.)

The cast is budgeted primarily on a favored-nations basis following the SAG low-budget agreement. The crew pay scale is significantly higher than on *Swingers* but still within low-budget parameters. Crew overtime is budgeted at 15%, and although this is low, it was all that the budget could sustain. Note that deals were made with some key crew people who were guaranteed higher pay than others (not strict favored nations).

Sample Budget 3

Sample budget 3, shown in Figure 6–6, is for a local, nonunion crew, paid on a flat weekly rate. However, overtime is accounted for within each crew member's line item and is applied at 20% of the total sum of his or her salary for the production period only. The script is set in a small desert town in California and in Las Vegas, neither of which is an expensive location to secure. The number of principal players is larger in this budget than in the *Swingers* budget or sample budget 2. The cast pay (SAG scale), travel, living, and necessary fringes amount to significantly more money in this budget than in the other two.

Sample budget 3 was prepared for fund-raising purposes and therefore has not been actualized. (The film hasn't been made yet.) All contractual costs were included because it was likely that with a budget of this level, financing would be secured at least partially from a film production company or a bank that would require both a contingency and a bond.

BUDGETING TERMS

Below you'll find definitions for key budgeting terms that will be helpful to know as you budget your film. All of the terms below are also cross-referenced in the Glossary in the back of the book.

Agency Fees

Each cast member must pay his or her agent a 10% fee. It is common practice within the industry for the production to pay the agency fee in addition to the actor's salary.

Completion Bond

A completion bond is required when a film's financing is secured through an independent film company or a bank. This insurance policy serves as a guarantee to the financing entity that the film will be completed. A completion bond is usually computed at 3% of the budget total. The bond company guarantees to pay for any cost overruns, thereby ensuring that the film will be completed. In the event that the bond company must actually kick in money to complete the film, it will virtually take over the set and own the film. The bond company can replace the director, the producer, and any crew member it chooses. Not only must the bond company approve the budget before you go into production, but it must also approve the people hired for key crew positions.

Contingency

Contingency was applied to all of the sample budgets at 10%, which is usual. Contingency serves as a cushion to protect against the uncertainty involved in making films. Contingency is applied to the below-the-line costs of the budget. A higher contingency may be required for larger-budget films depending on the nature of the financing.

Favored Nations

This term indicates that a cast or crew member will receive treatment on par with the best that the producer is offering anyone else on the set, but not better. It refers in particular to pay and perks (dressing rooms, travel, accommodations, and so on). We try to run our sets on a favored-nations basis and furnish everyone with an acceptable standard and no one with a lavish standard. Certain established cast or crew members may not accept this approach. Arrangements are always open to negotiation. You may, however, have to meet a particular actor's or crew member's request to keep him or her involved in the project.

Flat Fee

Crew compensation and equipment rentals can be arranged on the basis of a *flat fee* (as opposed to a daily or a weekly rate). There are potential advantages to this arrangement. When you agree to a flat fee, the cost remains the same regardless of how many days or weeks it ultimately takes to complete filming or of how much overtime is worked. An *allow* differs from a flat fee in that it is money allocated for a given expense, the exact cost of which has not yet been determined.

Kit Rental

A kit rental is a fee paid for equipment or supplies that a crew member provides to the production. For example, you may have to budget a kit rental fee for a makeup artist who has her own makeup supplies. The fee depends on the department and the budget of the show. It can be paid in a lump sum or budgeted for on a weekly basis. The kit rental fee is not subject to payroll taxes.

Overhead

On an independent film, overhead is applied as a percentage of the overall budget; it can range from 1% to 10%. Overhead is meant to cover certain preproduction costs, office rental, utility costs, nominal development costs, and out-of-pocket expenses of those who are involved with the project for some time before the film is financed.

Production Insurance

Typically, production insurance is calculated at 2% to 3.5% of the budget. All independent films must be insured to secure equipment, locations, transportation, props, wardrobe, cast, crew, and so on, and the policy must be purchased before the production period officially begins. Notice in sample budget 2 that the insurance is accounted for in line item 910-08, rather than as a percentage of the budget total, as in the other budgets included here.

Loan-Out Company

A loan-out company is a corporation that "loans" the services of its employee. Certain members of the above- and below-the-line staff may want to be paid as "loan-outs." When hiring a loan-out, the producer (or the producer's payroll company) does not deduct employee payroll taxes or add fringes to the loan-out's pay. Instead, the loan-out company is responsible for absorbing the tax liability on the income. This can be less costly for the production, but in some instances, an actor or crew person will require that the production cover the fringes. A word of warning: If the production doesn't pay the fringes on a loan-out crew or cast member and the IRS discovers during an audit of the loan-out company that employee taxes were not paid, the IRS could hold the production company responsible for the fringes or the payroll taxes. Any employee paid as a loan-out must provide papers of incorporation, a federal identification number or employee identification number (EIN), and proof of worker's compensation insurance so that in the event he or she is hurt on the set, the production company will be protected.

Loss and Damage

Loss and damage (L&D) is a line item that you should include for almost every department for which you are renting equipment or materials. The most conservative way to handle budgeting for L&D is to set aside an amount in each department's budget equal to the amount of the deductible on the production insurance policy. For example, if your deductible is $1,200, you would budget $1,200 for L&D in each department category. (Insurance deductibles must usually be met on a per-occurrence basis.) What low budgets often reflect is the equivalent of the deductible for the departments for which equipment is costly, such as camera, and less money for departments such as wardrobe. This money ensures that the production will be covered in the event that a lens is broken or a costume is irreparably damaged. You may never use this money, in which case it will be money saved when you actualize your budget.

DEALING WITH A BOND COMPANY

If the financing of your film is such that a completion bond is required, you will have to meet with a bond company representative and "defend" your budget. Prepare for this meeting carefully. The bond company rep will go through your budget line item by line item and ask how you arrived at each cost. If you have allows or flat fees in your budget, you will have to substantiate those numbers with actual quotes from vendors. The bond company will require that you budget overtime for both cast and crew. By and large, bond company reps know a great deal about line producing films and will ask solid questions. The difficult aspect for filmmakers whose budgets require them to "shoot from the hip" is that the bond company cannot approve a budget that is based on deals you *think* you may be able to secure.

Don't let the bond company get in the way of your making your film, but understand that you will have to abide by its rules and regulations. The bond company will require that you submit daily production reports as well as weekly cost reports. The bond company will require that you have an accountant, and the accountant and an assistant will be instrumental in preparing weekly cost reports.

THE BUDGETS AND THEIR LINE ITEMS

600-00 Story

Scripts evolve in different ways and that evolution will dictate how you budget the line items below. Be certain to adhere to any contractual obligations you may have when budgeting your story costs.

600-01 Rights Purchase

This line item covers the purchase of any underlying rights to property or material, such as the rights to someone's life story or the rights to a story, novel, or play on which the script is based. In sample budget 2 (Figure 6–5), $50,000 was budgeted for the purchase of the short story on which the script was based. This is relatively high for a low-budget endeavor, but because the story was written by a well-known writer, the cost was deemed worthwhile. Negotiate to the best of your ability to keep this number as low as possible.

600-03 Writers

Budget this category if you have a writer-for-hire (as opposed to a spec script), if you anticipate engaging a writer to assist with rewrites during the filming process, or if you have commissioned a writer to pen the script. If you have paid the writer out of your own pocket over the months or years taken to get the project to this point, budget appropriately so you will be reimbursed the costs. Notice that none of the sample budgets have money allocated in this category. None of the indie pictures we've worked on thus far have required that we engage a writer-for-hire.

600-04 Screenplay Purchase

At this stage, you should have an agreement with the writer that spells out the cost of the screenplay when you exercise your option. (See Chapter 2.) Include both the option price and the purchase price in this line item. If it's a percentage of the overall budget with a floor and a ceiling (the floor is the minimum cost; the ceiling the maximum cost), start by entering a middle amount. You will make it more exact when the budget is complete. You will need to apply fringes to this amount unless the writer is a loan-out. Generally, when a significant sum of money will be paid, it makes sense for the writer to incorporate and form a "loan-out" company to reduce his or her tax burden.

On *Swingers,* the agreement with the writer, Jon Favreau, was a $1,000 fee with contingent compensation guaranteed only if the film was sold. Therefore, in this category we budgeted $1,000 (see Figure 6–2). This was a bare-bones budget, reflecting the least amount of money we could make the movie for. It didn't include the amount guaranteed to Favreau if the film sold. Although the amount was specified in his contract, it was not money that had to be paid out of the production budget.

600-05 Research

This line item is for research costs for your screenplay. If you're buying a screenplay, you probably won't need to budget any money here. If you wrote the script and did the research yourself, or if you commissioned a writer to write the script and do the research, those costs need to be reimbursed.

600-11 Script Copying

Script photocopying costs are budgeted in this line item. For sample budget 2 (Figure 6–5), 100 script copies were budgeted. Over the course of the development period of this film, at least that many copies were generated.

610-00 Producer

610-01 Executive Producer

If you're raising money, this line item will initially be zero. You don't know what fee the executive producer (if you get one) will take, if any, beyond the money that he or she will invest or secure to make the film. Often, on independent pictures, the executive producer credit is given to people based on various types of involvement. Unless you know for sure that you will have an executive producer and what his or her fee will be, leave this line item blank. You can plug in the number later if necessary.

610-02 Producer

Producers' fees depend on the situation and on the overall budget. On *Swingers,* every crew member was paid $300 per week (favored nations), including the producer (see Figure 6–2). The producer is in the budget for a greater number of weeks than anyone else because the producer's job, in effect, spanned the largest time period. Sample budget 2 (Figure 6–5) has $2,500 allocated for each producer. Originally, this fee was higher, but due to budget limitations the fee was gradually reduced until it was whittled down to $2,500. Sample budget 1 (Figure 6–4) has a $5,000 flat fee for each producer, which, if broken down into an hourly rate, is still very low pay. Producers on independent films often waive their fees in order to get the movie made. More often than not, when a producer is paid, it is either a prenegotiated flat fee or a percentage of the total budget, not a weekly rate as with *Swingers.*

610-07 Producer's Entertainment

Depending on the type of show you're running and the source of your financing, you may want to allocate some money for entertainment. Will you be taking potential investors or cast members out for lunch? You may want to take department heads to see a film that relates to the film you're making. Even if it's a nominal amount, try to estimate your actual costs realistically. Account for all potential expenses, and add sales tax to purchases.

610-08 Preproduction Expenses

Inevitably, you will have preproduction expenses. If you're going with a bare-bones budget you can leave this line item blank, but everyone will need to eat (you will pick up the tab on meals), the office will need supplies, and you'll tip when necessary. You'll end up spending the money one way or another, and it's best to account for some expenses here and allow the film to cover these costs if possible.

620-00 Director

620-01 Director

On *Swingers,* everyone worked for a reduced rate and on a favored-nations basis. Note that the director was budgeted for $1,000 (see Figure 6–2). Remember that everything is negotiable. You might find a director who is willing to defer part or all of his or her fee. In sample budget 2 (Figure 6–5), the director was willing to do anything to get the picture

made and agreed to a nominal fee. She was not a director-for-hire. Your primary concern as the line producer is to be certain that those who agree to defer their fees have the financial wherewithal to survive and do the job 150%. If your director is a member of the Directors Guild of America (DGA), you will need to operate within the guild's rules. The DGA sets minimums for fees and the number of weeks a director must be paid. Contact the DGA for current information. (Newer versions of Movie Magic Budgeting list some of the guild's rates.)

620-05 Casting Director

Budget for a casting director if you can afford one. In addition to being a significant creative contributor, the casting director will oversee the casting process, negotiate talent deals, call the Station 12 department of SAG, and facilitate the casting process in other ways. (See Chapter 7 for information on Station 12.) Try to cut a deal with a casting director who will agree to a flat fee. Most casting directors are loan-outs, so it's up to you whether to apply fringes here.

620-08 Casting Expenses

In this line item, budget for casting expenses, including renting a space in which to hold auditions, photocopying script pages (sides), and providing some food and beverages. On *Swingers,* we budgeted $200 (see Figure 6–2). We held auditions in the producer's home and supplied food and drinks. In sample budget 2 (Figure 6–5), $300 was budgeted for casting expenses because it was necessary to rent a space for a nominal fee and provide some beverages and snacks.

630-00 Cast

630-01 Principal Players

Look at your day-out-of-days sheet for your cast. Any actor who is needed for more than three days in a row is considered a principal player and must be budgeted on a weekly rate. On *Swingers,* the core group of boys—Mike, Trent, Rob, and Sue—were all weekly players (see Figure 6–2). The SAG low-budget scale pay at the time was $1,558 (U.S. 1995) per week. In addition to government fringes, which include FICA, SUI, and FUI, you should also include an agency commission of 10% of each actor's earnings. (See "Budgeting Terms" above.) If it's a SAG production, the SAG Corp fringe is applied at 13.3% (1999). (Rates may change, so verify first.) Although it isn't mandatory that the production pay the 10% agency fee, it is an expected courtesy. It is safe to assume that government fringes will amount to approximately 18%.

Note how the character Rob was accounted for in the *Swingers* budget (Figure 6–2). We made a mistake here. At the time, we thought it would be less expensive to pay him as a daily player than as a weekly player because he worked few consecutive days. It turned out to be more expensive because Rob was put on hold and the production had to pay for hold days, even though he was not working. (See Chapter 5.) We didn't realize this at the time, so we ended up paying the actor more than if we had scheduled him as a weekly player. We also could have budgeted him as a drop-pickup, which means that if we needed him for two days in the beginning of the shoot but not again until the end, we could have dropped him and then picked him up again, without paying for hold days in between. The risk with a drop-pickup is that the actor is free to take other work in the meantime and could be unavailable to your production when next needed. In current SAG low-budget agreements, the consecutive employment requirement is often waived, so if your budget is low, the issue of hold days and a drop-pickups may be irrelevant. Check with SAG in order to budget for your cast properly.

SAG now has several agreements: a low-budget agreement (the budget must be under $2 million), an affirmative-action low-budget agreement (under $2.75 million), a modified low-budget agreement (under $500,000), a limited exhibition agreement (under $200,000), and an experimental film agreement (under $75,000). The *SAG Film Contracts Digest* specifies the parameters of these agreements. When we made *Swingers,* the low-budget agreement was the only contract option in effect. Had we shot only two months later, we would have qualified for the modified low-budget agreement and saved about one-half of our cast costs.

All three sample budgets include cast fees based on SAG low-budget scale rates. If you have an actor who demands more than scale, you will have to negotiate his or her fee. If yours is a non-SAG show, you can pay whatever rate you and your cast members agree to. If it's a SAG production but you have an actor who is not yet a member of the guild, you will have to submit a Taft-Hartley form to the guild within 15 days from the date of hire. (See Chapter 8.) The guild will charge you a preference claim, which is a penalty for having hired a nonguild actor, the cost of which is currently $400. (Call SAG to determine the current rate.) Budget for this cost if you anticipate having a mixed cast of SAG and non-SAG members. Make sure your actors know that they will have to pay dues to join the guild within 30 days of their start-work date.

630-02 Day Players
Look at your day-out-of-days sheet to determine which of your characters will be played by day players. Any actor who works a total of three consecutive days or fewer should be

budgeted as a day player. When preproduction begins, you will negotiate with SAG and become a guild signatory. Only then will you determine what the union scale rates will be at the time of your shoot for the SAG agreement that best fits your project. For now, a quick call to SAG for rates will suffice. You'll need to inform SAG of your total budget along with other information. Don't forget to apply fringes to day players' pay.

630-03 Rehearsal
In sample budget 2 (Figure 6–5), we separated shoot time and rehearsal time when budgeting principal players and created line item 630-03. We budgeted five cast members for three days of rehearsal. It's fine to include rehearsal time in line item 630-01 instead, adding estimated rehearsal time to the time you have budgeted each actor for filming. Rehearsal time is considered normal work time by the guild and is paid as such, fringes and all.

In sample budget 3 (Figure 6–6), the rehearsal time was included in line item 630-01. This is why the first two principal players are budgeted for six weeks of work, while the header on the budget states that it's a five-week shoot. The additional week is for rehearsal. Fringes were applied.

630-05 SAG Residuals
Residuals are money earned by an actor when a film sells and plays in foreign territories. SAG has recently started to request that low-budget productions put up money for SAG residuals in advance of filming in addition to the bond. This can be a large sum relative to the overall budget. Although everything is negotiable with SAG, you may want to budget up to $10,000 in this category as a contingency.

630-06 Looping/ADR
Looping, or additional dialogue replacement (ADR), sessions will take place after your shoot has wrapped and you have decided which lines of dialogue need to be rerecorded or added. SAG requires that actors be paid scale (or whatever their agreed-on rate above and beyond scale) for the days they attend a looping session. It is safe to assume that you will need some of your principal actors (and often day players) for looping, so budget each principal player for at least one day of looping. Most likely, you will not need all of them. Try to negotiate one day of looping into your initial contract with each actor.

630-07 Meal Penalties
All of the sample budgets (Figures 6–4 to 6–6) have a line item for meal penalties. If your cast is SAG, you will have to

pay meal penalties if you work cast members more than six hours in a row without providing a meal. For example, if lunch is served late, you will pay a meal penalty to any actor who breaks for lunch more than six hours after his or her call time. The meal penalty will be figured into the cast time cards and paid as part of their salary. Even if your shoot is nonunion, make every effort to abide by guild rules. These rules were created in the interest of workers and are important regulations to uphold.

630-08 Overtime

On a SAG production, weekly players are paid for a 44-hour workweek, and daily players are paid for an 8-hour day. If a weekly player works for more than 10 hours in one day, or a day player for more than 8 hours, the guild requires that you compensate the actor for overtime, which is usually paid as time and a half up to 12 hours, and double time for each hour thereafter. Overtime is likely to occur, so budget accordingly.

630-09 Medical Exams

Most companies that provide production insurance require that key cast members have a medical exam before beginning principal photography. The cost of several medical exams is included in all of the sample budgets (Figures 6–4 to 6–6). The director should be budgeted for an exam as well.

630-20 Side Deals

A side deal is money above and beyond scale that you anticipate paying one or more of your actors. This line item is used to account for any side deals you may make with cameo actors, extras, musicians, and so on. (See the *Swingers* budget, Figure 6–2.)

640-00 Fringes

A fringe is any cost above and beyond a central cost. For example, sales tax, employee taxes, and agency fees are all considered fringes.

None of the budgets included here has a fringes category per se; instead, the fringes are built into each relevant category. We have found that this is an easier way to organize the budget because it allows us to see the fringe costs for each line item and the total fringes for each category.

Adjust the fringe rates in Movie Magic Budgeting by choosing the Fringes command under the Set up heading. When you want to apply fringes to a given line item or category, click on the percent sign in the top-middle section of the screen. A box will appear with all established fringe costs. Select the fringe costs that apply to the given line item.

650-00 Travel and Living

Budget here for above-the-line travel and living costs (cast, producers, director, writer, and so on). When a production travels out of town (that is, when it shoots on location), the production is required to pay for the travel and living costs of cast and crew members who travel to work on the show. For example, if you're shooting in Park City, Utah, cast and crew members from Park City are considered local hires, and you need not pay for their travel and living expenses. However, if you need to bring employees from Los Angeles to Park City, Utah, you must provide them with travel, lodging, and a per diem (see Figures 6–5 and 6–6). If the employees in question are members of a union, check with the union for minimum per diem rates. If not, come up with a rate that is sufficient given the local cost of living, for employees to buy meals, do laundry, and so on. Don't forget gratuities and sales tax. Further, cast contracts often stipulate that the production provide certain accommodations (i.e., three-star hotel, a driver, etc.).

650-01 Producer Travel and Producer Living

In the *Swingers* budget (Figure 6–2), no money was allocated for producer travel because a production van, accounted for in the Transportation category (770-00), took most of the crew and the producer to Vegas. In sample budget 2 (Figure 6–5), the producers anticipated that the film would be shot on the East Coast but edited in Los Angeles, and they knew that one of the producers would have to make several trips across country; therefore, $1600 was allotted for the travel expenses.

If your production will be traveling to a location where you will have to sleep overnight, you must budget for living accommodations. For the producing unit on *Swingers*, we budgeted three nights in Las Vegas. We secured an inexpensive deal on hotel rooms, which cost us approximately $25 per night. Don't forget sales tax and gratuities.

650-02 Director

In all travel categories, refer to your schedule to determine how many locations above-the-line talent will travel to. Determine the mode of transportation required (plane, train, automobile). Make some phone calls to determine the cost, taking into consideration how each person will, or is required by contract to, travel (first class or economy).

Look at your schedule to determine how long you will be on location. Make some calls to determine what your hotel or motel costs will be. If your director is not a member of the DGA, establish a per diem rate that is reasonable for the locale so that the director can cover such expenses as transportation and food on days off.

650-03 Writer

In each of the three sample budgets (Figures 6–4 to 6–6), the writer was involved in the project in another capacity as well (either as an actor or director), so no extra money was allocated for the writer's travel. (The cost of his or her travel was accounted for under line item 650-02 or 650-06.) If you engage a writer-for-hire and require that the writer be on the set, budget travel and living expenses as you would for the director.

650-06 Cast Travel and Living/Per Diem

Refer to your schedule to determine which actors need to be where, when, and for how long. Find out the cost of the actors' required mode of transportation. If not stipulated in the actor's contract, budget for the safest and most affordable mode of transportation.

The guild has guidelines about how its members may travel. When you're budgeting your cast, remember that travel days are paid as regular workdays. High-profile actors may have specific requirements about their travel plans. If you don't know yet who your actors will be and how they must travel, pad this line item. If you have cast arriving from a foreign country, don't forget to budget for the necessary work visas and flights.

Look at your schedule and day-out-of-days sheet to determine how many actors will have to travel to distant locations and for how long. Assume that you will give cast members at least one night's rest before they start shooting and that you may wrap late the day they finish work. Budget for two extra hotel or motel and per diem days to cover the beginning and end of their shoot period. The guild breaks down per diem by breakfast, lunch, and dinner. For example, $60 per diem (1999) is $12 for breakfast, $18 for lunch, and $30 for dinner. Technically, you only need to pay per diem for those meals not provided on the set. If you serve breakfast and lunch on the set and break before a third meal, the per diem cannot be less than $30 but need not be more, pending any other arrangement you have with a given actor.

Categories 600-00 through 650-00 cover the above-the-line costs.

700-00 Extra Talent

An extra is anyone who is required in a shot but has no speaking role. Extras are important to the look and feel of a film. Unless your movie is two people sitting in a room for two hours, you will most likely need extras. It is particularly important to hire an extras' casting agency if you will be shooting on location; bringing all of your extras with you will be expensive, and it may be difficult to find extras without the help of a local agency. In general, an extra's casting agent will be invaluable if a large number of extras are required. You will also need to compensate extras for any wardrobe you ask them to bring to wear during filming.

700-02 Extras and Stand-ins

Look at your day-out-of-days sheet to determine how many extras you'll need, where, and for how long. If yours is a SAG show, call SAG for the extras' rate. (Rates depend on the state in which you are working.) When you become a SAG signatory, one point of negotiation will be the cost of extras and how many SAG extras you're required to have. (That is, SAG may require you to pay SAG rates for 30 extras who are SAG members, with the remainder of your extras paid whatever rate you agree on.) Under the modified low-budget agreement, extras are not covered at all, and you will need to determine the rate at which you will pay them.

Look at sample budget 2, line item 700-02 (Figure 6–5). Forty SAG extras were budgeted for one shoot day at the New York SAG rate, which was $102 per day. This met the required number of SAG extras per our negotiated contract. The remaining extras were budgeted at $25 and $40 per day. In sample budget 3 (Figure 6–6), 30 extras were budgeted at $90 dollars per day for seven days, which was the rate quoted by the Los Angeles SAG office when the budget was compiled, and an additional 20 extras were budgeted at $50 per day for five days.

None of the indie shows we've done thus far has required stand-ins, but it is something to consider if you have name actors. A stand-in would be most appropriate when shooting scenes MOS (without sound), when shooting background shots, or for blocking purposes when you have high-profile actors who shouldn't stand around while the lighting is being tweaked. It may be less expensive to hire stand-ins, and sometimes actors request them. The stand-in rate is usually the same as the extra rate. (Check with SAG for current rates.)

700-03 Welfare Workers/Teachers

If your shoot requires minors to be on the set during the school year, you will need to hire a set teacher. The set teacher can also fulfill the role of welfare worker because he

sidered overtime. On a low-budget nonunion feature you may be able to negotiate a rate that works for everyone. Establish at the outset whether overtime will be paid. If you can rent your equipment from someone on the crew, it's a good way to boost the allure of the job. Discuss with the key grip the number of crew members he or she feels is required for the show to run smoothly and to best do their job.

725-02 Best Boy Grip
The best boy grip is responsible for dealing with all of the department paperwork, expendables, time cards, and so on. He or she usually begins work a day or two before the shoot, at the earliest. Usually, the key grip will choose the best boy.

725-03 Crane/Dolly Grips
Ask the director and the DP how much crane and dolly work they anticipate. If you will have a crane or a dolly on the set, budget a crane operator who will be in charge of operating this machinery.

The dolly grip works with the camera department and the DP to move the dolly at the speed and for the distance that the DP desires. You may be able to use one of the grips you already have on the set if you can't afford to hire a special person. The primary concern is that there be someone who is solely responsible for operating the dolly; this is essential for both safety and efficiency.

The crane grip is another key technical person. Depending on the type of crane and how sophisticated it is, you may need to hire an outside person who is familiar and comfortable with the equipment. Some cranes come with their own operators.

725-04 Extra Grips/Company Grips
Grips perform a lot of the heavy-duty lifting, hauling, and set up on the set. It is better to budget for more than for less in this line item. If you're unsure, discuss with the key grip what his or her needs are. By and large, when you hire your key grip, you're committing to his or her team; it is best to allow the key grip and other top personnel to hire the people they know, trust, and like to work with. This will help ensure that your set runs smoothly and on schedule. You may want to bring on more grips for your heavier shoot days (day players). Discuss with the key grip which days could use a few extra grips to ensure that all runs as necessary.

725-05 Camera Dollies
Both dollies and cranes are costly. More likely than not, if your show is low-budget, you may not need or be able to afford this special equipment for the duration of the shoot. It

will keep your costs down considerably if you rent the equipment only for the days you will use it. If you need a crane once at the beginning of the shoot and not again until the end, you shouldn't pay for a three-week rental.

725-08 Grip Equipment Rentals
The most cost-efficient way to budget for grip rentals is to make a deal with a key grip who owns a grip truck or has his or her own equipment. Otherwise, try to make an all-in deal at a rental house that includes the truck that houses the equipment. If you can secure all of the lighting and grip equipment from one rental house, it's even better. You'll find that it's cheaper and easier in terms of pickup and returns. If you're not renting from your key grip, get a list of the necessary equipment from him or her.

725-09 Grip Equipment Purchases
Grip purchases can add up, so budget carefully. If you've little idea what to budget, discuss it with the key grip. You may need tape, cloth, gels, and duvetyn, among other things. Don't forget to include sales tax on all purchases. If the key grip has a relationship with a particular vendor, you may be able to purchase expendables at a discount. Your key grip may have his or her own items that can be bought by the production at a reduced cost.

725-10 Grip Box Rentals
Budget a box rental for the key grip if he or she will be renting items they own to the production. Don't apply fringes.

725-11 Craft Service
Craft service is absolutely imperative; keep everyone snacking and happy throughout the shoot day since they all need sustenance. The craft service person will need several days of prep to make purchases. He or she will also need a day or two of wrap for returns and paperwork.

Food always costs more than anticipated. Don't skimp when budgeting for craft service. To keep your crew from mutiny, give the craft service person ample funds to do more than just get chips, soda, and salsa. It is important to have healthful snacks, a first aid kit, vitamins, and aspirin on your craft service table.

Account for craft service rentals in the production expendables line item (775-07). Tables, thermoses, coffee urns, perhaps a hot plate or two, and chairs will be needed.

725-12 Cleanup and Trash
There may be times when you need to hire someone to come in, clean up, and take garbage away from a location. This is

often referred to as cartage. Budgeting this line item will ensure that you don't upset your crew members by making them work another two hours after a long day to clean; it will also ensure that the friend you rented the location from won't want to kill you. You won't always be able to afford cleanup and trash disposal, but the need may well arise, and it's best to budget for it.

725-19 First Aid
Have a first aid kit on the set at all times. You can rent one from expendables houses or buy one. If you will be doing any special effects or stunts, you should budget for an on-set medic, as well. The medic will be paid for these supplies. You can budget for the first aid kit in the production expendables line item (910-19) if you wish.

725-22 Heating/Air-Conditioning
Don't forget about the effect the weather will have on the comfort of the cast and crew and on the safety and workability of your equipment. If weather is a potential concern, price out the necessary heating or air-conditioning equipment. Look at your day-out-of-days sheet and figure out how long you'll be at a given location that might require a heating or air-conditioning unit. You will be responsible for these costs if you're on a stage or at a location where the heating or air-conditioning will be used.

725-24 Dressing Room Rentals
It may be necessary to budget for a trailer or two if you're shooting outside. You cannot expect your actors to change in the street, and you'll need a place to store wardrobe, apply makeup, and coif hair. On a low-budget film you may want to rent one vehicle that can serve as a honey wagon, dressing room, and production office, and is equipped with phones and a bathroom. Trailers or motor homes can be costly, so price them out first. (See "770-00 Transportation.") On larger budget shows, dressing rooms are usually rented for actors.

725-25 Miscellaneous Expenses
Use this line item to pad the budget (see sample budget 2 [Figure 6–5]). Unanticipated costs always arise. In sample budget 3 (Figure 6–6), we allocated money for walkie-talkies and beepers in this line item.

725-30 Location Load and Unload
If you anticipate that any of your locations will be particularly problematic because of heavy set dressing or strict time limitations, you may want to bring on additional PAs to assist with loading and unloading materials and equipment. Their help will ensure that all runs smoothly and on schedule.

730-00 Electrical

In this category you will budget for the electrical department personnel, all electrical equipment rentals and purchases (including a generator), carbons, power, and kit rentals if any. This category may account for a large portion of the budget, depending on the lighting needs of the show and the locations at which you will be filming.

730-01, 730-02, 730-03 Gaffer, Best Boy, and Electricians
Use these line items to allocate money for the gaffer (730-01), the best boy (730-02), and the electricians (730-03). Usually, the gaffer will have a crew with whom he or she likes to work. If the show is nonunion, you won't have to pay union rates, but you may need to budget for overtime (see sample budgets 2 and 3 [Figures 6–5 and 6–6]).

Try to hire a gaffer with his or her own truck, and budget the cost of the equipment rental in line item 730-08. This will save you money. If not, rent electrical equipment from a vendor with whom your gaffer has a relationship if this allows you to secure a better deal. Determine whether you will be paying the gaffer a kit rental (line item 730-10) for equipment or supplies that he or she provides to the production. Get a list of expendables that will be needed from the best boy and be sure to budget appropriately for electrical purchases (line item 730-09). Add fringes for the electrical crew and sales tax for purchases. When budgeting for loss and damage (line item 730-20), allocate enough money to cover the deductible on your production insurance policy.

730-06 Power
If you're on location or filming on a stage, you may have to cover power costs if they exceed whatever the norm is for the location or stage. Some locations will allow you to tie in for power rather than run power in from a generator. Tying in can be a convenient money saver, but be prepared to cover the cost because a tie-in will typically drive up the electric bill.

735-00 Special Effects

Special effects are often mechanical effects that are shot while filming rather than done optically in postproduction, such as an explosion, an earthquake, or the destruction of a building. Special effects of this type can be costly. Call an optical house for quotes. There were no special effects in *Swingers* or in sample budgets 1 or 2 (Figures 6–2, 6–4, and 6–5). Sample budget 3 (Figure 6–6), however, required a shooting star that needed to be optically placed in the film by computer graphics. If you will be creating special effects on the set, you may need to budget for a special effects person (line item 735-01);

775-02 Location Staff

Budget for the location manager and, if necessary and affordable, an assistant or two in this line item. There is a significant amount of paperwork, arrangements, and organizing related to shooting on location (such as posting notices, obtaining releases, scouting, securing permits, taking photos, and negotiating agreements and contracts). The number of scripted locations will determine how much prep time the location manager needs. Use your schedules to help you when budgeting this line item. Keep in mind that locations take time to find and secure and that they often fall through. Allow sufficient time for the location manager to secure (or replace) locations.

775-03 Site Rentals/Permits/Licenses

List each location by name in the budget, and include the cost of renting the locations in this line item. Refer to your schedule to ensure that you account for all of the locations and the amount of time (days or weeks) needed at each and that you properly budget for the costs.

Also include permit fees in this line item. Permits must be secured in order to film at many locations. Don't steal locations! Secure permits! You will need a permit if you have a generator on the set, if the space in which you are filming is open to the public, if equipment will be set up outside, or if the location is a public place or is used as a public thoroughfare. If you fail to secure the proper filming permits your show could be shut down, which will cost more money in the long run. The location manager should contact the appropriate city filming office to determine which locations require permits and to ascertain the fees involved. He or she should also file the necessary paperwork.

The costs of the site and the permit fees will depend on the location and the city in which you are filming. Certain cities are more lenient with permits. Often, you can secure a blanket permit for all of your locations if they are near one another, rather than permitting each location separately. A blanket permit will ultimately save you money. Have your proof of insurance and permits on the set at all times. (Securing locations and permits is discussed in Chapter 7.)

775-04 Hotel and Lodging

Account here for the cost of all below-the-line crew lodging when filming at a distant location. Use your schedule to help you determine the number of days and the number of crew members for whom you will need to budget hotel costs. Budget per diem for crew when filming at a distant location. No fringes are added to per diems. The per diem minimum varies from city to city. Contact the local film commission for the rates. Apply sales tax to any hotel costs, and be prepared to pay gratuities.

775-05 Catering Services

Don't skimp here! Most likely, your crew will work long hours at a reduced rate. Feeding crew members a hot, well-balanced meal is incredibly important for both morale and stamina. The schedule will help you determine how many days you will need to cater the shoot for and the number of people to be fed each day. Remember that any visitors and extras on the set will also need to eat. Err on the side of providing more meals rather than fewer. Call several catering companies to secure the best deal possible. If the catering company bids are too high, come up with a creative way to cater the shoot to keep costs down. (See Chapter 7.) Add sales tax on any food purchases. Refer to the sample budgets (Figures 6–4 to 6–6) to see how the catering costs were broken out.

775-06 Meal Allowances/Extra Meals

SAG and union rules require that the cast and crew be fed every six hours. Regardless of whether the cast is SAG and the crew is union, you should follow these union rules. Meal penalties are paid on both cast and crew members if lunch or dinner is not served within the six-hour interval. Second meals are often walkaway or wrap-out meals (though they can be sit-down meals also) that are served if a shoot day will go into overtime and it has been six hours since lunch was served. The craft service person should keep a list of affordable restaurants located near each location in case a second meal must be served. The first AD should alert both the line producer and the craft service person approximately three hours before the second meal must be served so that food can be ordered, delivered, or picked up and served on time.

Meals for the extras who will be filming on the set can be either box lunches or dinners ordered from restaurants, or extra meals ordered from the caterer. Often, if there are many extras, it is cheaper to order box meals than to have the caterer prepare more food.

775-07 Production Expendables

Budget this line item as an allowance. Include money for such items as a wardrobe steamer, wardrobe racks, cones, bullhorns, tables, chairs, desks, director's chairs, rope, bungee cord, coffee urns, coolers, craft service equipment, tablecloths, handcarts for carrying equipment, hangers, and makeup tables. Pad this line item a bit. You'll want to be covered when unanticipated costs arise. Production expendables are often charged on a three-day week (you pay for three days' worth of rental to secure the equipment for an entire week), and many of the items needed will be inexpensive. Remember to add sales tax if you plan to purchase any of these items.

775-11 Fire and Police

When permits are secured, the location manager, in conjunction with the permit office, will arrange for the proper fire and police personnel to be present at the necessary locations. If you plan to run a generator at your location or you'll be shooting on a sidewalk or a public thoroughfare, the film commission may require that a fire fighter or police officer be present. If you are filming at a location while it's open to the public, a police officer must be present. The city may check on the production and will shut it down if the proper officials are not present and the proper paperwork is not on hand. Fire fighters and police officers are paid an hourly fee that is established by the city you're filming in, and there is usually a four-hour minimum, even if the official is needed for only one hour. Check local film guides like *LA 411* or *NYPG (New York Production Guide),* or call the local permit office for the rates specific to the city in which you will be filming. Add the appropriate fringes to the rates.

775-18 Office Rent/Furniture

In this line item budget for office rent and overhead over the course of the show and for office furniture or equipment that you will need to rent. Alternatively, you may include office rent and furniture costs in the Administrative Expenses category under line item 910-17. Setting up a production office can be costly, so be as creative as possible. On *Swingers,* we ran the production out of our house; we budgeted a small amount for utilities and supplies in this line item, but not for rent. Find an inexpensive office with plenty of space, electrical outlets, and phone jacks.

You might also check out apartments for rent in a convenient and safe area. See if you can rent an apartment on a month-to-month basis. This is often cheaper than renting space that is specifically zoned for offices or businesses. Of course, if you have to install extra phone lines, outlets, and lights, rent a parking lot because there isn't enough parking available on the street, walk up and down many stairs with equipment, and risk disturbing the neighbors, it may not be worth it to rent an apartment instead of an office. Investigate and weigh your options carefully.

775-21 Location Security

Have security present to ensure the safety of equipment that is left overnight, during the filming of any scenes with many cast members and extras, to guard production vehicles with equipment on them, and when shooting in a dangerous neighborhood. Budget a small amount of money in this line item even if you don't anticipate hiring security personnel. If the money allocated here goes unused, you will have a pad to cover unexpected costs that arise.

775-22 Parking Lots

This line item is for parking lots that have to be rented for office or set parking for the cast and crew. If you have to rent a secure lot for the overnight parking of production vehicles or housing expensive rented equipment, include the cost here.

780-00 Process Photography

Budget in this category for shots that you plan to create in a process studio. Suppose, for example, that you need a shot of an actor standing in front of a river, but you don't want to travel to a river for that one shot. You can create the shot you need by projecting stock footage of a river onto a screen and positioning the actor in front of it. When you sync up the shot it will appear as if the actor is standing in front of the river. Today, blue screens are often used instead of process photography, and the images are combined in postproduction.

785-00 Production Dailies

This category covers developing the film, printing the dailies, transferring the sound, coding the dailies, and transferring the film to videotape. Call several labs for quotes to determine if they are able to accommodate your film's needs. If one of your crew members is a student, you can often obtain a discount on these costs.

785-01 Negative Raw Stock

Discuss with the director and the DP the type of film stock (35mm, 16mm, super 8, super 16), the speed, and the quantity they will need. Then check with film supply houses for current prices. Raw stock is priced by the foot. Remember to add sales tax to any purchase. (Refer to the sample budgets [Figures 6–4 to 6–6] to see how we broke out our costs.) Instead of factory unopened raw stock, you can purchase "recans" or short ends, which are less expensive. A recan is film that was loaded into a magazine but never shot, and then literally recanned. The disadvantage of using recanned film is that occasionally the film has been exposed or is bad, and you lose whatever footage you've shot. Test the film first. You can also purchase short ends at a reduced rate; these are partial rolls of film left over from someone else's shoot. Be aware that short ends are, by definition, short and you will there-

equipment, you may not be able to extend your stay at the facility. Having to change to a different cutting room can be costly and time-consuming.

800-12 Editorial Supplies

Budget in this line item for editing expendables, such as pens, paper, notebooks, splicing tape, and 1/2-inch and 3/4-inch videotape (or whatever format you may use for your masters, e.g., D2, Beta SP, etc.). Be sure to budget food costs, also. Keep in mind the length of time the editors will be cutting when budgeting for supplies and food. Include sales tax on these items.

800-14 Postproduction Supervisor

If the budget can't afford a postproduction supervisor for the entire postproduction period, it is advisable to hire one for a short time to help organize the film's postproduction needs. Postproduction is costly, and it pays to have someone on board who is familiar with the process, can secure the best deals, understands the timing of each of the processes, and will oversee all of the film's needs (such as sound mix, sound effects, ADR, looping, music, main and end titles, opticals, and color timing). Postproduction is time-consuming, and if you are the producer, you will be dealing with many other things during this period. (For more on postproduction, see Chapter 9.)

800-17 Other Costs

Budget a reasonable amount of money for this line item, even if just for padding. Unanticipated costs may arise during the editing process, and you'll want to be covered.

810-00 Music

In this category you will budget for all of the film's music needs, including the composer, musicians, and a supervisor. In the sample budgets (Figures 6–4 to 6–6) we allocated money for many of the line items in this category as an allowance because we were uncertain what the actual costs would be.

Music can be source music or score. Music that appears to be coming from a radio, television, jukebox, and so on, in the background of a given scene is source music. Score is any music that doesn't come from any visible source and that helps communicate the story or set the mood. Music can be composed specifically for the film, or the rights to existing songs can be licensed.

On a low-budget independent film, you may not be able to budget enough money in this category to cover all of the actual music costs. It will depend on how extensive your film's music needs are and how costly the music is. We usually budget this category as a package or an allowance that includes any festival music rights, some licensing, a composer, and a supervisor. Rarely, however, does the budgeted amount cover all costs. If you secure distribution, the distributor may either assume the costs, split them with you, or require that the music be changed to something more affordable. Music rights, composing, facilities, and licensing are very expensive, and deals are hard to come by. It is important to budget enough for a composer, a music supervisor, and any necessary rights, such as festival rights at the very least. (See Chapter 9 for more on costs.)

810-08 Composer

If you hire a composer to score the film, he or she will come on board during the editing process. Composers' rates vary, but for now, budget either a weekly rate for most of postproduction or an allowance. Give the composer and the music supervisor video transfers of the film along the way so that they can determine where music will be placed. The composer and the music supervisor (with the director, editor, and the producer) will choose the music that best communicates the mood of the film and helps tell the story.

810-09 through 810-23

These line items are for different types of musicians. On larger-budget shows, most of these line items will be budgeted.

810-25 Music Supervisor

Bring the music supervisor on board in late production or early postproduction. The music supervisor will spot the film with the director and producer for music cues and will suggest either source music or score for specific areas in the film. He or she will help secure the necessary rights and licenses for scripted songs or music, determine master use and sync licensing fees, and negotiate with the publishing company or the record company for the use of songs. The music supervisor will secure festival rights if needed and will work closely with the composer (if one has been hired), arranging for any facilities or musicians needed. The music supervisor will help determine the film's needs and what they will cost.

810-28, 810-29 Master Use Licenses, Music Publishing Licenses

The licensing fees involved with these two line items often cost more than the entire budget of *Swingers*. Depending on the songs chosen and how many of them there are, these licenses can be very costly. In sample budget 2 (Figure 6–5), the producers specifically requested that $8,000 be allocated in the music category. They needed to keep the budget under $1 million, so they chose to allocate a small sum of money in this category knowing that they'd have to figure out how to pay for rights and licenses later. Securing these rights is very important, and it may be difficult to get the songs you want for the money you have.

820-00 Postproduction Sound

In this line item budget for sound mixing, recording, rerecording, music, sound effects, dialogue, ADR, and foley. You can keep costs down in this category by making package deals at a sound facility and premixing some of the sound on an Avid if you are cutting on one. Sound package prices depend on the medium being used to mix the sound, the elements needed, and how many hours or days you will need to complete the mix. If there is a lot of usable dialogue on the production track, the film will require less ADR.

820-01 Dialogue Recording (ADR)
Budget in this line item for the cost of renting an ADR facility. The cast will report to the facility during postproduction to rerecord any lost lines they delivered during production or to record any additional lines. You should budget the actors' fees for recording ADR in the Cast category (630-00). (See Chapter 9 for information on low-budget ADR.)

820-02 Narration Recording
If the film requires narration or voice-over, budget for it in this line item. Narration and voice-over can be recorded on a stage, usually after the picture is shot and then synced up to the picture later. It usually makes sense to record voice-over during postproduction because it can be used to alter or enhance the film's narrative.

820-03 Sound Effects (Foley)
Budget here for foley artists and the sound stage they will use to add in any sound effects. Foley artists use props to create sounds that need to be added to a film to best communicate the full effect of a scene or replaced because they were not clean off the production track. They record sounds such as kissing, rain, and footsteps on a sound stage, matching each sound to the picture.

820-06 Dubbing Session
In the dubbing session, or mix, the various sound elements (dialogue, music, and effects) are mixed together on a dubbing stage while the film is projected. Try to make a flat deal with the dubbing facility. Be sure to dub on the largest stage you can afford. It makes a difference in the quality of the sound.

Most films are mixed into four analog channels (left, center, right, surround). This is referred to as matrix stereo. For a fee, the mix can be supervised by Dolby Laboratories or Ultra-stereo. Both companies require the use of their names in advertising the film. Dolby SR (or its generic equivalent) is the best analog format around. Recently, three digital formats have been introduced: Digital Theater Sound (DTS), Dolby Digital, and Sony Digital Dynamic Sound (SDDS). In these formats, the film is mixed to five or more channels (left, center, right, left surround, right surround). Most mixes are recorded onto 35mm full coat, although you can save money by recording onto digital tape, such as DAT or D88.

820-07 Sound Transfers
Budget in this line item for transferring sound (dialogue, music, and effects) to magnetic stripe film, creating the magnetic master composite mix. This magnetic soundtrack will be conformed to the answer print. Usually, the cost for transferring the sound is billed by the hour. Try to make an all-in package deal for the magnetic tape and the transfer. Have the sound editor arrange for the film's needs.

820-09 Purchased Sound Effects
Budget for any prerecorded sound effects that you will need to purchase to add to the film during the mix. Check with your editor and director.

820-12 Magnetic Tape for Edit
Budget this line item for magnetic stripe film. (The cost is quoted per foot.) The soundtrack of the film will be transferred to a 35mm magnetic master tape composed of three stripes, which contain the music, the sound effects, and the dialogue of the film. Try to make a package deal on the magnetic tape and the transfer. Add sales tax to any purchases.

830-00 Stock Shots

If you need a shot of an Egyptian tomb, for example, rather than building a replica of one or traveling to Egypt for the shot, you may want to purchase footage from a stock footage library. Stock footage can be expensive. Be careful to purchase stock that matches the type of film you're using in order that the film look and feel uniform. Call around for quotes.

840-00 Titles

Budget here for the main and end titles (840-01, 840-02, and 840-03) of the film. Main titles typically run at the beginning of the film, and the end titles at the end. We usually budget this category as an allowance until we determine the style of the titles and the total number of cards that we will have to run. Be accurate in your allowance by calling for some preliminary quotes. You can be as creative as you like when determining how to run the film's titles. The more intricate title cards you have and the more stylized they are, the more expensive they will be. Be sure to adhere to size requirements when crediting the cast and crew; these requirements are usually prenegotiated in the cast and crew contracts along with the placement of the credit in the film.

850-00 Opticals, Mattes, and Inserts

Most likely, you will have to budget an allowance for optical effects (850-01) until you can determine accurately how many opticals you will need, and you'll only know this once you begin to assemble the film. You may find that you have to correct or reposition shots optically or that you have to add elements that were not actually in the shot, such as creatures, volcanoes, windstorms, laser beams, and falling stars. On *Swingers,* we found some shots that were slightly out of focus and others that needed to be repositioned because the ground glass in the viewfinder of our camera was not positioned correctly on one of our filming days.

Also budget here for any inserts, fade-ins, or dissolves you may need. These types of shots are done optically and can be costly, but visually they may serve the film best. Arrange for both title and optical work at the same facility so that the negative isn't being shipped around to different title houses.

860-00 Laboratory Processing

This category includes the costs for the postproduction lab and related items.

860-01 Reprinting and Developing
Often, through simple wear and tear on the film, certain shots will have to be reprinted and developed. Budget this line item as an allowance because initially, you won't be able to determine what the film will need. This line item applies only if the film is being cut on a flatbed.

You may need prints of the locked picture so that the music and sound editors can be sure that the music and sound are properly synced to the picture. The most cost-effective way to do this is to strike "dirty dupes," which are black-and-white prints of the locked picture made from the cut.

860-02 First Trial Composite Print/Answer Print
This print reflects the first color timing pass combined with any opticals and the soundtrack. A color timer, together with the director and often the editor and the DP, makes color

corrections to the film so that the color values of the film are the same throughout and the color for each scene is correct. The first trial print allows you to view first-round color corrections and to find any spots within the film that need further correction. This is also the first time you will see the film projected from a print that marries image and sound, allowing you to check for sync problems. You may need to strike several prints before the color is correct. The corrected composite is called your answer print. For sample budgets 1 and 2 (Figures 6–4 and 6–5), the producers planned to strike only an answer print that they would screen in hopes of securing distribution.

860-07 Interpositive/Internegative
If you secure distribution you will need to strike both an interpositive print (IP) and an internegative print (IN). An interpositive is a timed print created directly from the original negative. It is used to create duplicate picture negatives called internegatives, which are used for striking additional release prints to prevent wear and tear on the original negative. Most low-budget films don't budget for an interpositive or an internegative, and answer prints can be struck without them. The sample budgets (Figures 6–4 to 6–6) do not allocate money for either an interpositive or an internegative but do include an answer print.

Categories 810-00 through 870-00 cover the postproduction period costs.

910-00 Administrative Expenses

Budget here for all of the film's administrative costs, including start-up costs, accounting supplies, office costs, party costs, and miscellaneous items or gifts. In the sample budgets (Figures 6–4 to 6–6), we created our own line items to account for certain costs in this category. Many of the line items were not included in the blank budget forms that come with Movie Magic Budgeting.

910-01 Accounting and Terminal Fees
Any accounting software, supplies, or forms you will purchase should be budgeted in this line item. If you will be preparing cast and crew payroll yourself rather than hiring an accountant or using a payroll company, budget for checks and any software programs you will use. If you are using an accountant, budget for checks and software costs here, but not for the accountant.

910-02 MPAA Certificate
The Motion Picture Association of America (MPAA) will view your finished film and assign it a rating. A rating is

required if the film is to be released. The certificate certifies that the film has been rated by the MPAA and that its production adhered to the MPAA's regulations and standards. The cost of the certificate will be based on the budget of the film.

910-03 Postage, Shipping, and FedEx
Budget an allowance for this line item. Try to estimate what your shipping needs will be and where items will be shipped to. Budget enough money for all three stages of the film: preproduction, production, and postproduction.

910-04 Photocopying
Either rent a photocopier, purchase one, or find one that you can borrow. You will need to make many copies every day, including call sheets, Exhibit G's, contracts, production reports, and the script supervisor's notes. If you don't get your own photocopier, ask someone you know who has access to one to run script copies if possible, or set up an account at a local print shop and try to make a deal with them. Renting a copier is not very costly and will prove to be well worth the expense.

910-05 Legal Expenses and Fees
You may not be able to afford an attorney, but with enough research you will be able to navigate through your contacts and paperwork. On *Swingers*, we did not have an attorney until after we sold the film and could afford one. Our attorney helped us with delivery paperwork for the distribution company. If you can afford an attorney, it will be money well spent. Usually, attorneys' fees are around 2% of the budget of the film, or the attorney will bill on an hourly basis. He or she will help with any financing and partnership contracts, production insurance, errors-and-omission insurance, and other paperwork. If you can't afford an attorney, seek advice regarding any contracts, music licenses, or paperwork you need help with. You can refer to books about contracts, film guides, and organizations like California Lawyers for the Arts. (See the resource guide at the back of this book.)

910-06 Telephone/Facsimile
When budgeting this line item, keep in mind where you will be calling. If you are on location, you may be making many long-distance calls and sending long-distance faxes. The crew will be making long-distance calls, also. Don't skimp on this line item. A large part of your job will be done on the phone, and the cost of calls adds up. Make sure that you get the best rate from the local phone company and long-distance carrier and that your office has a sufficient number of phone lines.

910-12 Preview Expense/Distribution Screening
If your film is not accepted at any festivals, you may want to set up your own distribution screening. Budget for the cost of a theater or screening room, press kits, invitations and flyers, and whatever else you need to make sure that distributors attend the screening. The cost of renting a projection room is rarely less than $250. Sometimes, universities and film archives will screen a film inexpensively. (Chapter 9 explains how we organized the distribution screening for *Swingers*.) You may want to include in this line item costs for research screenings, preview screenings, cast and crew screenings, and any press or agent screenings that you plan in order to get feedback or to generate buzz about the film.

910-15 Cellular Phones
As the line producer, you must be reachable at all times, even when you are away from the office and the set. Cellular phones are costly, however, so beware. It is less expensive to wear a beeper and then find a pay phone, but this is less convenient, as well. Be sure to budget enough money for the rental or purchase of the phone, the long-distance charges, and the fees included in your cellular plan.

910-16 Festival Expenses
We created this line item in sample budgets 1 and 3 (Figures 6–4 and 6–6). Often, festival costs, application fees, transferring the film to video, and shipping costs are overlooked when compiling a budget for a film. If the film is being submitted to any festivals, be sure to budget for all of these costs. Assume that each festival will require an application fee, still photographs, and at least a video dub of the film. (See Chapter 9.) If you are planning to apply to festivals overseas, budget for international shipping costs.

910-18 Research Report/E&O Report
A research report is a safeguard that verifies that there are no illegal usages in the script; the researcher makes sure that the script doesn't portray a living person or use actual phone numbers and that the names of all characters and locations are fictitious. A research report will identify any potential problems. The researcher will also verify whether the title of the film has been used before, and if it has, where it originated and whether it is advisable that it be changed. Research reports can cost anywhere from $1,000 to $2,000. Call around for quotes. If you have absolutely no money for this report, a distribution company may file for a research report when it picks up the film.

Distributors also require errors-and-omissions (E&O) insurance on the film. They may assume the cost if you can't afford it and haven't secured it before distribution; this, however, is not ideal. E&O insurance protects the production company or distributor from liability lawsuits for slander, unauthorized use of the film's title, use of living people's names, and copyright infringement. To secure E&O coverage you must provide the carrier with a copy of the research report described earlier.

910-20 Corporate Filing
Create a corporate entity that will be used for the sole purpose of making the film. The bank account for the funds used to make the film will be set up in this name as well as all vendor accounts. The entity may be structured in a variety of ways, including an s-corporation or a limited liability partnership. Discuss with your partners and investors how they want to structure the company. Forming a corporation or a limited liability partnership limits the liability of all investors. It can be expensive to do this through an attorney, and there are yearly and state fees involved. When making *Swingers,* we filed for our corporate status over the Internet, which was far cheaper (approximately $300) than using an attorney. The state and federal fees for corporations remained the same, and we had an accountant sort out the taxes that the corporation needed to pay. If you are inexperienced in this area, speak with an attorney or an accountant to make sure you cover all the bases.

910-21 Polaroid and B/W Still Film
Budget for both Polaroid film and black-and-white and color film for still photos. The art, set dressing, prop, wardrobe, location, and makeup and hair departments and the script supervisor will want to take photos as records (the photos will be placed in continuity notebooks) to ensure the continuity of the film in case scenes have to be recreated and reshot.

910-22 Payroll Company
Hire a payroll company to pay the cast and crew. Payroll companies usually charge a small percentage of the total payroll or a small fee per check issued. The payroll company will compute and deduct the appropriate government taxes from each employee's check and will report withholdings to the proper government agencies. On *Swingers,* we hired a payroll company to pay the cast only. We totaled each cast member's hours each week, including any overtime or meal penalties, and sent the calculations to the payroll company. (We also sent the calculations to SAG at the end of each week.)

910-23 Storage Facility
We created this line item because when a show is wrapped (or during production), items sometimes have to be stored. Some borrowed or rented items will be used again, and the production will own other things when the show is over. When budgeting this line item, consider such things as props,

wardrobe, gels, expendables, and craft service equipment. We allowed $500 for this line item in sample budgets 1 and 3 (Figures 6–4 and 6–6).

910-35 Wrap Party
We created this line item in sample budgets 1 and 3 (Figures 6–4 and 6–6). It is safe to assume that even if you can't afford to have a wrap party, you'll want to do something to thank the cast and crew and to celebrate having completed the film. We recommend that you budget even a small amount of money for a wrap party of some kind.

920-00 Publicity

Unit publicity on a film is very important. Ideally, the film will attract a distributor and generate buzz. Whether you hire a unit publicist or generate buzz about the film in other ways, it is important that you promote your film to the public. Publicity is often overlooked on low-budget films. Don't make this mistake. At the very least, have still photographs taken during production, and ask a friend to videotape some behind-the-scenes footage of the film. Then, when the time comes to put the film out to the world, you will have the materials you need to promote it (refer to the interviews on the accompanying CD-ROM). We couldn't afford a publicist on *Swingers* until after we sold the film, but we did have several talent agency contacts to whom we showed the film before securing a distributor. These contacts helped create a positive buzz about the film within the industry. Call around to publicists to determine the costs involved in hiring their services. See if you can put up a small retainer or work out a deferral arrangement.

920-02 Still Photographer
Budget here for a still photographer for after the picture is completed and during any publicity or marketing of the film. Create a press kit of photos of the cast and core team of filmmakers to help create buzz about the film and attract a distributor.

920-03 Still Film and Processing
Budget in this line item for supplies and processing for the still photographer. Call around to photo labs for costs. If you plan to purchase and process the film at the same place, it may save you money. If the still photographer has a relationship with a particular lab, see if he or she can secure a reduced rate on processing.

950-00 Finance Charges

You may have to create this category to account for finance charges on a loan taken by the company. The production budget should ultimately cover charges applied to the loan. This will not be an expense you can foresee prior to knowing how your film will be financed.

970-00 Delivery Expenses

In sample budget 2 (Figure 6–5), this category was created for any paperwork, approvals, reports, prints, and so on, that would have to be delivered if film distribution was secured. On low-budget films, financial problems often arise when distribution is secured but certain delivery items cannot be paid for because there is no money left in the budget.

Insurance

Insurance was applied to the sample budgets (Figures 6–4 to 6–6) at 2%. Typically, insurance is calculated at 2% to 3.5% of the budget. All independent films must be insured in order to secure equipment, locations, transportation, props, wardrobe, cast, crew, and so on, and the policy must be paid for before the production period officially begins.

The insurance cost is applied to the total above- and below-the-line costs, not to the grand total of the budget. Sample budget 3 (Figure 6–6), for instance, has an insurance cost of $26,125, which is 2% of the above- and below-the-line total of $1,306,237. If you are using Movie Magic Budgeting, it will automatically apply the percentage you allocate to the above- and below-the-line total. You'll want to insure the production for up to $1 million, which is the standard liability limit; this is the amount that is usually required to rent equipment and expendables and to secure locations.

WHEN YOUR BUDGET IS WAY TOO HIGH

If your budget is accurate but higher than you had anticipated, you'll have to go back and make changes. However, do not go through your budget and randomly slash numbers! If you do, you will have a final number that meets your needs, but you will not have a budget that reflects how much money you actually require to make the movie. Here are some things to reconsider if your budget is too high. (They do not appear in order of priority.)

- Film format: Using 16mm film instead of 35mm film will keep your costs down, allowing you to get your movie in the can, but if you shoot on 16mm film stock, will you limit the possibilities for the movie and its release? You may have to have the film blown up to 35mm for its release, which is expensive, but still 16mm may save you money. Similarly, shooting on

mini digital video (mini DV) has become a real option (refer to the interviews on the accompanying CD-ROM). Shooting on DV may reduce your costs by half. If you purchase the equipment needed to shoot and edit your film, you will be able to make many movies and have your own edit facility. (See the Resource Guide at the back of this book for more information on digital filmmaking.)

- Crew rates: Have you budgeted too much for your crew? Perhaps you can reduce everyone's weekly pay by $100.
- Non-SAG actors: Can you make the movie you want with non-SAG actors? If so, it will significantly reduce your cast expenses. On every indie film we've been involved with, the SAG cast members were the highest paid of anyone on the set. Keep in mind that this may not be the place to save money because you don't want to make significant compromises insofar as the talent level of the cast is concerned.
- Casting agent: Can you get by without a casting agent? Perhaps you can find an able person who needs a first shot at casting and is willing to work at a reduced rate.
- Catering: Catering companies are expensive. Do you know anyone who would be willing to cook or donate meals for the production? Can you make a deal with several restaurants in town at $5 per person in exchange for a production credit? (See Chapter 7 for more catering ideas.)
- Locations: The right locations are important to the look of the movie and shouldn't be compromised, but you might find an innovative way to deal with locations. Can you get a different bar, a different house, or a different store that will be cheaper? Can you use a friend's or a relative's house? Can you find locations that are near one another so that you're eligible for a blanket permit? (See Chapter 7 for more on permits.)
- Recans versus factory unopened raw stock: Recans are much less expensive than factory unopened film. Discuss your options carefully with the DP and the director.
- Kit rentals: Can you eliminate kit rentals from your budget, or can you negotiate lower fees? Make sure to still be fair and considerate of your crew.
- Travel: Can you eliminate travel expenses by rethinking a given location? Look for something within driving distance that can serve the same purpose.
- Equipment Rentals: Can you limit the number of weeks or days that you rent equipment? Can you trim down your camera and lighting packages? Ask the DP and the gaffer what they can do without. (Do they really need that Steadi-Cam or that crane?)

- Editing process: Can you shorten postproduction by several weeks without rushing too much? (Refer to the interview on the accompanying CD-ROM.) Alternatively, can you rent an Avid and have the editor cut in your apartment or in an inexpensive facility?
- Transportation: Reduce the number of production vehicles or at least the number of days you need some of them. Try to rent a cube truck that will accommodate several, or even all, of the departments. Can you borrow picture vehicles rather than rent them?

BUDGETING WITHOUT MOVIE MAGIC BUDGETING

Movie Magic Budgeting makes life a lot easier, but there are other ways to deal with budgeting an independent film. The $62,000 budget reproduced in Figure 6–7 was originally done by hand. You can use any spreadsheet program that tallies numbers for you, or you can use a pencil and a calculator. If you don't have the Movie Magic Scheduling program you will need to be careful to include all of the necessary elements specific to your script when you break it down and schedule it. Refer to your schedule as you budget.

The $62,000 film was shot on 16mm film. It was a feature-length, dialogue-driven piece, shot in seven different interior locations and as many exterior locations. The shoot was 18 days long (three six-day weeks). Neither the non-SAG cast nor the 15-person crew received any pay. Instead, we signed deferral contracts with the cast and crew. Unfortunately, we were never able to pay out the deferral contracts.

We had student status at the time, which allowed for significant cost reductions at the lab, the permit office, and some of our equipment rental houses. Student status usually requires that a key member of your crew be enrolled full-time in a film school. Generally, a letter from the film department and a valid student identification will allow you access to student rates. Despite the corners we cut, we did have production insurance and permits, and we fed the cast and crew real meals.

We did not have Movie Magic Budgeting at the time, and we couldn't have afforded it. To budget, we used a calculator and entered the numbers into a word processor. Ideally, you should purchase a simple spreadsheet program so that you don't have to continually retally your numbers.

This film was financed through a combination of personal savings, credit cards, and a private investor. The film traveled the festival circuit and was picked up for distribution by Turbulent Arts, a small San Francisco–based arthouse distributor.

The crew, although unpaid, had varying degrees of experience. Each wanted an opportunity to work on a feature film. In many instances, crew members had had a lesser credit on previous films and wanted a key credit. Some of the crew had never worked on a film before but had some other qualifying experience. For example, our makeup artist had worked at a makeup counter in a department store and was eager to break into film work.

Some of the locations were secured at no cost, and several were rented for a nominal fee. For almost every interior location we had to pay repair fees for items that were broken or damaged during the production. For one location, a local café, we agreed to pay any electrical charges that were above and beyond the restaurant's usual electrical bill (we gave them a deposit as a guarantee), and we also agreed to reimburse the café for the difference between what they usually earned during a morning shift and what they earned while we were shooting. The café fell short of its regular earnings by approximately $50.

The cost through the production period was $26,215, postproduction came in at $36,410, and the grand total was $62,625. Preproduction was four weeks long, and the production period was three weeks. You'll see when referring to the budget that we made most of our equipment deals based on a two-day week. This is not standard, but it can be done with a great deal of persuasion and patience. Crew members who used their cars extensively during preproduction and production were reimbursed for their gas receipts. We turned our apartment into the production office, so we had no added rental expense. We installed two extra phone lines, purchased office supplies, and bought a large table that served as multiple workstations.

Our lighting, grip, camera, and sound equipment packages were modest. We shot a combination of factory unopened 16mm film stock and recans.

Most of the meals were prepared by the craft service person in our kitchen. We also purchased meals from restaurants on several occasions for convenience and variety. For breakfast, we solicited donations of bagels and cream cheese and morning pastries from several cafés and were given a weekly donation of coffee in exchange for a thank-you in the film's credits.

We cut the film on a flatbed over a period of three months. We rented the flatbed from an ad we found in the back of the monthly publication of the Film Arts Foundation, a film-support organization based in San Francisco. A cutting room with the essential equipment was rented at the Saul Zaentz Film Center.

BLANK BUDGET (PARAMOUNT FORM)

PRODUCTION NUMBER: DATE:
PRODUCER: LOCATIONS:
DIRECTOR: DAYS:
SCRIPT DATE: WEEKS:
START DATE:
FINISH DATE: NOTE:

Acct#	Category Title	Page	Total
600-00	STORY	1	$0
610-00	PRODUCER	1	$0
620-00	DIRECTOR	1	$0
630-00	CAST	1	$0
640-00	FRINGES	2	$0
650-00	TRAVEL & LIVING	2	$0
	Total Above-The-Line		**$0**
700-00	EXTRA TALENT	2	$0
705-00	PRODUCTION STAFF	2	$0
710-00	CAMERA	2	$0
715-00	SET DESIGN	3	$0
720-00	SET CONSTRUCTION	3	$0
721-00	SET STRIKING	3	$0
722-00	MINIATURES	3	$0
725-00	SET OPERATIONS	3	$0
730-00	ELECTRICAL	4	$0
735-00	SPECIAL EFFECTS	4	$0
740-00	SPECIAL SHOOTING UNITS	4	$0
745-00	SET DRESSING	4	$0
750-00	PROPERTIES	5	$0
755-00	WARDROBE	5	$0
760-00	MAKEUP & HAIRSTYLISTS	6	$0
765-00	PRODUCTION SOUND	6	$0
770-00	TRANSPORTATION	6	$0
775-00	LOCATION EXPENSE	7	$0
780-00	PROCESS PHOTOGRAPHY	7	$0
785-00	PRODUCTION DAILIES	7	$0
790-00	LIVING EXPENSE	8	$0
795-00	FRINGES	8	$0
797-00	TESTS	8	$0
798-00	FACILITIES FEES	8	$0
	Total Production		**$0**
800-00	EDITING	8	$0
810-00	MUSIC	9	$0
820-00	POSTPRODUCTION SOUND	9	$0
830-00	STOCK SHOTS	10	$0
840-00	TITLES	10	$0
850-00	OPTICALS, MATTES, INSERTS	10	$0

Figure 6–1   Sample budget form

Acct#	Description	Amount	Units	X	Rate	Subtotal	Total
785-00	**PRODUCTION DAILIES (CONT'D)**						
785-07	CODING DAILIES						$0
785-08	SCREEN DAILIES						$0
785-09	VIDEO TAPE TRANSFERS						$0
785-10	TAPE STOCK						$0
						Total For 785-00	**$0**
790-00	**LIVING EXPENSES**						
790-01	LIVING EXPENSES-CONTR...						$0
790-02	OTHER LIVING EXPENSES						$0
790-03	FARES-OTHER THAN TO L...						$0
						Total For 790-00	**$0**
795-00	**FRINGES**						
						Total For 795-00	**$0**
797-00	**TESTS**						
797-01	TEST #1						$0
797-02	TEST #2						$0
797-03	TEST #3						$0
797-04	TEST #4						$0
						Total For 797-00	**$0**
798-00	**FACILITIES FEES**						
798-01	STAGE CONSTRUCTION						$0
798-02	STAGE SHOOTING						$0
798-03	STAGE HOLDING						$0
798-04	OFFICE SPACE						$0
798-05	TESTS/INSERTS/PROMOS						$0
						Total For 798-00	**$0**
	Total Production						**$0**
800-00	**EDITING**						
800-01	FILM EDITOR						$0
800-02	SOUND EFFECTS EDITING						$0
800-03	MUSIC EDITING						$0
800-04	NEGATIVE CUTTING						$0
800-06	PROJECTION						$0
800-07	CONTINUITY SCRIPTS						$0
800-11	EDITORIAL FACILITIES						$0
800-12	EDITORIAL SUPPLIES						$0
800-14	POSTPROD. SUPERVISION						$0
800-17	OTHER COSTS						$0
800-18	ASSISTANT EDITOR						$0

(continued)

Figure 6–1   Sample budget form (continued)

Acct#	Description	Amount	Units	X	Rate	Subtotal	Total
800-00	**EDITING (CONT'D)**						
800-19	APPRENTICE EDITOR						$0
						Total For 800-00	$0
810-00	**MUSIC**						
810-08	COMPOSER						$0
810-09	CONDUCTOR						$0
810-10	SONGWRITER						$0
810-11	LYRICIST						$0
810-21	RECORDING MUSICIANS						$0
810-22	SINGERS & VOCAL COAC...						$0
810-23	ORCHESTRATORS & ARRA...						$0
810-24	COPYISTS & PROOFREAD...						$0
810-25	MUSIC SUPERVISOR						$0
810-26	MUSIC CLEARANCE SALA...						$0
810-27	MUSIC CLERICAL						$0
810-28	MASTER USE LICENSES						$0
810-29	MUSIC PUBLISHING LICEN...						$0
810-30	PRESCORE						$0
810-31	REHEARSAL MUSICIANS						$0
810-32	DEMO COSTS						$0
810-33	SCORE (FACILITIES)						$0
810-34	STUDIO EQUIPMENT RENT...						$0
810-35	MUSIC INSTRUMENT RENT...						$0
810-36	MUSIC INSTRUMENT CART...						$0
810-37	MUSIC TRANSFERS						$0
810-38	NEW USE/REUSE (MUSICI...						$0
810-39	NEW USE/REUSE (SINGERS)						$0
810-40	TRAVEL & PER DIEM						$0
810-41	PAYROLL TAXES/FRINGES						$0
810-42	PHONO						$0
810-43	MUSIC RESEARCH REPOR...						$0
						Total For 810-00	$0
820-00	**POSTPRODUCTION SOUND**						
820-01	DIALOGUE RECORDING (A...						$0
820-02	NARRATION RECORDING						$0
820-03	SOUND EFFECTS (FOLEY)						$0
820-06	DUBBING SESSION						$0
820-07	SOUND TRANSFERS						$0
820-09	PURCHASED SOUND EFFE...						$0
820-11	SOUND TRANSFER 35 & 3...						$0
820-12	MAGNETIC TAPE FOR EDIT						$0
820-13	OPTICAL NEG 35 & 35/32						$0
820-14	PREVIEW EXPENSES						$0
						Total For 820-00	$0

Figure 6–1 Sample budget form (continued)

"SWINGERS" BUDGET

PRODUCTION NO.:
PRODUCER:
DIRECTOR:
SCRIPT DATE:
START DATE: 8/31/95
FINISH DATE: 9/22/95

DATE: AUGUST 31, 1995
LOCATIONS: HLYWD/VEGAS
BASED ON: 3 WEEK SHOOT
6 DAY WEEK
SAG

NOT A FINAL SHOOTING BUDGET

Acct#	Description	Amount	Units	X	Rate	Subtotal	Total
600-00	STORY						
600-01	RIGHTS PURCHASED						
	Writer		ALLOW		1,000	1,000	$1,000
600-03	WRITERS						$0
600-04	SCREENPLAY PURCHASE						$0
						Total For 600-00	$1,000
610-00	PRODUCER						
610-01	EXECUTIVE PRODUCER						$0
610-02	PRODUCER						
	PRODUCER	15	WEEKS		300	4,500	$4,500
610-03	ASSOCIATE PRODUCER						$0
610-07	PRODUCER'S ENT.						
	Producer's Entertainment		ALLOW		209	209	$209
610-08	PREPRODUCTION EXPEN...						
	Ent./food/film/Supplies		ALLOW		1,000	1,000	
	SALES TAX	8.25%			1,000	83	$1,083
						Total For 610-00	$5,792
620-00	DIRECTOR						
620-01	DIRECTOR						
	DIRECTOR	1	FLAT		1,000	1,000	$1,000
620-05	CASTING DIRECTOR						
	CASTING FEES/EXPENSE...	1	FLAT		2,000	2,000	$2,000
620-08	CASTING EXPENSES						
	CASTING EXPENSES		ALLOW		200	200	$200
						Total For 620-00	$3,200
630-00	CAST						
630-01	PRINCIPAL PLAYERS						
	SUE	1	WEEK		1,558	1,558	
	pro-rata	3	DAYS		343	1,029	
	MIKE	3	WEEKS		1,558	4,674	
	TRENT	2	WEEKS		1,558	3,116	
	pro-rata	3	DAYS		343	1,029	
	ROB	8	Days		448	3,584	

(continued)

Figure 6–2 Swingers *budget ($279,577) (continued)*

Acct#	Description	Amount	Units	X	Rate	Subtotal	Total
630-00	**CAST (CONT'D)**						
630-01	PRINCIPAL PLAYERS (CONT'D)						
	CHARLES	1	WEEK		1,558	1,558	
	Pro-rata	1	DAY		343	343	
	SAG CORP	12.8%			16,891	2,162	
	FICA #1	6.2%			16,891	1,047	
	FICA #2	1.45%			16,891	245	
	SUI	5.4%			7,000	378	
	FUI	0.8%			7,000	56	
	AGENCY COMMISS.	10.0%			16,891	1,689	$22,468
630-02	DAY PLAYERS						
	BLUE HAIR	1	DAY		448	448	
	DEALER	1	DAY		448	448	
	PIT BOSS						
	CASINO WAITRESS	1	DAY		50	50	
	PARTY BLONDE						
	GIRL IN HAT	1	DAY		448	448	
	LISA	2	DAYS		448	896	
	CHRISTY	3	DAYS		448	1,344	
	NIKKI	1	DAY		448	448	
	LORRAINE	3	DAYS		448	1,344	
	BALD GUY	1	DAY		448	448	
	SAG CORP	12.8%			5,874	752	
	FICA #1	6.2%			5,874	364	
	FICA #2	1.45%			5,874	85	
	SUI	5.4%			5,874	317	
	FUI	0.8%			5,874	47	
	AGENCY COMMISS.	10.0%			5,874	587	$8,027
630-06	LOOPING/ADR (INCL. 1 DA...						$0
630-08	OVERTIME						
	OVERTIME		ALLOW		500	500	
	SAG CORP	12.8%			500	64	
	FICA #1	6.2%			500	31	
	FICA #2	1.45%			500	7	
	SUI	5.4%			500	27	
	FUI	0.8%			500	4	$633
630-09	MEDICAL EXAMS						
	Medical Exams		ALLOW	5	100	500	$500
630-20	SIDE DEALS						
	SIDE DEALS		ALLOW		1,500	1,500	$1,500
						Total For 630-00	**$33,128**
650-00	**TRAVEL & LIVING**						
650-03	WRITER'S TRAVEL						$0
650-03	WRITER'S LIVING						$0
650-01	PRODUCER'S TRAVEL						$0

Figure 6–2 Swingers *budget ($279,577) (continued)*

Acct#	Description	Amount	Units	X	Rate	Subtotal	Total
710-00	**CAMERA (CONT'D)**						
710-06	STILL PHOTOGRAPHER (CONT'D)						
	STILL PHOTGRAPHER	5	DAYS		100	500	
	SUPPLIES/DEVELOPING		ALLOW		500	500	$1,000
710-08	CAMERA RENTALS						
	Camera Package	4	WEEKS		2,000	8,000	$8,000
710-09	CAMERA SUPPLIES						
	Camera Expendables		ALLOW		350	350	
	SALES TAX	8.25%			350	29	$379
710-11	CAM ACCESSORIES/VIDE...						
	Camera Accessories		ALLOW		280	280	$280
710-20	LOSS, DAMAGE & REPAIR						
	Loss and damage		ALLOW		1,000	1,000	$1,000
						Total For 710-00	$12,819
715-00	**ART/SET DESIGN(MATERIALS IN PROPS)**						
715-01	PRODUCTION DESIGNER						
	Prod. Designer - PREP	3	WEEKS		300	900	
	SHOOT	3	WEEKS		300	900	
	WRAP	1	WEEK		300	300	$2,100
715-02	ART/SET DIRECTOR						
	PREP	2	WEEKS		300	600	
	SHOOT	3	WEEKS		300	900	$1,500
715-03	SET DESIGNERS						$0
						Total For 715-00	$3,600
725-00	**SET OPERATIONS**						
725-01	1ST COMPANY GRIP/KEY ...						
	PREP	0.6	WEEKS		300	180	
	SHOOT	3	WEEKS		300	900	$1,080
725-02	BEST BOY GRIP						
	PREP	0.6	WEEKS		300	180	
	SHOOT	3	WEEKS	2	300	1,800	$1,980
725-03	CRANE/DOLLY GRIPS						
	CRANE/DOLLY GRIP	1	WEEK		1,000	1,000	$1,000
725-04	EXTRA GRIPS/COMPANY ...						
	EXTRA GRIP	1	WEEK		300	300	$300
725-05	CAMERA DOLLIES						
	Dolly W/ TRACK	3	DAYS		150	450	$450
725-06	CAMERA CRANES						$0
725-08	GRIP EQUIPMENT RENTALS						
	GRIP EQUIPMENT(TRUCK I...	3	WEEKS		2,000	6,000	
	CAR MOUNTS	3	DAYS		50	150	
	EXPENDABLES	3	WEEKS		200	600	$6,750
725-09	GRIP EQUIPMENT PURCH...						
	Grip Purchases		ALLOW		500	500	
	SALES TAX	8.25%			500	41	$541

(continued)

Figure 6–2 Swingers *budget ($279,577) (continued)*

IFP/WEST INDEPENDENT FILMMAKER'S MANUAL

ll66– IFP/WEST INDEPENDENT FILMMAKER'S MANUAL

Acct#	Description	Amount	Units	X	Rate	Subtotal	Total
725-00	**SET OPERATIONS (CONT'D)**						
725-10	GRIP BOX RENTALS						$0
725-11	CRAFT SERVICE/SERVICE...						
	CRAFT SERVICEMAN-PREP	0.6	WEEKS		300	180	
	SHOOT	3	WEEKS		300	900	
	CRAFT SERVICE FOOD	3	WEEKS		400	1,200	
	SALES TAX	8.25%			1,200	99	$2,379
725-12	SET CLEANUP & TRASH DI...						
	SET CLEANUP & TRASH DI...		ALLOW		200	200	$200
725-19	FIRST AID						
	First Aid		ALLOW		500	500	$500
725-20	LOSS & DAMAGE						
	L&D		Allow		1,000	1,000	$1,000
725-24	DRESSING ROOM RENTALS						$0
725-30	LOCATION LOAD AND UNL...						$0
						Total For 725-00	**$16,180**
730-00	**ELECTRICAL**						
730-01	GAFFER						
	PREP	0.6	WEEKS		300	180	
	SHOOT	3	WEEKS		300	900	$1,080
730-02	BEST BOY						
	PREP	0.6	WEEKS		300	180	
	SHOOT	3	WEEKS	2	300	1,800	$1,980
730-05	GLOBES/CARBONS/SUPP...						
	GLOBES/CARBONS/SUPP...		ALLOW		200	200	$200
730-07	GENERATOR RENTAL						
	Generator	3	WEEKS		600	1,800	
	Gas and oil	3	WEEKS		200	600	$2,400
730-08	ELEC. EQUIP. RENTALS						
	ELECTRICAL PACKAGE	3	WEEKS		1,700	5,100	
	KINO FLOWS/PRACTICALS	3	WEEKS		300	900	
	TRUCK INCLUDED						$6,000
730-09	ELEC. EQUIP. PURCHASE						
	ELEC. PURCHASE/EXPEN...		ALLOW		500	500	
	SALES TAX	8.25%			500	41	$541
730-10	BOX RENTAL						$0
730-20	LOSS, DAMAGE, & REPAIR						
	LOSS & DAMAGE		ALLOW		1,000	1,000	$1,000
						Total For 730-00	**$13,201**
745-00	**SET DRESSING**						
						Total For 745-00	**$0**
750-00	**PROPERTIES**						
750-01	PROPERTY MASTER(SEE ...						$0
750-04	PICTURE VEHICLES LABO...						

Figure 6–2 Swingers *budget ($279,577) (continued)*

Acct#	Description	Amount	Units	X	Rate	Subtotal	Total
800-00	**EDITING**						
800-01	FILM EDITOR						
	FILM EDITOR	10	WEEKS		300	3,000	$3,000
800-02	SOUND EFFECTS EDITING						$0
800-03	MUSIC EDITING						$0
800-04	NEGATIVE CUTTING						
	NEGATIVE CUTTING	10	REELS		500	5,000	$5,000
800-06	PROJECTION						
	PROJECTION		ALLOW		500	500	$500
800-11	EDITORIAL FACILITIES						
	EDIT BAY	1	FLAT		12,000	12,000	$12,000
800-12	EDITORIAL SUPPLIES						
	SUPPLIES/FOOD	15	Weeks		200	3,000	
	SALES TAX	8.25%			3,000	248	$3,248
800-14	POSTPROD. SUPERVISION						$0
800-18	ASSISTANT EDITOR						
	ASSISTANT EDITOR	8	WEEKS		300	2,400	$2,400
800-19	APPRENTICE EDITOR (INT...						$0
						Total For 800-00	**$26,148**
810-00	**MUSIC**						
810-08	COMPOSER						
	COMPOSER	5	WEEKS		300	1,500	$1,500
810-25	MUSIC SUPERVISOR						
	MUSIC SUPERVISOR	5	WEEKS		300	1,500	$1,500
810-26	MUSIC CLEARANCE SALA...						$0
810-27	MUSIC CLERICAL						$0
810-28	MASTER USE LICENSES						$0
810-29	MUSIC PUBLISHING LICEN...						$0
810-30	PRESCORE						$0
810-31	REHEARSAL MUSICIANS						$0
810-32	DEMO COSTS						$0
810-33	SCORE (FACILITIES)						$0
810-34	STUDIO EQUIPMENT RENT...						$0
810-35	MUSIC INSTRUMENT RENT...						$0
810-37	MUSIC TRANSFERS						$0
						Total For 810-00	**$3,000**
820-00	**POSTPRODUCTION SOUND**						
820-01	DIALOGUE RECORDING/ADR						
	ADR FACILITY/FOOD		Allow		300	300	$300
820-02	NARRATION RECORDING						$0
820-03	SOUND EFFECTS (FOLEY)						
	FOLEY	1	FLAT		1,000	1,000	$1,000
820-06	DUBBING SESSION						
	SOUND MIX	1	FLAT		5,000	5,000	$5,000
820-07	SOUND TRANSFERS						
	SOUND TRANSFERS		ALLOW		2,000	2,000	$2,000
						Total For 820-00	**$8,300**

(continued)

Figure 6–2 Swingers *budget ($279,577) (continued)*

Acct#	Description	Amount	Units	X	Rate	Subtotal	Total
840-00	**TITLES**						
840-01	TITLES (MAIN & END)						
	MAIN AND END TITLES	1	FLAT		1,000	1,000	$1,000
840-02	MAIN TITLES						$0
840-03	END TITLES						$0
840-04	MISCELLANEOUS TITLES						$0
840-05	LABORATORY PROCESSING						$0
						Total For 840-00	$1,000
850-00	**OPTICALS, MATTES, INSERTS**						
850-01	OPTICAL EFFECTS/DUPE ...						
	OPTICALS		ALLOW		1,000	1,000	$1,000
850-02	MASTER POSITIVES						$0
850-03	LABORATORY PROCESSING						$0
850-04	SPECIAL PHOTO EFFECTS						$0
850-11	PURCHASES						$0
						Total For 850-00	$1,000
860-00	**LABORATORY PROCESSING**						
860-01	REPRINTING & DEVELOPING						$0
860-02	1ST TRIAL COMPOSITE P...						
	WORK PRINT		ALLOW		2,000	2,000	$2,000
860-03	MASTER POSITIVE PRINT						$0
860-06	DEVELOP SOUND NEGATI...						$0
860-07	ANSWER PRINT						
	Answer Print	8,500	FEET		1.1	9,350	$9,350
						Total For 860-00	$11,350
	TOTAL COMPLETION PERIOD						$50,798
910-00	**ADMINISTRATIVE EXPENSES**						
910-01	ACCOUNTING & TERMINAL...						
	ACCOUNTING PACKAGE		ALLOW		100	100	
910-02	MPAA CERTIFICATE						
	MPAA CERTIFICATE		ALLOW		900	900	
910-03	POSTAGE & SHIPPING & F...						
	POSTAGE & SHIPPING & F...		ALLOW		300	300	
910-04	PHOTOCOPYING (NO SCRI...						
	PHOTOCOPYING		ALLOW		400	400	
910-05	LEGAL EXPENSES & FEES						
	LEGAL FEES & EXPENSES		ALLOW	0	5,000	0	
910-00	**ADMINISTRATIVE EXPENSES (CONT'D)**						
910-06	TELEPHONE/FACSIMILE						
	TELEPHONE & FAX		ALLOW		1,200	1,200	$1,200
910-12	PREVIEW EXPENSE/DIST. ...						
	PREVIEW		ALLOW		2,000	2,000	$2,000
910-18	RESEARCH REPORT/TITLE...						
	RESEARCH REPORT		Allow		1,000	1,000	$1,000
910-19	PRODUCTION EXPENDABL...						
910-20	CORPORATE FILING						
	Filing over Internet	1			300	300	
910-21	POLAROID & B/W STILL FI...						
	POLAROID & STILL FILM		ALLOW		300	300	
910-22	PAYROLL CO.						
	PAYROLL COMPANY	3	WEEKS	12	3	108	
						Total For 910-00	$6,608
	TOTAL OTHER						$6,608
	Completion Bond: 0.00%						
	Contingency: 10.00%						$25,018
	Overhead: 0.00%						
	Insurance: 1.75%						$4,378
	TOTAL ABOVE-THE-LINE						$45,173
	TOTAL BELOW-THE-LINE						$205,008
	TOTAL ABOVE & BELOW-THE-LINE						$250,181
	GRAND TOTAL						$279,577

Figure 6–2 Swingers *budget ($279,577) (continued)*

"SWINGERS"

ACTUALIZED BUDGET
PRODUCTION NO.:
PRODUCER:
DIRECTOR:
SCRIPT DATE:
START DATE:8/31/95
FINISH DATE:9/22/95

DATE: AUGUST 31, 1995
LOCATIONS: HLYWD/VEGAS
BASED ON: 3 WEEK SHOOT
6 DAY WEEK
  SAG

NOT FINAL SHOOTING BUDGET

Acct#	Category Title	Page	Original	Total	Variance
600-00	STORY	1	$1,000	$1,000	$0
610-00	PRODUCER	1	$5,983	$5,792	($191)
620-00	DIRECTOR	1	$3,200	$3,200	$0
630-00	CAST	1	$33,708	$33,128	($580)
650-00	TRAVEL & LIVING	2	$1,891	$2,053	$162
	TOTAL ABOVE-THE-LINE		**$45,781**	**$45,173**	**($608)**
700-00	EXTRA TALENT	3	$4,253	$5,589	$1,336
705-00	PRODUCTION STAFF	4	$20,940	$18,360	($2,580)
710-00	CAMERA	4	$12,711	$12,819	$108
715-00	ART/SET DESIGN(MATERIALS IN PROPS)	5	$3,600	$3,600	$0
725-00	SET OPERATIONS	5	$15,580	$16,180	$600
730-00	ELECTRICAL	6	$12,701	$13,201	$500
750-00	PROPERTIES	6	$6,665	$5,965	($700)
755-00	WARDROBE	7	$8,637	$9,937	$1,300
760-00	MAKEUP & HAIRSTYLISTS	8	$1,680	$1,780	$100
765-00	PRODUCTION SOUND	8	$9,333	$9,160	($173)
770-00	TRANSPORTATION	8	$6,430	$4,977	($1,453)
775-00	LOCATION EXPENSE	9	$26,094	$28,282	$2,188
785-00	PRODUCTION DAILIES	10	$21,836	$17,753	($4,083)
	TOTAL SHOOTING PERIOD		**$150,460**	**$147,603**	**($2,857)**
800-00	EDITING	11	$21,983	$26,148	$4,165
810-00	MUSIC	11	$3,000	$3,000	$0
820-00	POST PRODUCTION SOUND	11	$8,000	$8,300	$300
840-00	TITLES	11	$1,500	$1,000	($500)
850-00	OPTICALS, MATTES, INSERTS	12	$1,000	$1,000	$0
860-00	LABORATORY PROCESSING	12	$11,350	$11,350	$0
	TOTAL COMPLETION PERIOD		**$46,833**	**$50,798**	**$3,965**
910-OO	ADMINISTRATIVE EXPENSES	12	$7,257	$6,608	($649)
	TOTAL OTHER		**$7,257**	**$6,608**	**($649)**
	Completion Bond: 0.00%		$0	$0	$0
	Contingency: 10.00%		$25,033	$25,018	($15)
	Overhead: 0.00%		$0	$0	$0
	Insurance: 1.75%		$4,381	$4,378	($3)

(continued)

Figure 6–3 Swingers *actualized budget*

SWINGERS

Acct#	Category Title	Page	Original	Total	Variance
	TOTAL ABOVE-THE-LINE		$45,781	$45,173	($608)
	TOTAL BELOW-THE-LINE		$204,549	$205,008	$459
	TOTAL ABOVE & BELOW-THE-LINE		$250,331	$250,181	($149)
	GRAND TOTAL		$279,745	$279,577	($168)

Figure 6–3 Swingers *actualized budget (continued)*

SAMPLE BUDGET 1

PRODUCTION NO.:

PRODUCER:

DIRECTOR:

SCRIPT DATE:

START DATE:

FINISH DATE:

DATE:

LOCATION: LOCAL SHOOT

BASED ON: 5 WEEK PREPRODUCTION

3 WEEK SHOOT- 6 DAY WEEK

SAG - UNDER $2 MILLION AGRMT.

LOCAL/NONUNION CREW/FLAT

NOT A FINAL SHOOTING BUDGET

Acct#	Category Title	Page	Total
600-00	STORY	1	$2,500
610-00	PRODUCER	1	$12,165
620-00	DIRECTOR	1	$12,541
630-00	CAST	1	$84,541
650-00	TRAVEL & LIVING	3	$0
	TOTAL ABOVE-THE-LINE		**$111,747**
700-00	EXTRA TALENT/STUNTS	3	$9,240
705-00	PRODUCTION STAFF	4	$40,922
710-00	CAMERA	5	$26,587
715-00	ART/SET DESIGN	6	$27,535
725-00	SET OPERATIONS	6	$23,257
730-00	ELECTRICAL	7	$19,262
745-00	SET DRESSING(see PROPS/ART)	8	$0
750-00	PROPERTIES	8	$21,069
755-00	WARDROBE	9	$22,881
760-00	MAKEUP & HAIR	9	$8,714
765-00	PRODUCTION SOUND	10	$11,044
770-00	TRANSPORTATION	10	$25,350
775-00	LOCATION EXPENSES	11	$75,720
785-00	PRODUCTION DAILIES	12	$85,633
	TOTAL SHOOTING PERIOD		**$397,213**
800-00	EDITING	13	$62,036
810-00	MUSIC	13	$22,694
820-00	POSTPRODUCTION SOUND	13	$19,403
840-00	TITLES	14	$2,500
850-00	OPTICALS, MATTES, INSERTS	14	$3,000
860-00	LABORATORY PROCESSING	14	$16,723
	TOTAL COMPLETION PERIOD		**$126,355**
910-00	ADMINISTRATIVE EXPENSES	14	$26,328
920-00	PUBLICITY	15	$0
	TOTAL OTHER		**$26,328**
	Completion Bond: 0.00%		$0
	Contingency: 10.00%		$66,164
	Overhead: 0.00%		$0
	Insurance: 2.00%		$13,233

(*continued*)

Figure 6–4   Sample budget 1 ($741,040)

Acct#	Category Title	Page	Total
	TOTAL ABOVE-THE-LINE		$111,747
	TOTAL BELOW-THE-LINE		$549,896
	TOTAL ABOVE & BELOW-THE-LINE		$661,643
	GRAND TOTAL		$741,040

Figure 6–4   Sample budget 1 ($741,040) (continued)

SAMPLE BUDGET 1

PRODUCTION NO.:   DATE:
PRODUCER: LOCATION: LOCAL SHOOT
DIRECTOR: BASED ON: 5 WEEK PREPRODUCTION
SCRIPT DATE: 3 WEEK SHOOT- 6 DAY WEEK
START DATE: SAG - UNDER $2 MILLION AGRMT.
FINISH DATE: LOCAL/NONUNION CREW/FLAT
                                 NOT A FINAL SHOOTING BUDGET

Acct#	Description	Amount	Units	X	Rate	Subtotal	Total
600-00	**STORY**						
600-01	RIGHTS PURCHASED						
	OPTION PRICE	1	Flat		500	500	$500
600-03	WRITERS						$0
600-04	SCREENPLAY PURCHASE						
	SCREENPLAY PURCHASE	1	Flat		2,000	2,000	$2,000
						Total For 600-00	$2,500
610-00	**PRODUCER**						
610-01	EXECUTIVE PRODUCER						$0
610-02	PRODUCER						
	PRODUCERS - LOAN-OUT	1	Flat	2	5,000	10,000	$10,000
610-03	ASSOCIATE PRODUCER						$0
610-07	PRODUCER'S ENT.						$0
610-08	PREPRODUCTION EXPEN...						
	ENT./FOOD/FILM/SUPPLIES		ALLOW		2,000	2,000	
	SALES TAX	8.25%			2,000	165	$2,165
						Total For 610-00	$12,165
620-00	**DIRECTOR**						
620-01	DIRECTOR						
	DIRECTOR - LOAN-OUT	1	FLAT		7,500	7,500	$7,500
620-05	CASTING DIRECTOR						
	CASTING FEES (loan-out)	3	Weeks		1,500	4,500	$4,500
620-08	CASTING EXPENSES						
	CASTING EXPENSES		ALLOW		500	500	
	SALES TAX	8.25%			500	41	$541
						Total For 620-00	$12,541
630-00	**CAST**						
630-01	PRINCIPAL PLAYERS						
	DAVE	3	Weeks		1,620	4,860	
	JANE	3	Weeks		1,620	4,860	
	SCOTT	2	Weeks		1,620	3,240	
	MATT	1	Week		1,620	1,620	
	JONATHAN	1	Week		1,620	1,620	

(continued)

Figure 6–4 Sample budget 1 ($741,040) (continued)

Acct#	Description	Amount	Units	X	Rate	Subtotal	Total
630-00	**CAST (CONT'D)**						
630-01	PRINCIPAL PLAYERS (CONT'D)						
	MARK	1	Week		1,620	1,620	
	BROOKE	2	Weeks		1,620	3,240	
	MARCI	2	Weeks		1,620	3,240	
	OVERTIME	20%			24,300	4,860	
	SAG CORP	13.3%			24,300	3,232	
	FICA #1	6.2%			24,300	1,507	
	FICA #2	1.45%			24,300	352	
	SUI	5.4%			7,000	378	
	FUI	0.8%			7,000	56	
	AGENCY COMMISS.	10.0%			24,300	2,430	$37,115
630-02	DAY PLAYERS						
	MR. TULLY	3	Days		466	1,398	
	JENSEN	3	Days		466	1,398	
	BOBBY MARTEL	2	Days		466	932	
	JOSH	1	Day		466	466	
	STEPHANIE	1	Day		466	466	
	CARRIE	1	Day		466	466	
	MRS. JOHNSON	2	Days		466	932	
	TUSTIN GREEN	1	Day		466	466	
	HARRY	1	Day		466	466	
	JUSTINE	2	Days		466	932	
	DANCERS	2	Days	4	466	3,728	
	VALETS	1	Day	3	466	1,398	
	ELIZABETH	1	Day		466	466	
	CHRISTOPHER	1	Day		466	466	
	KYLE	2	Days		466	932	
	BARTENDERS	3	2	3	466	4,194	
	AMANDA	1	Day		466	466	
	OVERTIME	20%			19,572	3,914	
	SAG CORP	13.3%			19,572	2,603	
	FICA #1	6.2%			19,572	1,213	
	FICA #2	1.45%			19,572	284	
	SUI	5.4%			14,922	806	
	FUI	0.8%			14,922	119	
	AGENCY COMMISS.	10.0%			19,572	1,957	$30,469
630-03	REHEARSAL						
	DAVE	3	Days		466	1,398	
	JANE	3	Days		466	1,398	
	SCOTT	2	Days		466	932	
	BROOKE	2	Days		466	932	
	MARCI	2	Days		466	932	
	OVERTIME	20%			5,592	1,118	
	SAG CORP	13.3%			5,592	744	
	FICA #1	6.2%			5,592	347	
	FICA #2	1.45%			5,592	81	

Figure 6–4   Sample budget 1 ($741,040) (continued)

Acct#	Description	Amount	Units	X	Rate	Subtotal	Total
770-00	**TRANSPORTATION**						
770-01	MESSENGER SERVICE						
	MESSENGER SERVICE		Allow		300	300	$300
770-02	TRANSPORTATION COORD.						$0
770-05	MILEAGE ALLOWANCE						$0
770-06	FUEL						
	FUEL/CARS/TRUCKS	8	Weeks	10	50	4,000	
	SALES TAX	8.25%			4,000	330	$4,330
770-09	EXTRA DRIVERS						
	DRIVERS	5	Weeks	2	400	4,000	
	DRIVERS	3	Weeks	2	400	2,400	
	NON-UNION	18%			6,400	1,152	$7,552
770-10	LOC. VEHICLES/PROD. TR...						
	CUBE VANS (SCOUT/P/U'S)	6	Weeks		300	1,800	
	CAMERA/SOUND	3	Weeks		400	1,200	
	PRODUCTION CUBE	5	Weeks		350	1,750	
	WARDROBE CUBE	5	Weeks		350	1,750	
	PR0P/ART CUBE	5	Weeks		350	1,750	
	GRIP/ELECTRIC TRUCK	3	Weeks		800	2,400	
	SALES TAX	8.25%			10,650	879	
	CITY TAX	6.0%			10,650	639	$12,168
770-20	LOSS, DAMAGE, REPAIRS						
	LOSS & DAMAGE		ALLOW		1,000	1,000	$1,000
						Total For 770-00	**$25,350**
775-00	**LOCATION EXPENSES**						
775-01	SURVEY EXPENSE						
	LOCATION MGR. SCOUT -F...	20	Days		15	300	
	GAS	5	Weeks		100	500	
	TIPS		Allow		100	100	
	FILM/PROCESS/SUPPLIES	5	Weeks		200	1,000	
	PHONE/CELL	5	Weeks		100	500	
	SCOUTING WITH CREW						
	FOOD	3	Days	10	12	360	
	POLAROID FILM		Allow		200	200	
	CELLULAR	3	Days		50	150	
	FUEL		Allow		150	150	
	sales tax	8.25%			2,510	207	$3,467
775-02	LOCATION STAFF						
	LOCATION MANAGER - PR...	5	Weeks		600	3,000	
	SHOOT	3	Weeks		600	1,800	
	WRAP	1	Week		600	600	
	NON-UNION	18%			5,400	972	$6,372
775-03	SITE RENTALS/PERMITS/L...						
	HOUSE	3	Days		750	2,250	
	MAIN STREET (PERMIT RO...		Allow		200	200	

(continued)

Figure 6–4   Sample budget 1 ($741,040) (continued)

Acct#	Description	Amount	Units	X	Rate	Subtotal	Total
775-00	**LOCATION EXPENSES (CONT'D)**						
775-03	SITE RENTALS/PERMITS/LIC. (CONT'D)						
	HOUSE	3	Days		500	1,500	
	BAR	5	Days		1,000	5,000	
	PARK (PERMIT ONLY)		Allow		150	150	
	DINER	1	Day		500	500	
	CLUB + (PARK LOT)	3	Days		1,500	4,500	
	STORE	2	Days		300	600	
	ICE CREAM PARLOR	1	Day		300	300	
	PERMITS/SITE RENTALS		Allow		750	750	$15,750
775-04	CREW TRAVEL & LODGING						$0
775-05	CATERING SERVICES						
	CATERING - B'FAST	18	Days	60	5	5,400	
	LUNCH (INCL. EXTRAS)	18	Days	75	10	13,500	
	SALES TAX	8.25%			18,900	1,559	$20,459
775-06	2ND MEALS/EXTRA MEALS						
	2ND MEALS	8	MEALS	50	8	3,200	
	SALES TAX	8.25%			3,200	264	$3,464
775-07	PRODUCTION EXPENDABL...						
	EXPENDABLES	3	Weeks		500	1,500	
	SALES TAX	8.25%			1,500	124	$1,624
775-11	FIRE/POLICE						
	FIREMAN	80	Hours		52	4,160	
	POLICE OFFICER	60	Hours		48	2,880	
	IA	33.0%			7,040	2,323	
	FICA #1	6.2%			4,160	258	
	FICA #2	1.45%			4,160	60	
	SUI	5.4%			4,160	225	
	FUI	0.8%			4,160	33	$9,939
775-13	A/C & HEAT FEES						
	A/C HEAT FEES (OFFICE)	8	Weeks		100	800	$800
775-14	AIRPORT PICKUP/DELIVE...						$0
775-15	LOCATION LOCK & UNLOAD						$0
775-17	GRATUITIES						
	TIPS		ALLOW		200	200	$200
775-18	OFFICE RENT/FURNITURE/...						
	OFFICE RENT/OVERHEAD/...	2	Months		1,000	2,000	
	SUPPLIES		Allow		2,000	2,000	
	SALES TAX	8.25%			2,000	165	$4,165
775-20	LOSS & DAMAGE						
	LOSS & DAMAGE		Allow		1,000	1,000	$1,000
775-21	LOCATION SECURITY						
	LOCATION SECURITY(BAR...	2	Weeks		3,000	6,000	
	NON-UNION	18%			6,000	1,080	$7,080
775-22	PARKING LOTS(FOR CREW)						
	PARKING LOT FOR CREW/...	2	Weeks		700	1,400	$1,400

Figure 6–4   Sample budget 1 ($741,040) (continued)

Acct#	Description	Amount	Units	X	Rate	Subtotal	Total
775-00	LOCATION EXPENSES (CONT'D)						
							$0
						Total For 775-00	$75,720
785-00	PRODUCTION DAILIES						
785-01	NEGATIVE RAW STOCK						
	RAW STOCK(5298 RE-CAN...	90,000	FEET		0.40	36,000	
	SALES TAX	8.25%			36,000	2,970	$38,970
785-02	DEVELOPING						
	80,000 FT DEVELOP	90,000	FEET		0.12	10,800	
	PREP @ 80,000 FEET	90,000	FEET		0.07	6,300	$17,100
785-03	TRANSFER DAILIES						
	TRANSFER TO VIDEO - 3/4"	90,000	FEET		0.24	21,600	$21,600
785-05	TRANSFER SOUND DAILIES						
	TRANSFER SOUND DAILIES		ALLOW		5,000	5,000	$5,000
785-08	SCREEN DAILIES						
	SCREEN DAILIES		Allow		500	500	$500
785-10	TAPE STOCK						
	TAPE STOCK - BETA 3/4" - ...	25	TAPES		24	600	
	BETA SP TAPES	25	TAPES		41	1,025	
	VHS TAPES	50	TAPES		13	650	
	sales tax	8.25%			2,275	188	$2,463
						Total For 785-00	$85,633
	TOTAL SHOOTING PERIOD						$397,213
800-00	EDITING						
800-01	FILM EDITOR						
	FILM EDITOR	16	Weeks		600	9,600	
	NON-UNION	18%			9,600	1,728	$11,328
800-02	SOUND EFFECTS/MUSIC E...						
	SOUND EFFECTS EDIT		Allow		5,000	5,000	$5,000
800-03	MUSIC EDITING						$0
800-04	NEGATIVE CUTTING						
	NEGATIVE CUTTING	10	REELS		500	5,000	$5,000
800-06	PROJECTION						
	PROJECTION		ALLOW		500	500	$500
800-11	EDITORIAL FACILITIES/AVID						
	EDIT BAY	16	Weeks		1,500	24,000	$24,000
800-12	EDITORIAL SUPPLIES						
	SUPPLIES/FOOD	16	Weeks		200	3,200	
	SALES TAX	8.25%			3,200	264	$3,464
800-14	POST PROD. SUPERVISION						
	POST. SUPER	8	Weeks		600	4,800	
	NON-UNION	18%			4,800	864	$5,664
800-18	ASSISTANT EDITOR						
	ASSISTANT EDITOR	12	Weeks		500	6,000	

(continued)

Figure 6–4   Sample budget 1 ($741,040) (continued)

Acct#	Description	Amount	Units	X	Rate	Subtotal	Total
800-00	**EDITING (CONT'D)**						
800-18	ASSISTANT EDITOR (CONT'D)						
	NON-UNION	18%			6,000	1,080	$7,080
800-19	APPRENTICE EDITOR (INT...						$0
						Total For 800-00	$62,036
810-00	**MUSIC**						
810-08	COMPOSER						
	COMPOSER	8	Weeks		600	4,800	
	NON-UNION	18%			4,800	864	$5,664
810-25	MUSIC SUPERVISOR						
	MUSIC SUPERVISOR	10	Weeks		600	6,000	
	NON-UNION	18%			6,000	1,080	$7,080
810-26	MUSIC CLEARANCE SALA...						$0
810-27	MUSIC CLERICAL						$0
810-28	MASTER USE LICENSES/F...						
	FESTIVAL LICENSES		Allow		1,000	1,000	$1,000
810-29	MUSIC PUBLISHING LICEN...						$0
810-30	PRESCORE						$0
810-31	REHEARSAL MUSICIANS						
	MUSICIANS	5	PEOP...		500	2,500	
	NON-UNION	18%			2,500	450	$2,950
810-32	DEMO COSTS						$0
810-33	SCORE (FACILITIES)						
	SCORE FACILITIES	2	Days		1,500	3,000	$3,000
810-34	STUDIO EQUIPMENT RENT...						$0
810-35	MUSIC INSTRUMENT RENT...						$0
810-37	MUSIC TRANSFERS						
	MUSIC TRANSFERS		Allow		3,000	3,000	$3,000
						Total For 810-00	$22,694
820-00	**POSTPRODUCTION SOUND**						
820-01	DIALOGUE RECORDING (A...						
	ADR FACILITY		ALLOW		2,500	2,500	$2,500
820-03	SOUND EFFECTS (FOLEY)						
	SOUND EFFECTS/FOLEY		Allow		3,000	3,000	$3,000
820-06	DUBBING SESSION						
	SOUND MIX-TEMP AND FI...		ALLOW		10,000	10,000	$10,000
820-09	PURCHASED SOUND EFFE...						
	PURCHASED SOUND EFFE...		Allow		1,500	1,500	$1,500
820-12	MAGNETIC TAPE FOR EDIT						
	Mag Tape		ALLOW		1,000	1,000	
	sales tax	8.25%			1,000	83	$1,083
820-13	OPTICAL NEG 35 & 35/32						
	DEVELOP OPTICAL NEG. ...	12,000	FEET		0.11	1,320	$1,320

Figure 6–4   Sample budget 1 ($741,040) (continued)

Acct#	Description	Amount	Units	X	Rate	Subtotal	Total
820-00	POSTPRODUCTION SOUND (CONT'D)						
							$0
						Total For 820-00	$19,403
840-00	TITLES						
840-01	TITLES (MAIN & END)						
	MAIN AND END TITLES		Allow		1,500	1,500	$1,500
840-02	MAIN TITLES						$0
840-03	END TITLES						$0
840-04	MISCELLANEOUS TITLES						$0
840-05	LABORATORY PROCESSING						
	TITLE PROCESSING FILM		Allow		1,000	1,000	$1,000
						Total For 840-00	$2,500
850-00	OPTICALS, MATTES, INSERTS						
850-01	OPTICAL EFFECTS/DUPE ...						
	OPTICALS		ALLOW		3,000	3,000	$3,000
850-02	MASTER POSITIVES						$0
850-03	LABORATORY PROCESSING						$0
850-04	SPECIAL PHOTO EFFECTS						$0
850-11	PURCHASES						$0
						Total For 850-00	$3,000
860-00	LABORATORY PROCESSING						
860-01	REPRINTING & DEVELOPING						
	REPRINT & DEVELOP	3,000	FEET		0.22	660	$660
860-02	1ST TRIAL COMPOSITE P...						$0
860-07	ANSWER PRINT/COLOR TI...						
	ANSWER PRINT	10,000	FEET		0.86	8,600	$8,600
860-08	SYNC REEL CHARGE						
	SYNC REEL CHARGE	10	REELS		38	380	$380
860-09	TELECINE						
	TELECINE	30	Hours		200	6,000	$6,000
860-17	LEADER & MISCELLANEOUS						
	LEADER & TAPE		Allow		1,000	1,000	
	sales tax	8.25%			1,000	83	$1,083
						Total For 860-00	$16,723
	TOTAL COMPLETION PERIOD						$126,355
910-00	ADMINISTRATIVE EXPENSES						
910-01	ACCOUNTING & TERMINAL...						
	ACCOUNTING PACKAGE		ALLOW		200	200	$200
910-02	MPAA CERTIFICATE						
	MPAA CERTIFICATE		ALLOW		1,000	1,000	$1,000
910-03	POSTAGE & SHIPPING & F...						
	POSTAGE & SHIPPING		ALLOW		1,000	1,000	$1,000

(continued)

Figure 6–4   Sample budget 1 ($741,040) (continued)

Acct#	Description	Amount	Units	X	Rate	Subtotal	Total
910-00	**ADMINISTRATIVE EXPENSES (CONT'D)**						
910-04	PHOTOCOPYING (NO SCRI...						
	XEROX & FAX RENTAL	20	Weeks	2	150	6,000	$6,000
910-05	LEGAL EXPENSES & FEES						
	LEGAL FEES & EXPENSES		ALLOW		5,000	5,000	$5,000
910-06	TELEPHONE/FACSIMILE						
	TELEPHONE & FAX	20	Weeks		300	6,000	
	SALES TAX	8.25%			6,000	495	$6,495
910-10	SCRIPT COPYRIGHT						
	SCRIPT COPYRIGHT		Allow		50	50	$50
910-12	PREVIEW EXPENSE/DIST. ...						
	PREVIEW SCREEN & MAT...		ALLOW		1,500	1,500	$1,500
910-16	FESTIVAL EXPENSES						
	FESTIVAL EXPENSES		ALLOW		200	200	$200
910-18	RESEARCH REPORT/TITLE...						$0
910-20	CORPORATE FILING						
	Filing over Internet	1			300	300	$300
910-21	POLAROID & B/W STILL FI...						
	POLAROID & STILL FILM		ALLOW		1,000	1,000	
	SALES TAX	8.25%			1,000	83	$1,083
910-22	PAYROLL COMPANY						
	PAYROLL COMPANY	1	Flat		2,000	2,000	$2,000
910-23	STORAGE						
	STORAGE FACILITY		ALLOW		500	500	$500
910-35	WRAP PARTY						
	WRAP PARTY		ALLOW		1,000	1,000	$1,000
						Total For 910-00	**$26,328**

TOTAL OTHER		**$26,328**

Completion Bond: 0.00%	**$0**

Contingency: 10.00%	**$66,164**

Overhead: 0.00%	**$0**

Insurance: 2.00%	**$13,233**

TOTAL ABOVE-THE-LINE	**$111,747**
TOTAL BELOW-THE-LINE	**$549,896**
TOTAL ABOVE & BELOW-THE-LINE	**$661,643**
GRAND TOTAL	**$741,040**

Figure 6–4   Sample budget 1 ($741,040) (continued)

SAMPLE BUDGET 2

PRODUCTION NO.:   DATE:
PRODUCER: LOCATIONS: N. Y. State/AtlanticCity
DIRECTOR: Based on 23-day shoot
SCRIPT DATE: 5 weeks prep
START DATE: SAG/NON-UNION CREW
FINISH DATE: FAVORED NATIONS
                             NOTE:

Acct#	Category Title	Page	Total
600-00	STORY	1	$52,934
610-00	PRODUCER	1	$5,500
620-00	DIRECTOR	1	$10,000
630-00	CAST	1	$96,739
650-00	TRAVEL & LIVING	2	$21,340
	TOTAL ABOVE-THE-LINE		$186,513
700-00	EXTRA TALENT	3	$20,796
705-00	PRODUCTION STAFF	4	$52,842
710-00	CAMERA	5	$43,331
715-00	SET DESIGN/DRESSING	5	$38,867
725-00	SET OPERATIONS	6	$26,957
730-00	ELECTRICAL	7	$30,640
750-00	PROPERTIES	7	$11,647
755-00	WARDROBE	8	$18,355
760-00	MAKEUP & HAIRSTYLISTS	8	$9,594
765-00	PRODUCTION SOUND	9	$15,110
770-00	TRANSPORTATION	9	$33,622
775-00	LOCATION EXPENSES	10	$107,891
785-00	PRODUCTION DAILIES	12	$80,677
797-00	TESTS	12	$350
	TOTAL SHOOTING PERIOD		$490,679
800-00	EDITING	13	$41,168
810-00	MUSIC	13	$8,000
820-00	POSTPRODUCTION SOUND	13	$25,000
840-00	TITLES	14	$3,600
850-00	OPTICALS, MATTES & INSERTS	14	$1,900
860-00	LABORATORY PROCESSING	14	$10,799
	TOTAL COMPLETION PERIOD		$90,467
910-00	ADMINISTRATIVE EXPENSES	14	$64,970
920-00	PUBLICITY	15	$2,802
970-00	DELIVERY EXPENSES	15	$47,579
	TOTAL OTHER		$115,351
	Completion Bond: 3.00%		$26,490
	Contingency: 10.00%		$88,301
	Overhead: 0.00%		$0

(continued)

Figure 6–5   Sample budget 2 ($997,800)

Acct#	Category Title	Page	Total
	TOTAL ABOVE-THE-LINE		$186,513
	TOTAL BELOW-THE-LINE		$696,496
	TOTAL ABOVE & BELOW-THE-LINE		$883,009
	GRAND TOTAL		$997,800

Figure 6–5   Sample budget 2 ($997,800) (continued)

SAMPLE BUDGET 2

PRODUCTION NO.:	**DATE:**
PRODUCER:	**LOCATIONS: N.Y. State/Atlantic City**
DIRECTOR:	Based on 23-day shoot
SCRIPT DATE:	5 weeks prep
START DATE:	SAG/NON-UNION CREW
FINISH DATE:	FAVORED NATIONS
	NOTE:

Acct#	Description	Amount	Units	X	Rate	Subtotal	Total
600-00	**STORY**						
600-01	RIGHTS PURCHASED						
	Purchase Price	1			50,000	50,000	$50,000
600-04	SCREENPLAY PURCHASE						
	Screenplay purchase	1			2,500	2,500	$2,500
600-11	SCRIPT COPYING						
	Script copies	100	SCRI...		4	400	$400
600	Total Fringes						
	Sales Tax	8.5%			400	34	$34
						Total For 600-00	$52,934
610-00	**PRODUCER**						
610-01	EXECUTIVE PRODUCER						
	EXEC PROD		Allow		500	500	$500
610-02	PRODUCER						
	PRODUCER FEE #1		ALLOW		2,500	2,500	
	PRODUCER FEE #2		ALLOW		2,500	2,500	$5,000
						Total For 610-00	$5,500
620-00	**DIRECTOR**						
620-01	DIRECTOR						
	DIRECTOR'S FEE		ALLOW		2,500	2,500	$2,500
620-04	RESEARCH CONSULTANT						
	Choreographer Expenses	1	day		200	200	$200
620-05	CASTING DIRECTOR						
	Casting Director		Allow		7,000	7,000	$7,000
620-08	CASTING EXPENSES		allow		300	300	$300
						Total For 620-00	$10,000
630-00	**CAST**						
630-01	PRINCIPAL PLAYERS						
	HILDA NURSE	4	WEEKS		1,890	7,560	
	EDWIN NURSE	1	Week		1,890	1,890	
	KARL	2.4	Weeks		1,890	4,536	
	JILL	1.2	WEEKS		1,890	2,268	
	MARY	1	Week		1,890	1,890	

(continued)

Figure 6–5 Sample budget 2 ($997,800) (continued)

Acct#	Description	Amount	Units	X	Rate	Subtotal	Total
630-00	**CAST (CONT'D)**						
630-01	PRINCIPAL PLAYERS (CONT'D)						
	LISA	1	Week		1,890	1,890	
	MARGARET	1	Day		466	466	
	TOMMY	1	WEEK		1,890	1,890	
	URSULA NURSE	1	Week		1,890	1,890	
	XAVIER NURSE	3	Weeks		1,890	5,670	
	MIKE QUACK JR	1	Week		1,890	1,890	
	MIKE QUACK SR	1	Week		1,890	1,890	
	OFFICER DRUID	5	DAYS		466	2,330	
	HOMELESS WOMAN	1	WEEK		1,890	1,890	
	Overtime	1	%	20	37,950	7,590	
	LOOPING ALLOWANCE	5	DAYS		466	2,330	
	TRAVELING ALLOWANCE	13	Days		466	6,058	$53,928
630-02	DAY PLAYERS						
	TICKET MAN	2	Days		466	932	
	FAT WOMAN	1	Day		466	466	
	OLD MAN	1	DAY		466	466	
	CHARLIE	2	Days		466	932	
	DEALER	2	Days		466	932	
	SCOTT CARLSON	2	Days		466	932	
	NICK	1	Day		466	466	
	BUFFY TOMSON	1	Day		466	466	
	DR. CLARKE	1	Day		466	466	
	Overtime	1	%	20	6,058	1,212	
	TRAVELLING ALLOWANCE	2	DAYS		466	932	$8,202
630-03	REHEARSAL						
	Rehearsal -principal players	3	Days	5	466	6,990	$6,990
630-06	SAG PER DIEM						
	See 650 Account						$0
630-07	MEAL PENALTIES						
	MEAL PENALTIES		ALLOW		500	500	$500
630-09	MEDICAL EXAMS						
	med exams		allow		300	300	$300
630-10	TUTOR/WELFARE WORKER						$0
630	Total Fringes						
	SAG CORP	13.3%			69,120	9,193	
	NONUNION	15.5%			69,120	10,714	
	Agency Fee	10.0%			69,120	6,912	$26,819
						Total For 630-00	**$96,739**
650-00	**TRAVEL & LIVING**						
650-01	PRODUCER'S TRAVEL						
	Roundtrip airfare LA-NYC	4	flights		400	1,600	$1,600
650-03	WRITER'S TRAVEL						$0
650-03	WRITER'S LIVING						$0
650-04	PRODUCER'S LIVING						

Figure 6–5   Sample budget 2 ($997,800) (continued)

Acct#	Description	Amount	Units	X	Rate	Subtotal	Total
650-00	**TRAVEL & LIVING (CONT'D)**						
650-04	PRODUCER'S LIVING (CONT'D)						
	PRODUCER'S LIVING-ASB...	26	DAYS	2	16	832	
	NEW JERSEY	3	DAYS	2	30	180	$1,012
650-06	CAST TRAVEL/PER DIEM						
	LA -NY/first class	3	fares		800	2,400	
	LA -NY/first class	1	Flat		2,500	2,500	
	HILDA NURSE	24	Days		53	1,272	
	EDWIN NURSE	20	Days		53	1,060	
	KARL	13	Days		53	689	
	JILL	8	Days		53	424	
	MARY	6	Days		53	318	
	MARGARET	7	Days		53	371	
	TOMMY	6	Days		53	318	
	URSULA NURSE	6	Days		53	318	
	XAVIER NURSE	7	Days		53	371	
	MIKE QUACK JR	6	Days		53	318	
	MIKE QUACK SR	6	Days		53	318	
	OFFICER DRUID	6	Days		53	318	
	HOMELESS WOMAN	6	Days		53	318	
	TICKET MAN	3	Days		53	159	
	FAT WOMAN	3	Days		53	159	
	OLD MAN	1	DAY		53	53	
	CHARLIE	1	Day		53	53	
	DEALER	2	Days		53	106	
	SCOTT CARLSON	2	Days		53	106	
	NICK	1	Day		53	53	
	BUFFY TOMSON	1	Day		53	53	
	DR. CLARKE	1	Day		53	53	$12,108
650-08	CAST TRAVEL						
	Cast to set Train/Car	30	Trips		70	2,100	$2,100
650-09	CAST LIVING						
	Cast living	1	Day	145	16	2,320	
	New Jersey	3	Days	5	30	450	
	Cast Living New York	5	Days		150	750	
	Star Cast Living	7	Days		100	700	$4,220
650	Total Fringes						
	N.J. sales tax	6.0%			2,950	177	
	Sales Tax	8.5%			1,450	123	
	A.P. sales tax	0%			1,012	0	$300
						Total For 650-00	$21,340
	TOTAL ABOVE-THE-LINE						**$186,513**

(continued)

Figure 6–5   Sample budget 2 ($997,800) (continued)

Acct#	Description	Amount	Units	X	Rate	Subtotal	Total
700-00	**EXTRA TALENT**						
700-02	EXTRAS & STAND-INS						
	SAG EXTRAS	1	Day	40	102	4,080	
	DAY PLAY EXTRAS Man D...	1	Day	20	25	500	
	CONTINUITY EXTRAS	1	Day	130	40	5,200	
	Travel Time/Expenses	10	Allow		70	700	$10,480
700-03	WELFARE WORKER						
	TUTOR/WELFARE WORKER	17	Days		200	3,400	$3,400
700-05	EXTRAS CASTING						
	Extras Casting Agent	8	Weeks		250	2,000	
	Extras advertisement	2	Ads		135	270	$2,270
700-08	ALLOWANCES-CAR						
	miles/report to location		allow		200	200	$200
700-09	STUNT COORDINATOR						
	STUNT COORDINATOR	2	Days		871	1,742	$1,742
700	Total Fringes						
	SAG CORP	13.3%			5,822	774	
	NONUNION	15.5%			11,222	1,739	
	N.J. sales tax	6.0%			270	16	
	Agency Fee	10.0%			1,742	174	$2,704
						Total For 700-00	**$20,796**
705-00	**PRODUCTION STAFF**						
705-01	LINE PRODUCER/UPM						
	LINE PRODUCER/UPM	9	Weeks		1,000	9,000	
	kit rental		allow		75	75	$9,075
705-02	PRODUCTION COORDINAT...						
	COORDINATOR	44	Days		125	5,500	$5,500
705-03	1ST ASSISTANT DIRECTOR						
	AD	42	Days		125	5,250	$5,250
705-04	2ND ASSISTANT DIRECTOR						
	2nd AD	28	Days		100	2,800	$2,800
705-05	2ND 2ND ASSISTANT DIR						
	2nd 2nd AD	25	Days		80	2,000	$2,000
705-06	SCRIPT SUPERVISOR						
	script supervisor	29	Days		125	3,625	$3,625
705-07	APOC						
	Coordinator #2	41	Days		80	3,280	$3,280
705-08	PRODUCT PLACEMENT						
	PRODUCT PLACEMENT		Allow		200	200	$200
705-10	PRODUCTION ASSISTANTS						
	Key Set PA	28	Days		80	2,240	
	Set PA	26	Days		50	1,300	
	Set PA	26	Days		50	1,300	
	Set PA	10	Days		50	500	
	PA/Talent Driver	23	Days		50	1,150	
	Office PA	15	Days		70	1,050	

Figure 6–5   Sample budget 2 ($997,800) (continued)

Acct#	Description	Amount	Units	X	Rate	Subtotal	Total
705-00	**PRODUCTION STAFF (CONT'D)**						
705-10	PRODUCTION ASSISTANTS (CONT'D)						
	Office PA	50	Days		50	2,500	
	Car Rental Allowance	4	Weeks	2	50	400	$10,440
705-11	PREPRODUCTION EXPEN...						
	Meals		Allow		1,400	1,400	
	Office Supplies		Allow		1,400	1,400	$2,800
705	Total Fringes						
	Crew Overtime	15.0%			19,175	2,876	
	NONUNION	15.5%			30,695	4,758	
	Sales Tax	8.5%			2,800	238	$7,872
						Total For 705-00	**$52,842**
710-00	**CAMERA**						
710-01	DIRECTOR OF PHOTOGRA...						
	Prep	19	DAYS		150	2,850	
	Shoot	24	DAYS		300	7,200	
	Kit Rental	4	Weeks		100	400	$10,450
710-03	1ST ASST CAMERAMAN						
	1ST AC	27	Days		125	3,375	$3,375
710-04	2ND ASST CAMERAMAN						
	2ND AC	27	Days		100	2,700	$2,700
710-05	FILM LOADER						
	LOADER	23	DAYS		80	1,840	$1,840
710-06	STILL PHOTOGRAPHER						
	PHOTOGRAPHER		Allow		500	500	
	EXPENDABLES/SUPPLIES		ALLOW		700	700	$1,200
710-08	CAMERA RENTALS						
	Camera Package (vid tap inc)	4	Weeks		4,500	18,000	$18,000
710-09	CAMERA SUPPLIES						
	Camera SUPPLIES		Allow		500	500	$500
710-11	CAM ACCESORIES/VIDEO ...						
	other toys		Allow		250	250	$250
710-20	LOSS, DAMAGE & REPAIR		Allow		1,200	1,200	$1,200
710	Total Fringes						
	Crew Overtime	15.0%			6,075	911	
	NONUNION	15.5%			18,465	2,862	
	Sales Tax	8.5%			500	43	$3,816
						Total For 710-00	**$43,331**
715-00	**SET DESIGN/DRESSING**						
715-01	PRODUCTION DESIGNER						
	PROD. DESIGNER	54	Days		125	6,750	$6,750
715-02	ART DIRECTOR						
	ART DIRECTOR	40	Days		125	5,000	$5,000
715-03	SET DESIGNER/LEAD MAN						
	LEAD MAN	23	Days		100	2,300	$2,300

(*continued*)

Figure 6–5   Sample budget 2 ($997,800) (continued)

Acct#	Description	Amount	Units	X	Rate	Subtotal	Total
715-00	SET DESIGN/DRESSING (CONT'D)						
715-04	SET DRESSER						
	DRESSER	54	Days		80	4,320	
	Carpenters/local hire	26	Days		80	2,080	
	Additional Carpenter	5	DAYS		80	400	
	Painters/local hire	20	Days		80	1,600	$8,400
715-05	RENTALS						
	Rentals/non taxed		Allow		2,000	2,000	$2,000
715-06	SUPPLIES						
	Materials		ALLOW		4,500	4,500	
	Purchases		allow		2,500	2,500	$7,000
715-10	KIT RENTAL		ALLOW		975	975	$975
715-11	ART PAs						
	PA	28	Days		50	1,400	$1,400
715	Total Fringes						
	Crew Overtime	15.0%			5,000	750	
	NONUNION	15.5%			23,850	3,697	
	Sales Tax	8.5%			7,000	595	$5,042
						Total For 715-00	$38,867
725-00	SET OPERATIONS						
725-01	1ST COMPANY GRIP						
	key grip	28	Days		125	3,500	$3,500
725-02	BEST BOY GRIP						
	GRIP	26	Days		100	2,600	
	COMPANY GRIP	26	Days	0	80	0	$2,600
725-03	GRIPS						
	GRIP	23	Days		80	1,840	
	ADDITIONAL LABOR	10	Days		80	800	$2,640
725-05	CAMERA DOLLIES						
	DOLLY/W/ALL ACCES.	4	WEEKS	0	1,200	0	$0
725-08	GRIP EQUIPMENT RENTALS						
	GRIP RENTALS		ALLOW		8,500	8,500	$8,500
725-09	GRIP PURCHASES						
	PURCHASES		allow		500	500	
	TRUCK BUILD		allow		500	500	$1,000
725-10	KIT RENTAL						
	KIT RENTAL		ALLOW		400	400	$400
725-11	CRAFT SERVICE						
	CRAFT PERSON	24	Days		50	1,200	
	CRAFT FOOD	5	WEEKS		600	3,000	$4,200
725-25	MISCELLANEOUS EXPENSE						
	Miscellaneous		allow		250	250	$250
725-20	LOSS, DAMAGE & REPAIR		ALLOW		750	750	$750
725	Total Fringes						
	Crew Overtime	15.0%			8,740	1,311	
	NONUNION	15.5%			9,940	1,541	

Figure 6–5   Sample budget 2 ($997,800) (continued)

Acct#	Description	Amount	Units	X	Rate	Subtotal	Total
725-00	**SET OPERATIONS (CONT'D)**						
725	Total Fringes (CONT'D)						
	N.J. sales tax	6.0%			3,000	180	
	Sales Tax	8.5%			1,000	85	$3,117
						Total For 725-00	**$26,957**
730-00	**ELECTRICAL**						
730-01	GAFFER						
	Gaffer	28	Days		125	3,500	$3,500
730-02	BEST BOY						
	Best Boy	23	Days		100	2,300	$2,300
730-03	ELECTRICIANS						
	ELECTRIC	23	Days		80	1,840	
	SWING/DRIVER	25	Days		80	2,000	$3,840
730-04	LOCATION RIGGING/STRIKE		ALLOW		250	250	$250
730-05	GLOBES/CARBONS/SUPP...		ALLOW		2,000	2,000	$2,000
730-06	POWER						
	POWER		ALLOW		1,000	1,000	$1,000
730-07	GENERATOR RENTAL						
	Rental	4	WEEKS		1,000	4,000	$4,000
730-08	ELECTRICAL EQUIP RENT...		Allow		8,500	8,500	$8,500
730-10	KIT RENTAL						
	KIT RENTAL		ALLOW		400	400	$400
730-13	MISCELLANEOUS EXPENSE						
	MISC.		ALLOW		250	250	$250
730-20	LOSS, DAMAGE, & REPAIR		Allow		1,200	1,200	$1,200
730	Total Fringes						
	Crew Overtime	15.0%			9,640	1,446	
	NONUNION	15.5%			9,640	1,494	
	N.J. sales tax	6.0%			2,000	120	
	Sales Tax	8.5%			4,000	340	$3,400
						Total For 730-00	**$30,640**
750-00	**PROPERTIES**						
750-01	PROPERTY MASTER						
	Prop Master	12	Days		125	1,500	
	Prop Master	26	Days		80	2,080	$3,580
750-02	ASSISTANT PROPERTY M...						
	PROP PA	32	Days		50	1,600	$1,600
750-05	PICTURE VEHICLE RENTALS						
	Ambulance (Product Placed)						
	Police Car (Product Placed)						
	Academy Bus (Product Plac...						
	Old Cadillac		allow		150	150	
	Lincoln Continental		allow		150	150	
	'77 Gray Cadillac		Allow		150	150	
	'79 Gr Chevy Nova		Allow		150	150	
	'86 White Caddy Seville		Allow		150	150	$750

(continued)

Figure 6–5 Sample budget 2 ($997,800) (continued)

Acct#	Description	Amount	Units	X	Rate	Subtotal	Total
750-00	**PROPERTIES (CONT'D)**						
750-08	PROP RENTALS						
	RENTALS		Allow		1,500	1,500	$1,500
750-09	PROP PURCHASES						
	PURCHASES		Allow		1,500	1,500	$1,500
750-10	KIT RENTALS						
	KIT RENTALS		ALLOW	0	150	0	$0
750-12	EXPENDABLES		allow		500	500	$500
750-20	LOSS, DAMAGE & REPAIRS		Allow		750	750	$750
750	Total Fringes						
	Crew Overtime	15.0%			3,580	537	
	NONUNION	15.5%			5,180	803	
	Sales Tax	8.5%			1,500	128	$1,467
						Total For 750-00	**$11,647**
755-00	**WARDROBE**						
755-04	COSTUME DESIGNER						
	COSTUME DESIGNER	41	Allow		125	5,125	$5,125
755-03	ASSISTING WARDROBE P...						
	WARD. ASST.	35	Days		100	3,500	
	WARDROBE PA/SWING	21	Days		50	1,050	$4,550
755-06	ALTERATIONS - L&M		Allow		100	100	$100
755-07	CLEANING & DYEING		Allow		500	500	$500
755-08	WARDROBE RENTALS		Allow		2,200	2,200	$2,200
755-09	WARDROBE PURCHASES						
	PURCHASES		Allow		2,200	2,200	$2,200
755-10	KIT RENTAL						
	KIT RENTALS		ALLOW		200	200	$200
755-20	LOSS, DAMAGE & REPAIRS						
	L&D		Allow		500	500	$500
755	Total Fringes						
	Crew Overtime	15.0%			8,625	1,294	
	NONUNION	15.5%			9,675	1,500	
	Sales Tax	8.5%			2,200	187	$2,980
						Total For 755-00	**$18,355**
760-00	**MAKEUP & HAIRSTYLISTS**						
760-01	MAKEUP & HAIR ARTIST						
	M/U/HAIR STYLIST	27	Days		125	3,375	$3,375
760-02	ASSISTANT MAKE-UP/HAI...						
	ASST. HAIR AND M/U	24	Days		100	2,400	$2,400
760-03	MAKEUP/HAIR PA						
	Makeup/Hair PA Bus Station	5	Days		100	500	$500
760-06	WIG & HAIR PURCHASE						
	WIG/HAIR PURCHASE		ALLOW		350	350	$350
760-09	MAKEUP SUPPLIES/APPLI...						
	M/U SUPPLIES		Allow		700	700	$700

Figure 6–5   Sample budget 2 ($997,800) (continued)

Acct#	Description	Amount	Units	X	Rate	Subtotal	Total
760-00	**MAKEUP & HAIRSTYLISTS (CONT'D)**						
760-10	MAKEUP/HAIR KIT RENTALS						
	KIT RENTAL	4	Weeks	2	50	400	$400
760-11	BLOOD/GORE		ALLOW	0	1,200	0	$0
760	Total Fringes						
	Crew Overtime	15.0%			5,775	866	
	NONUNION	15.5%			6,275	973	
	Sales Tax	8.5%			350	30	$1,869
						Total For 760-00	**$9,594**
765-00	**PRODUCTION SOUND**						
765-01	SOUND MIXER						
	SOUND MIXER	24	Days		125	3,000	$3,000
765-02	BOOM MAN						
	BOOM MAN	23	Days		100	2,300	$2,300
765-06	SOUND EQUIP RENTALS						
	FULL PACKAGE	23	Days		175	4,025	
	SPECIAL RENTALS		Allow		400	400	
	WalkieTalkies	4	Weeks		410	1,640	$6,065
765-11	PURCHASES						
	408 Ampex Rolls	23	Days	3	7	483	
	DAT Tapes	10	Tapes		10	100	
	BATTERIES AND MISC	23	Days		15	345	$928
765-20	LOSS & DAMAGE						
	L&D		ALLOW		1,200	1,200	$1,200
765	Total Fringes						
	Crew Overtime	15.0%			5,300	795	
	NONUNION	15.5%			5,300	822	$1,617
						Total For 765-00	**$15,110**
770-00	**TRANSPORTATION**						
770-01	MESSENGER SERVICE						
	MESSENGER SERVICE		ALLOW		275	275	$275
770-02	TEAMSTERS						
	Teamsters	3	DAYS	2	500	3,000	
	Teamster Per Diem	3	Allow	2	25	150	$3,150
770-06	FUEL & TOLLS						
	FUEL		ALLOW		5,000	5,000	
	TOLLS		Allow		500	500	$5,500
770-10	PRODUCTION VEHICLES						
	PRODUCTION CUBE	6	Weeks		275	1,650	
	ART CUBE	8	Weeks		275	2,200	
	G/E TRUCK	4.5	Weeks	0	275	0	
	CAMERA TRUCK	4.5	Weeks		275	1,238	
	PROPS CARGO	6	Weeks		250	1,500	
	WARDROBE TRUCK	4.5	Weeks		275	1,238	
	Lumber & Labor - Truck Guts		Allow		500	500	

(continued)

Figure 6–5   Sample budget 2 ($997,800) (continued)

Acct#	Description	Amount	Units	X	Rate	Subtotal	Total
770-00	**TRANSPORTATION (CONT'D)**						
770-10	PRODUCTION VEHICLES (CONT'D)						
	Production Car	8	Weeks		170	1,360	
	Production 15-pass.	5	Weeks		270	1,350	
	Production 15-pass.	5	Weeks		270	1,350	
	Location Car	8	Weeks		170	1,360	
	Production Minivan	4	Weeks		250	1,000	
	Producer's Car	4.5	Weeks		170	765	
	Executive Producer Car	5	Weeks		170	850	
	3 Vehicle Weekly Allowance	8	Weeks	4	50	1,600	
	Additional Car	2.5	Weeks		170	425	$18,386
770-20	LOSS, DAMAGE, REPAIRS		allow		1,500	1,500	$1,500
770-28	ALL OTHER TRANSPORTA...						
	Cab Allowance		allow		500	500	$500
770-30	PREPRO/NONLOCAL CRE...						
	PrePro Crew Travel time	50			25	1,250	
	Crew Travel time (N.J.)	50			25	1,250	$2,500
770	Total Fringes						
	Teamster Fring	29.0%			3,150	914	
	Crew Overtime	15.0%			3,150	473	
	Sales Tax	8.5%			5,000	425	$1,811
						Total For 770-00	**$33,622**
775-00	**LOCATION EXPENSES**						
775-01	SURVEY EXPENSE						
	Tech Scout/Expenses		Allow		1,200	1,200	$1,200
775-02	LOCATION STAFF						
	LOCATION MANAGER	48	Days		125	6,000	
	LOCATION PA	38	DAYS		50	1,900	$7,900
775-03	SITE RENTALS/PERMITS/L...						
	Newman House		Allow		1,500	1,500	
	Holding & Lunch Site Newman		Allow		1,000	1,000	
	Quib House		Allow		1,500	1,500	
	Holding & Lunch Site Quib ...		Allow		900	900	
	Jackie & Mary's Rm - Holida...		Allow		500	500	
	Holding & Lunch Site Hotel		Allow		200	200	
	Bob'sTV Store		Allow		50	50	
	City Boardwalk		Allow	0	400	0	
	Bus Station		Allow		4,000	4,000	
	Bus Station - Women's Bath...		Allow		300	300	
	Holding & Lunch Site Bathro...		Allow		200	200	
	Casino - Interiors		Allow		500	500	
	Church (Incl. Holding)		Allow		400	400	
	Cocktail Lounge		Allow		150	150	
	Pawn Shop		Allow	0	400	0	
	Holding & Lunch Site Pawn		Allow		200	200	
	Donut shop		Allow		500	500	

Figure 6–5 Sample budget 2 ($997,800) (continued)

Acct#	Description	Amount	Units	X	Rate	Subtotal	Total
775-00	**LOCATION EXPENSES (CONT'D)**						
775-03	SITE RENTALS/PERMITS/LIC. (CONT'D)						
	Hospital		Allow		250	250	
	Exterior Liquor Store		Allow		300	300	
	High School		Allow	0	500	0	
	Holding & Lunch Site High S...		Allow		200	200	
	Movie Theater		Allow		300	300	
	Holding & Lunch Site Theater		Allow		200	200	
	Holding Bus Station	12	DAYS		50	600	
	PERMITS		Allow	0	500	0	
	Electricity & Water		Allow		800	800	
	Dumpster		Allow		600	600	
	Location Supplies		Allow		500	500	$15,650
775-04	HOTEL & LODGING						
	CREW LIVING NJ PART PR...	20	NIGHTS	10	16	3,200	
	CREW LIVING NJ PARK PR...	27	NIGHTS	38	16	16,416	
	CREW LIVING NJ PARK-W...	7	NIGHTS	7	16	784	
	CREW LIVING-other NJ	3	NIGHTS	30	30	2,700	
	ADDITIONAL HOUSING		ALLOW		500	500	$23,600
775-05	CATERING SERVICES						
	CATERING - 60 @ $12/DAY	23	Days	60	12	16,560	
	EXTRAS CATERING Man D...	200	Days		6	1,200	$17,760
775-06	MEAL ALLOWANCES/2ND ...						
	Prepro Per Diem	24	DAYS	7	10	1,680	
	PerDiem - Weekend crew m...	5	days	40	15	3,000	
	Per Diem Shoot	23	Days	50	10	11,500	
	SECOND MEALS	10	Days	40	10	4,000	
	EVENING CRAFT SERVICES		ALLOW		800	800	$20,980
775-07	PRODUCTION EXPENDABL...		Allow		1,200	1,200	$1,200
775-11	FIRE/POLICE						
	FIREMAN/POLICE		ALLOW		2,100	2,100	$2,100
775-21	LOCATION SECURITY						
	Prepro	12	Nights		192	2,304	
	Shoot	28	Nights		100	2,800	
	Additional Man Days	10	Nights		120	1,200	
	Hotel Security	26	Nights		100	2,600	$8,904
775-14	AIRPORT PICKUP/DELIVERY						
	CREW/CAST	10	Allow		95	950	$950
775-17	GRATUITIES		Allow		300	300	$300
775-18	OFFICE FURNITURE		Allow		250	250	$250
775-19	LOCATION MEDICAL EXPE...		Allow		100	100	$100
775-23	PHOTO SHOOT		Allow		1,200	1,200	$1,200
775-25	SHIPPING		Allow		250	250	$250
775-20	LOSS & DAMAGE						
	L&D		Allow		500	500	$500
775	Total Fringes						
	Teamster Fring	29.0%			2,100	609	

(continued)

Figure 6–5   Sample budget 2 ($997,800) (continued)

Acct#	Description	Amount	Units	X	Rate	Subtotal	Total
775-00	**LOCATION EXPENSES (CONT'D)**						
775	Total Fringes (CONT'D)						
	NONUNION	15.5%			7,900	1,225	
	N.J. sales tax	6.0%			28,400	1,704	
	Sales Tax	8.5%			17,760	1,510	$5,047
						Total For 775-00	**$107,891**
785-00	**PRODUCTION DAILIES**						
785-01	NEGATIVE RAW STOCK						
	5293 KODAK STOCK	25,875	FEET		0.46	11,903	
	5279 FACTORY SEALED	77,625	FEET		0.48	37,260	
	SHIPPING FILM TO LOCAT...		Allow		750	750	$49,913
785-02	DEVELOPING						
	PROCESS NORMAL/PREP	103,500	FEET		0.105	10,868	
	Shipping Film To Lab	23	Days		75	1,725	$12,593
785-03	TRANSFER DAILIES						
	TRANSFER TO BETA (64 H...	103,500	Feet	0.85	0.1284	11,296	
	PREP FOR TRANSFER		ALLOW	0	375	0	$11,296
785-05	TRANSFER SOUND DAILIES						
	NO COSTS PER LAB						$0
785-08	SCREEN DAILIES						
	PROJECTED DAILIES (8,00...	8,000	FEET		0.186	1,488	
	SCREENING		Allow		500	500	
	DATA DISK	30	DISK		10	300	$2,288
785-09	VIDEOTAPE TRANSFERS						
	Dub 3 VHS Tapes from Beta	23	DAYS	3	15	1,035	
	Shipping Dailies from L/A	23		2	50	2,300	$3,335
785-10	TAPE STOCK						
	BETA SP TAPES	25	TAPES		32.47	812	
	DAT TAPES	25	TAPES		10.83	271	$1,083
785	Total Fringes						
	Sales Tax	8.5%			1,988	169	$169
						Total For 785-00	**$80,677**
797-00	**TESTS**						
797-01	TEST #1						
	TEST		ALLOW		350	350	$350
						Total For 797-00	**$350**
	TOTAL SHOOTING PERIOD						**$490,679**
800-00	**EDITING**						
800-01	FILM EDITOR						
	Editor	14	Weeks		700	9,800	$9,800
800-18	ASSISTANT EDITOR						
	Assistant Editor	6	Weeks		500	3,000	$3,000
800-03	MUSIC EDITING						$0
800-04	NEGATIVE CUTTING						

Figure 6–5   Sample budget 2 ($997,800) (continued)

Acct#	Description	Amount	Units	X	Rate	Subtotal	Total
800-00	**EDITING (CONT'D)**						
800-04	NEGATIVE CUTTING (CONT'D)						
	NEGATIVE CUTTING		ALLOW		5,500	5,500	$5,500
800-05	DIALOGUE EDITING						
	DIALOGUE EDITING		ALLOW		1,750	1,750	$1,750
800-11	EDITORIAL FACILITIES						
	EDIT SUITE	3.5	MON...		378	1,323	
	EDIT SYSTEM	14	Weeks		1,000	14,000	
	SET UP CHARGE		ALLOW		350	350	
	DIGITAL DECK	5	WEEKS	0	150	0	
	PARKING		Allow		100	100	
	MEAL ALLOWANCE	12	WEEKS		75	900	$16,673
800-12	EDITORIAL SUPPLIES						
	Supplies		allow		750	750	$750
800-17	VIDEO TAPES/MISC.						
	Video Tapes		allow		1,200	1,200	
	Messenger	23	Days		15	345	$1,545
800	Total Fringes						
	NONUNION	15.5%			12,800	1,984	
	Sales Tax	8.5%			1,950	166	$2,150
						Total For 800-00	**$41,168**
810-00	**MUSIC**						
810-00	MUSIC						
	MUSIC		ALLOW		8,000	8,000	$8,000
						Total For 810-00	**$8,000**
820-00	**POSTPRODUCTION SOUND**						
820-01	DIALOGUE RECORDING (A...						
	ADR		ALLOW		4,000	4,000	$4,000
820-02	NARRATION RECORDING						
	NARRATION RECORDING		ALLOW		1,000	1,000	$1,000
820-03	SOUND EFFECTS (FOLEY)		ALLOW		4,000	4,000	$4,000
820-06	DUBBING SESSION						
	DUBBING/MIX		ALLOW		8,000	8,000	$8,000
820-07	SOUND TRANSFER 35 & 3...						
	SOUND TRANSFER		allow		5,000	5,000	$5,000
820-09	PURCHASED SOUND EFFE...						
	PURCHASED SOUND EFFE...		ALLOW		1,500	1,500	$1,500
820-13	PRINT MASTER TO DA88		ALLOW		1,000	1,000	$1,000
820-14	PREVIEW EXPENSES		ALLOW		500	500	$500
						Total For 820-00	**$25,000**
840-00	**TITLES**						
840-01	TITLES (MAIN & END)						
	16 Cards White over Black		Allow		1,120	1,120	
	3 Minute End Crawl (Title Ho...		Allow		1,480	1,480	$2,600

(continued)

Figure 6–5   Sample budget 2 ($997,800) (continued)

Acct#	Description	Amount	Units	X	Rate	Subtotal	Total
840-00	**TITLES (CONT'D)**						
840-02	MISCELLANEOUS TITLES		ALLOW		200	200	$200
840-05	LABORATORY PROCESSING						
	LAB PROCESSING		ALLOW		800	800	$800
						Total For 840-00	**$3,600**
850-00	**OPTICALS, MATTES & INSERTS**						
850-01	OPTICAL EFFECTS/DUPE ...						
	5 Dissolves (Tilte House Bid)		Allow		1,400	1,400	$1,400
850-03	LABORATORY PROCESSING		allow		500	500	$500
						Total For 850-00	**$1,900**
860-00	**LABORATORY PROCESSING**						
860-01	REPRINTING & DEVELOPING						
	REPRINTING & DEVELOPING		ALLOW		1,000	1,000	$1,000
860-07	ANSWER PRINT						
	Answer print	9,700	feet		0.842	8,167	
	2 Ck Prints/No Cost Per Fot...						$8,167
860-08	SYNC REEL CHARGE						
	sync reel charge	11	reel		38	418	$418
860-09	DYNAMIC LIGHT CONTROL...						
	DYNAMIC LIGHT COTROL ...		ALLOW		400	400	$400
860-17	LEADER & MISCELLANEOUS						
	video tape/other		allow		750	750	$750
860	Total Fringes						
	Sales Tax	8.5%			750	64	$64
						Total For 860-00	**$10,799**
	TOTAL COMPLETION PERIOD						**$90,467**
910-OO	**ADMINISTRATIVE EXPENSES**						
910-01	ACCOUNTING & TERMINAL...						
	ACCOUNTANT (PRODUCTI...	9	WEEKS		800	7,200	
	ACCOUNTANT (POST-1 day...	15	WEEKS		175	2,625	
	COMPUTER RENTAL	2.5	Months	0	100	0	$9,825
910-02	MPAA CERTIFICATE						$0
910-03	POSTAGE/STATIONERY/S...						
	SHIPPING		ALLOW		2,000	2,000	$2,000
910-04	PHOTOCOPYING (No Scripts)						
	PHOTOCOPYING (Production)		allow		1,500	1,500	$1,500
910-05	LEGAL EXPENSE & FEES						
	Legal Fee		Allow		15,000	15,000	
	Vetting screenplay		Allow		400	400	
	Clearance Research		Allow		1,000	1,000	
	Clearance Checks		Allow		1,000	1,000	$17,400
910-06	TELEPHONE/FACSIMILE/T...						
	TELEPHONE/FAX		Allow		7,250	7,250	

Figure 6–5 Sample budget 2 ($997,800) (continued)

Acct#	Description	Amount	Units	X	Rate	Subtotal	Total
910-00	**ADMINISTRATIVE EXPENSES (CONT'D)**						
910-06	TELEPHONE/FACSIMILE/TELEX (CONT'D)						
	PAGERS	5	Pagers		60	300	$7,550
910-08	INSURANCE						
	Bid (Including E&O)		Allow		18,792	18,792	$18,792
910-14	PARKING LOT EXPENSES						
	PARKING		Allow		1,500	1,500	$1,500
910-17	OFFICE RENT & OTH EXPE...						
	OFFICE RENT (NEW JERS...	30	Days		16	480	
	Office Rent (New York)	2	MON...		500	1,000	
	Office Supplies		Allow		750	750	
	Polaroid		Allow		800	800	
	Temporary Office Expenses		ALLOW		300	300	
	PRODUCTION SOFTWARE		ALLOW		630	630	$3,960
910-22	PAYROLL EXPENSE						
	Payroll Expense (incl fring		Allow		500	500	
	Additional Payroll Exp (P&W...	1		60	7	420	$920
910	Total Fringes						
	NONUNION	15.5%			9,825	1,523	$1,523
						Total For 910-00 $64,970	
920-00	**PUBLICITY**						
920-01	UNIT PUBLICIST						
	Unit Publicist		ALLOW		1,000	1,000	$1,000
920-02	SPECIAL STILL PHOTOGR...						
	Special Publicity Still Photog	1	FLAT		500	500	$500
920-03	STILL FILM & PROCESSING						
	Publicity Materials		ALLOW		1,200	1,200	$1,200
920	Total Fringes						
	Sales Tax	8.5%			1,200	102	$102
						Total For 920-00 $2,802	
970-00	**DELIVERY EXPENSES**						
970-00	Film and Audio Elements						
	35mm Interpostive	9,700	Allow		0.964	9,351	
	35mm Internegative	9,700	Allow		0.842	8,167	
	Textless interpo/titles						
	Check Print	9,700	Allow		0.202	1,959	
	35mm Release Print	9,700	Allow		0.105	1,019	
	35mm Optical Sound track	9,700	Allow		0.39	3,783	
	M&E (on DAT)		Allow		5,000	5,000	
	3-track mono D-M-E on DA88		Allow		400	400	
	Video Transfer (film to tape w		Allow		12,500	12,500	
	D1 NTSC Video master		Allow		900	900	
	D1 PAL Master		Allow		1,800	1,800	
	Stereo (Dolby) License		Allow		2,500	2,500	
	VHS Screeners		Allow		200	200	$47,579

(continued)

Figure 6–5 Sample budget 2 ($997,800) (continued)

Acct#	Description	Amount	Units	X	Rate	Subtotal	Total
970-00	**DELIVERY EXPENSES (CONT'D)**						
970-50	Advertising and Pub Materials						
	20 Color Slide Dupes	20	slides	2	0	0	
	Black & White Copy Negs/Pr...	20	negs	2	0	0	$0
						Total For 970-00	**$47,579**
	TOTAL OTHER						**$115,351**
	Completion Bond: 3.00%						$26,490
	Contingency: 10.00%						$88,301
	Overhead: 0.00%						$0
	TOTAL ABOVE-THE-LINE						$186,513
	TOTAL BELOW-THE-LINE						$696,496
	TOTAL ABOVE & BELOW-THE-LINE						$883,009
	GRAND TOTAL						$997,800

Figure 6–5   Sample budget 2 ($997,800) (continued)

SAMPLE BUDGET 3

PRODUCTION NO.:   DATE:
PRODUCERS: LOCATION: LOS ANGELES
DIRECTOR: 5 WEEK SHOOT - 5 DAY WEEK
SCRIPT DATE: LOCAL NONUNION CREW
START DATE: SAG LOW-BUDGET AGRMT.
FINISH DATE:

NOT FINAL SHOOTING BUDGET

Acct#	Category Title	Page	Total
600-00	STORY	1	$5,000
610-00	PRODUCER	1	$52,452
620-00	DIRECTOR	1	$34,083
630-00	CAST	1	$135,165
650-00	TRAVEL & LIVING	3	$17,258
	Total Above-The-Line		**$243,957**
700-00	EXTRA TALENT	5	$41,076
705-00	PRODUCTION STAFF	5	$79,578
710-00	CAMERA	6	$60,712
715-00	SET DESIGN	7	$48,835
720-00	SET CONSTRUCTION	8	$14,019
725-00	SET OPERATIONS	8	$59,521
730-00	ELECTRICAL	9	$51,138
735-00	SPECIAL EFFECTS	10	$7,500
740-00	SPECIAL SHOOTING UNITS	10	$16,846
745-00	SET DRESSING (included in 715)	11	$0
750-00	PROPERTIES	11	$37,635
755-00	WARDROBE	12	$39,035
760-00	MAKEUP & HAIRSTYLISTS	12	$31,180
765-00	PRODUCTION SOUND	13	$22,075
770-00	TRANSPORTATION	13	$37,613
775-00	LOCATION EXPENSE	14	$162,155
785-00	PRODUCTION DAILIES	16	$74,513
797-00	TESTS	17	$500
	Total Production		**$783,931**
800-00	EDITING	17	$115,226
810-00	MUSIC	18	$35,200
820-00	POSTPRODUCTION SOUND	18	$41,383
840-00	TITLES	19	$7,000
850-00	OPTICALS, MATTES, INSERTS	19	$10,000
860-00	LABORATORY PROCESSING	19	$20,103
	Total PostProduction		**$228,911**
910-00	ADMINISTRATIVE EXPENSES	19	$43,439
920-00	PUBLICITY	20	$6,000
	Total Other		**$49,439**
	Completion Bond: 3.00%		$39,187

(continued)

Figure 6–6   Sample budget 3 ($1.5 million)

Acct#	Category Title	Page	Total
	Contingency: 10.00%		$130,624
	Overhead: 1.00%		$13,062
	Insurance: 2.00%		$26,125
	TOTAL ABOVE-THE-LINE		**$243,957**
	TOTAL BELOW-THE-LINE		**$1,062,280**
	TOTAL ABOVE & BELOW-THE-LINE		**$1,306,237**
	GRAND TOTAL		**$1,515,235**

Figure 6–6   Sample budget 3 ($1.5 million) (continued)

SAMPLE BUDGET 3

PRODUCTION NO.:   DATE:
PRODUCERS: LOCATION: LOS ANGELES
DIRECTOR: 5 WEEK SHOOT - 5 DAY WEEK
SCRIPT DATE: LOCAL NONUNION CREW
START DATE: SAG LOW-BUDGET AGRMT.
FINISH DATE:

NOT FINAL SHOOTING BUDGET

Acct#	Description	Amount	Units	X	Rate	Subtotal	Total
600-00	**STORY**						
600-01	RIGHTS/OPTION PURCHAS...						$0
600-03	WRITERS						$0
600-04	SCREENPLAY PURCHASE						
	SCREENPLAY PURCHASE	1	Flat		5,000	5,000	$5,000
600-05	RESEARCH						$0
600-11	SCRIPT COPY						$0
						Total For 600-00	**$5,000**
610-00	**PRODUCER**						
610-01	EXECUTIVE PRODUCER						$0
610-02	PRODUCER						
	PRODUCERS - LOAN -OUT	1	Flat	2	20,000	40,000	$40,000
610-06	PRODUCER'S ASST.						
	PRODUCER'S ASSISTANT-...	5	WEEKS		600	3,000	
	SHOOT	5	WEEKS		600	3,000	
	WRAP	3	WEEKS		600	1,800	
	NONUNION	18.0%			7,800	1,404	$9,204
610-08	PREPRO EXPENSES/ENT.						
	PRE-PRO EXPENSES	6	Weeks		500	3,000	
	sales tax	8.25%			3,000	248	$3,248
						Total For 610-00	**$52,452**
620-00	**DIRECTOR**						
620-01	DIRECTOR						
	DIRECTOR (per contract) - L...	1	Flat		25,000	25,000	$25,000
620-02	STORYBOARD ARTIST						$0
620-04	RESEARCH CONSULTANT						$0
620-05	CASTING DIRECTOR						
	CASTING DIRECTOR - LOA...	4	Weeks		2,000	8,000	$8,000
620-08	CASTING EXPENSES						
	CASTING FEES/FACILITY/F...		Allow		1,000	1,000	
	sales tax	8.25%			1,000	83	$1,083
						Total For 620-00	**$34,083**

(continued)

Figure 6–6   Sample budget 3 ($1.5 million) (continued)

Acct#	Description	Amount	Units	X	Rate	Subtotal	Total
630-00	**CAST**						
630-01	PRINCIPAL PLAYERS (OT ...						
	JOHNSON	6	Weeks		1,620	9,720	
	TRAVIS	6	Weeks		1,620	9,720	
	L.D.	3	Weeks		1,620	4,860	
	GEOFFREY	3	Weeks		1,620	4,860	
	CALLIE	4	WEEKS		1,620	6,480	
	ROXANNE	1	WEEK		1,620	1,620	
	MARCUS	1.6	WEEKS		1,620	2,592	
	OREN	1.6	WEEKS		1,620	2,592	
	LEO	1	WEEK		1,620	1,620	
	ERIC	1	Week		1,620	1,620	
	JERRY	1	Week		1,620	1,620	
	URSULA	1	WEEK		1,620	1,620	
	FLOOR BOSS	1	WEEK		1,620	1,620	
	PIT BOSS	2	Weeks		1,620	3,240	
	ROSS	2	WEEKS		1,620	3,240	
	FUI	1.0%			57,024	570	
	overtime	20%			57,024	11,405	
	AGENCY FEE	10.0%			57,024	5,702	
	SAG CORP	13.3%			57,024	7,584	
	FICA	6.2%			57,024	3,535	
	FICA 2	1.45%			57,024	827	
	SUI	5.4%			57,024	3,079	$89,727
630-02	DAY PLAYERS						
	STERNS	2	DAYS		466	932	
	ELSON	2	DAYS		466	932	
	CAR MAN	2	DAYS		466	932	
	CAR WOMAN	2	DAY		466	932	
	CAR KID	2	DAYS		466	932	
	ROBERT H.	2	DAYS		466	932	
	HARRY	2	DAYS		466	932	
	MOTO COP	2	DAYS		466	932	
	VALETS	2	Days	3	466	2,796	
	CONCIERGE	1	Day		466	466	
	HUSBAND	2	DAYS		466	932	
	WIFE	2	DAYS		466	932	
	SECURITY GUARDS	3	DAYS	2	466	2,796	
	BARTENDER	1	DAY		466	466	
	FLOOR BOSS	4	DAYS		466	1,864	
	ARCHIE	2	DAYS		466	932	
	GAMING MANAGER	2	DAYS		466	932	
	MASON	1	DAYS		466	466	
	FUI	1.0%			20,038	200	
	overtime	20%			20,038	4,008	
	AGENCY FEE	10.0%			20,038	2,004	
	SAG CORP	13.3%			20,038	2,665	

Figure 6–6   Sample budget 3 ($1.5 million) (continued)

Acct#	Description	Amount	Units	X	Rate	Subtotal	Total
630-00	**CAST (CONT'D)**						
630-02	DAY PLAYERS (CONT'D)						
	FICA	6.2%			20,038	1,242	
	FICA 2	1.45%			20,038	291	
	SUI	5.4%			20,038	1,082	$31,530
630-06	LOOPING/ADR						
	JOHNSON	2	Days		466	932	
	TRAVIS	2	Days		466	932	
	L.D.	1	Day		466	466	
	GEOFFREY	1	Day		466	466	
	CALLIE	1	Day		466	466	
	OREN	1	Day		466	466	
	LEO	1	Day		466	466	
	URSULA	1	Day		466	466	
	RAMONA	1	Day		466	466	
	FUI	1.0%			5,126	51	
	AGENCY FEE	10.0%			5,126	513	
	SAG CORP	13.3%			5,126	682	
	FICA	6.2%			5,126	318	
	FICA 2	1.45%			5,126	74	
	SUI	5.4%			5,126	277	$7,041
630-07	MEAL PENALTIES						
	MEAL PENALTIES		Allow		5,000	5,000	
	FUI	1.0%			5,000	50	
	SAG CORP	13.3%			5,000	665	
	FICA	6.2%			5,000	310	
	FICA 2	1.45%			5,000	73	
	SUI	5.4%			5,000	270	$6,368
630-09	MEDICAL EXAMS						
	Key Cast Medical Exams	1	EXAMS	5	100	500	$500
						Total For 630-00	$135,165
650-00	**TRAVEL & LIVING**						
650-01	PRODUCERS						
	PRODUCERS - TRAVEL	2	FLIG...		170	340	
	LIVING	14	Days		60	840	
	sales tax	8.25%			840	69	$1,249
650-02	DIRECTOR						
	DIRECTOR/LEAD ACTOR	1	FLIG...		170	170	
	HOTEL	14	Days		100	1,400	
	sales tax	8.25%			1,400	116	$1,686
650-06	CAST TRAVEL/LIVING & P...						
	JOHNSON-FLIGHT (FROM ...		ALLOW		550	550	
	HOTEL	14	NIGHTS		60	840	
	JOHNSON - PERDIEM	14	DAYS		53	742	
	TRAVIS - PER DIEM	14	DAYS		53	742	
	L.D. -FLIGHT		ALLOW		170	170	

(continued)

Figure 6–6   Sample budget 3 ($1.5 million) (continued)

Acct#	Description	Amount	Units	X	Rate	Subtotal	Total
650-00	**TRAVEL & LIVING (CONT'D)**						
650-06	CAST TRAVEL/LIVING & PER DIEM (CONT'D)						
	HOTEL	8	NIGHTS		60	480	
	L. D. - PER DIEM	10	Days		53	530	
	GEOFFREY-FLIGHT		ALLOW		170	170	
	HOTEL	5	Days		60	300	
	GEOFFREY - PER DIEM	7	DAYS		53	371	
	CALLIE-FLIGHT		ALLOW		170	170	
	HOTEL	8	Days		60	480	
	CALLIE - PER DIEM	14	Days		53	742	
	ROXANNE-FLIGHT		ALLOW		170	170	
	HOTEL	3	DAYS		60	180	
	ROXANNE - PER DIEM	3	DAYS		53	159	
	OREN-FLIGHT		ALLOW		170	170	
	HOTEL	4	Days		60	240	
	OREN - PER DIEM	5	DAYS		53	265	
	MARCUS-FLIGHT		ALLOW		170	170	
	HOTEL	4	Days		60	240	
	MARCUS - PER DIEM	5	DAYS		53	265	
	LEO-FLIGHT		ALLOW		170	170	
	HOTEL	3	DAYS		60	180	
	LEO - PER DIEM	5	DAYS		53	265	
	ERIC-FLIGHT		ALLOW		170	170	
	HOTEL	4	DAYS		60	240	
	ERIC - PER DIEM	5	DAYS		53	265	
	JERRY-FLIGHT		ALLOW		170	170	
	HOTEL	4	DAYS		60	240	
	JERRY - PER DIEM	5	DAYS		53	265	
	URSULA-FLIGHT		ALLOW		170	170	
	HOTEL	5	Days		60	300	
	URSULA - PER DIEM	5	Days		53	265	
	GLADYS-FLIGHT		ALLOW		170	170	
	HOTEL	3	Days		60	180	
	GLADYS - PER DIEM	3	Days		53	159	
	STERNS - HOTEL	2	DAYS		60	120	
	STERNS - FLIGHT		Allow		170	170	
	STERNS - PER DIEM	2	DAYS		53	106	
	ELSON - HOTEL	2	Days		60	120	
	ELSON - FLIGHT		Allow		170	170	
	ELSON - PER DIEM	2	DAYS		53	106	
	CAR MAN - HOTEL	1	Day		60	60	
	CAR MAN - FLIGHT		Allow		170	170	
	CAR MAN - PER DIEM	2	DAYS		53	106	
	CAR WOMAN - HOTEL	1	DAY		60	60	
	CAR WOMAN - FLIGHT		Allow		170	170	
	CAR WOMAN - PER DIEM	2	DAY		53	106	
	CAR KID - HOTEL	1	Day		60	60	

Figure 6–6   Sample budget 3 ($1.5 million) (continued)

Acct#	Description	Amount	Units	X	Rate	Subtotal	Total
650-00	**TRAVEL & LIVING (CONT'D)**						
650-06	CAST TRAVEL/LIVING & PER DIEM (CONT'D)						
	CAR KID - FLIGHT		Allow		170	170	
	CAR KID - PER DIEM	2	DAYS		53	106	
	MASON - HOTEL	2	DAYS		60	120	
	MASON - FLIGHT		Allow		170	170	
	MASON - PER DIEM	2	Days		53	106	
	ARCHIE - HOTEL	2	DAYS		60	120	
	ARCHIE - FLIGHT		Allow		170	170	
	ARCHIE - PER DIEM	2	DAYS		53	106	
	sales tax	8.25%			4,560	376	$14,323
						Total For 650-00	**$17,258**
	Total Above-The-Line						**$243,957**
700-00	**EXTRA TALENT**						
700-02	ALL EXTRA TALENT & STA...						
	CASINO EXTRAS	7	Days	30	90	18,900	
	CASINO EXTRAS	5	Days	20	50	5,000	
	EXTRAS - DINER	2	Days	15	90	2,700	
	FUI	1.0%			26,600	266	
	AGENCY FEE	10.0%			26,600	2,660	
	SAG CORP	13.3%			26,600	3,538	
	FICA	6.2%			26,600	1,649	
	FICA 2	1.45%			26,600	386	
	SUI	5.4%			26,600	1,436	$36,535
700-05	EXTRAS CASTING						
	EXTRAS CASTING	2	Weeks		2,000	4,000	
	EXTRAS CASTING EXPEN...	1	Week		500	500	
	sales tax	8.25%			500	41	$4,541
						Total For 700-00	**$41,076**
705-00	**PRODUCTION STAFF**						
705-01	LINE PRODUCER/UPM						
	PREP	6	Weeks		800	4,800	
	SHOOT	5	WEEKS		800	4,000	
	WRAP	2	WEEKS		800	1,600	
	NONUNION	18.0%			10,400	1,872	$12,272
705-02	PRODUCTION COORDINAT...						
	PREP	5	WEEKS		600	3,000	
	SHOOT	5	WEEKS		600	3,000	
	WRAP	1	WEEK		600	600	
	NONUNION	18.0%			6,600	1,188	
	overtime	20%			3,000	600	$8,388
705-03	1ST ASSISTANT DIRECTOR						
	PREP	3	WEEKS		800	2,400	
	SHOOT	5	WEEKS		800	4,000	

(continued)

Figure 6–6   Sample budget 3 ($1.5 million) (continued)

Acct#	Description	Amount	Units	X	Rate	Subtotal	Total
705-00	**PRODUCTION STAFF (CONT'D)**						
705-03	1ST ASSISTANT DIRECTOR (CONT'D)						
	WRAP	0.6	WEEKS		800	480	
	NONUNION	18.0%			6,880	1,238	
	overtime	20%			4,000	800	$8,918
705-04	2ND ASSISTANT DIRECTOR						
	PREP	2	WEEKS		600	1,200	
	SHOOT	5	WEEKS		600	3,000	
	WRAP	0.6	Weeks		600	360	
	NONUNION	18.0%			4,560	821	
	overtime	20%			3,360	672	$6,053
705-05	2ND 2ND ASSISTANT DIRE...						
	2ND 2ND ASSITANT DIREC...	5	Weeks		500	2,500	
	NONUNION	18.0%			2,500	450	
	overtime	20%			2,500	500	$3,450
705-06	SCRIPT SUPERVISOR						
	PREP	0.6	Weeks		800	480	
	SHOOT	5	WEEKS		800	4,000	
	WRAP	0.6	WEEKS		800	480	
	NONUNION	18.0%			4,960	893	
	overtime	20%			4,000	800	$6,653
705-08	PRODUCTION ACCOUNTANT						
	ACCOUNTANT - PREP	4	Weeks		800	3,200	
	SHOOT	5	Weeks		800	4,000	
	WRAP	2	Weeks		800	1,600	
	NONUNION	18.0%			8,800	1,584	$10,384
705-10	PRODUCTION ASSISTANTS						
	PA 1 (OFFICE PA) - PREP	5	WEEKS		500	2,500	
	SHOOT	5	Weeks		500	2,500	
	WRAP	1	Week		500	500	
	PA 2 - PREP	3	Weeks		500	1,500	
	SHOOT	5	WEEKS		500	2,500	
	WRAP	1	WEEK		500	500	
	PA 3 - PREP	2	Weeks		500	1,000	
	SHOOT	5	Weeks		500	2,500	
	WRAP	1	Week		500	500	
	PA 4-PREP	1	Week		500	500	
	SHOOT	5	Weeks		500	2,500	
	NONUNION	18.0%			17,000	3,060	
	overtime	20%			17,000	3,400	$23,460
						Total For 705-00	**$79,578**
710-00	**CAMERA**						
710-01	DIRECTOR OF PHOTOGRA...						
	DP-LOAN OUT	6	Weeks		2,500	15,000	$15,000
710-03	1ST AC						
	PREP	0.6	WEEKS		800	480	

Figure 6–6   Sample budget 3 ($1.5 million) (continued)

Acct#	Description	Amount	Units	X	Rate	Subtotal	Total
710-00	**CAMERA (CONT'D)**						
710-03	1ST AC (CONT'D)						
	SHOOT	5	WEEKS		800	4,000	
	NONUNION	18.0%			4,480	806	
	overtime	20%			4,000	800	$6,086
710-04	2ND CAMERA ASST./LOAD...						
	PREP	0.6	WEEKS		600	360	
	SHOOT	5	WEEKS		600	3,000	
	NONUNION	18.0%			3,360	605	
	overtime	20%			3,000	600	$4,565
710-06	STILL PHOTOGRAPHER						
	STILL PHOTOGRAPHER	1	FLAT		2,000	2,000	
	NONUNION	18.0%			2,000	360	$2,360
710-08	CAMERA RENTALS						
	All Camera Package	5	Weeks		2,500	12,500	$12,500
710-09	CAMERA SUPPLIES						
	CAMERA PURCHASES		Allow		500	500	
	sales tax	8.25%			500	41	$541
710-11	CAMERA ACCESORIES						
	MONITOR	5	Weeks		1,200	6,000	
	MONITOR OPERATOR	5	Weeks		800	4,000	
	STEADI-CAM	2	Weeks		1,500	3,000	
	STEADI-CAM OPERATOR	2	Weeks		1,500	3,000	
	NONUNION	18.0%			7,000	1,260	
	overtime	20%			7,000	1,400	$18,660
710-20	LOSS & DAMAGE						
	LOSS & DAMAGE		ALLOW		1,000	1,000	$1,000
						Total For 710-00	**$60,712**
715-00	**SET DESIGN**						
715-01	PRODUCTION DESIGNER						
	PROD. DESIGNER - PREP	4	WEEKS		800	3,200	
	SHOOT	5	WEEKS		800	4,000	
	WRAP	0.6	WEEKS		800	480	
	NONUNION	18.0%			7,680	1,382	
	overtime	20%			4,000	800	$9,862
715-02	ART DIRECTOR						
	ART DIRECTOR - PREP	3	Weeks		800	2,400	
	SHOOT	5	WEEKS		800	4,000	
	WRAP	0.6	WEEKS		800	480	
	NONUNION	18.0%			6,880	1,238	
	overtime	20%			4,000	800	$8,918
715-03	SET DESIGNER/LEADMAN						
	PREP	3	Weeks		600	1,800	
	SHOOT	5	Weeks		600	3,000	
	WRAP	1	Week		600	600	
	NONUNION	18.0%			5,400	972	

(continued)

Figure 6–6   Sample budget 3 ($1.5 million) (continued)

Acct#	Description	Amount	Units	X	Rate	Subtotal	Total
715-00	**SET DESIGN (CONT'D)**						
715-03	SET DESIGNER/LEADMAN (CONT'D)						
	overtime	20%			3,000	600	$6,972
715-04	SWING GANG						
	PREP	1	Week	2	500	1,000	
	SHOOT	5	Weeks	2	500	5,000	
	WRAP	1	Week		500	500	
	NONUNION	18.0%			6,500	1,170	
	overtime	20%			5,000	1,000	$8,670
715-05	ART RENTALS						
	RENTALS	5	Weeks		1,500	7,500	$7,500
715-06	PURCHASE SUPPLIES						
	ART PURCHASE		ALLOW		5,000	5,000	
	sales tax	8.25%			5,000	413	$5,413
715-10	KIT RENTAL						
	KIT RENTAL	5	Weeks	2	50	500	$500
715-20	LOSS & DAMAGE						
	ART DEPT L& D		ALLOW		1,000	1,000	$1,000
						Total For 715-00	**$48,835**
720-00	**SET CONSTRUCTION**						
720-01	CONSTRUCTION LABOR						
	CONSTRUCTION LABOR		Allow		5,000	5,000	
	NONUNION	18.0%			5,000	900	$5,900
720-02	CONSTRUCTION MATERIA...						
	MATERIALS/PURCHASES		ALLOW		7,500	7,500	
	sales tax	8.25%			7,500	619	$8,119
						Total For 720-00	**$14,019**
725-00	**SET OPERATIONS**						
725-01	KEY GRIP						
	PREP	1	WEEK		800	800	
	SHOOT	5	WEEKS		800	4,000	
	NONUNION	18.0%			4,800	864	
	overtime	20%			4,000	800	$6,464
725-02	BEST BOY GRIP						
	PREP	0.4	Days		600	240	
	SHOOT	5	WEEKS		600	3,000	
	NONUNION	18.0%			3,240	583	
	overtime	20%			3,000	600	$4,423
725-03	CRANE/DOLLY GRIPS						
	Dolly Grip	4	WEEKS		600	2,400	
	NONUNION	18.0%			2,400	432	
	overtime	20%			2,400	480	$3,312
725-04	EXTRA COMPANY GRIPS						
	COMPANY GRIPS	5	Weeks	2	500	5,000	
	NONUNION	18.0%			5,000	900	

Figure 6–6   Sample budget 3 ($1.5 million) (continued)

Acct#	Description	Amount	Units	X	Rate	Subtotal	Total
725-00	**SET OPERATIONS (CONT'D)**						
725-04	EXTRA COMPANT GRIPS (CONT'D)						
	overtime	20%			5,000	1,000	$6,900
725-05	CAMERA DOLLY						
	DOLLY W/ACCESSORIES/...	4	Weeks		1,200	4,800	$4,800
725-06	CAMERA CRANE						
	CRANE	2	DAYS		1,500	3,000	
	CRANE OPERATOR	2	Days		200	400	
	NONUNION	18.0%			400	72	$3,472
725-08	GRIP EQUIPMENT RENTALS						
	RENTALS	5	WEEKS		1,500	7,500	
	Car Mounts	2	WEEKS		300	600	$8,100
725-09	GRIP PURCHASES						
	EXPENDABLES/GELS/BUB...	5	Weeks		1,000	5,000	
	sales tax	8.25%			5,000	413	$5,413
725-10	KIT RENTALS						
	KEY GRIP KIT RENTAL	5	Weeks		50	250	$250
725-11	CRAFT SERVICE/SERVICE...						
	Craft Service Person - PREP	1	Week		600	600	
	SHOOT	5	Weeks		600	3,000	
	PURCHASES	5	Weeks		750	3,750	
	Rentals	5	Weeks		250	1,250	
	KIT RENTAL	5	Weeks		50	250	
	sales tax	8.25%			3,750	309	
	NONUNION	18.0%			3,600	648	
	overtime	20%			3,000	600	$10,407
725-10	KIT RENTAL						$0
725-20	LOSS & DAMAGE						
	ALL L&D		Allow		1,000	1,000	$1,000
725-25	MISCELLANEOUS						
	WALKIES	5	Weeks	12	50	3,000	
	BEEPERS	10	Weeks	6	8	480	$3,480
725-30	LOCATION LOAD & UNLOAD						
	LOCATION LOAD & UNLOAD	2	Weeks		750	1,500	$1,500
						Total For 725-00	$59,521
730-00	**ELECTRICAL**						
730-01	GAFFER						
	KEY ELEC. - PREP	1	Week		800	800	
	SHOOT	5	WEEKS		800	4,000	
	NONUNION	18.0%			4,800	864	
	overtime	20%			4,000	800	$6,464
730-02	BEST BOY						
	BEST BOY - SHOOT	5	WEEKS		600	3,000	
	NONUNION	18.0%			3,000	540	
	overtime	20%			3,000	600	$4,140
730-03	ELECTRICS						

(continued)

Figure 6–6   Sample budget 3 ($1.5 million) (continued)

Acct#	Description	Amount	Units	X	Rate	Subtotal	Total
730-00	**ELECTRICAL (CONT'D)**						
730-03	ELECTRICS (CONT'D)						
	ELECTRICIANS	5	WEEKS	2	600	6,000	
	NONUNION	18.0%			6,000	1,080	
	overtime	20%			6,000	1,200	$8,280
730-05	GLOBES/CARBONS						
	GLOBES & CARBONS	5	Weeks		100	500	
	sales tax	8.25%			500	41	$541
730-06	POWER						
	POWER/TIE-IN	3	Weeks		100	300	$300
730-07	GENERATOR RENTAL						
	GENERATOR	5	WEEKS		1,200	6,000	
	FUEL FOR GENERATOR	5	WEEKS		300	1,500	$7,500
730-08	ELECTRICAL RENTAL PACK						
	ELEC. PACK RENTAL	5	WEEKS		3,000	15,000	$15,000
730-09	ELECTRICAL PURCHASES						
	ELECTRICAL PURCHASES	5	Weeks		1,000	5,000	
	sales tax	8.25%			5,000	413	$5,413
730-10	KIT RENTAL						
	KIT RENTAL	5	Weeks		500	2,500	$2,500
730-20	LOSS & DAMAGE						
	All L&D	1			1,000	1,000	$1,000
						Total For 730-00	**$51,138**
735-00	**SPECIAL EFFECTS**						
735-01	SPECIAL EFFECTS						
	SPECIAL EFFECTS (CGI)		ALLOW		7,500	7,500	$7,500
						Total For 735-00	**$7,500**
740-00	**SPECIAL SHOOTING UNITS**						
740-01	UNIT #1/PICKUPS INSERTS						
	2ND UNIT EXTERIORS- CR...						
	DP	0.6	Weeks		2,500	1,500	
	AD	0.6	Weeks		800	480	
	2ND AD	0.6	Days		600	360	
	KEY GRIP	0.6	Weeks		800	480	
	BEST BOY	0.6	Weeks		600	360	
	GAFFER	0.6	Weeks		800	480	
	ELECTRICIAN	0.6	Days		600	360	
	1ST AC	0.6	Weeks		800	480	
	2ND AC/LOADER	0.6	Weeks		500	300	
	SCRIPT SUPERVISOR	0.6	Weeks		800	480	
	PA	0.6	Weeks	2	500	600	
	LOCATION MANAGER	0.6	Weeks		800	480	
	LEADMAN	0.6	Weeks		600	360	
	EQUIPMENT & MATERIALS	3	Days		2,000	6,000	
	MEALS - BREAKFAST	3	Days	16	5	240	

Figure 6–6   Sample budget 3 ($1.5 million) (continued)

Acct#	Description	Amount	Units	X	Rate	Subtotal	Total
740-00	**SPECIAL SHOOTING UNITS (CONT'D)**						
740-01	UNIT #1/PICKUPS INSERTS (CONT'D)						
	MEALS - DINNER	3	Days	16	10	480	
	HOTELS (SHARE)	10	ROOMS	3	40	1,200	
	15 PASS VAN	1	Week		300	300	
	city tax	6.0%			300	18	
	sales tax	8.25%			8,220	678	
	NONUNION	18.0%			6,720	1,210	$16,846
						Total For 740-00	$16,846
745-00	**SET DRESSING (included in 715)**						
745-01	SET DECORATOR						$0
745-02	LEADMAN						$0
745-02	SWING GANG						$0
745-04	SET DRESSING PURCHASED						$0
745-05	SET DRESSING RENTALS						$0
745-07	SET DRESSING CLEAN & ...						$0
745-08	DRAPERY RENTALS						$0
745-09	DRAPERY PURCHASES						$0
745-20	LOSS, DAMAGE & REPAIR						$0
745-25	MISCELLANEOUS EXPENSE						$0
						Total For 745-00	$0
750-00	**PROPERTIES**						
750-01	PROPERTY MASTER						
	PROP MASTERS-PREP	3	Weeks		800	2,400	
	SHOOT	5	WEEKS		800	4,000	
	WRAP	0.6	WEEKS		800	480	
	NONUNION	18.0%			6,880	1,238	
	overtime	20%			4,000	800	$8,918
750-02	ASST. PROP MASTER						
	ASST. PROP MASTER - PR...	2	Weeks		600	1,200	
	SHOOT	5	Weeks		600	3,000	
	WRAP	1	Week		600	600	
	NONUNION	18.0%			4,800	864	
	overtime	20%			3,000	600	$6,264
750-05	PICTURE VEHICLES						
	NEW LEXUS	1	DAY		200	200	
	PICK-UP TRUCK	1	DAY	2	300	600	
	INDIAN MOTORCYCLE	1	DAY		500	500	
	JEEP	3	DAYS		100	300	
	POLICE BIKE	1	DAY		1,000	1,000	
	CADILLAC	1	FLAT		7,500	7,500	
	city tax	6.0%			500	30	
	sales tax	8.25%			8,000	660	$10,790
750-08	PROP RENTALS						
	PROP RENTALS	5	Weeks		1,000	5,000	$5,000

(continued)

Figure 6–6   Sample budget 3 ($1.5 million) (continued)

Acct#	Description	Amount	Units	X	Rate	Subtotal	Total
750-00	**PROPERTIES (CONT'D)**						
750-09	PROP PURCHASES						
	PROP PURCHASE	5	Weeks		1,000	5,000	
	sales tax	8.25%			5,000	413	$5,413
750-10	PROP BOX RENTALS						
	PROP KIT RENTALS	5	Weeks		50	250	$250
750-20	LOSS, DAMAGE & REPAIRS						
	L&D		ALLOW		1,000	1,000	$1,000
						Total For 750-00	**$37,635**
755-00	**WARDROBE**						
755-04	COSTUME DESIGNER						
	PREP	4	WEEKS		800	3,200	
	SHOOT	5	WEEKS		800	4,000	
	WRAP	1	Week		800	800	
	NONUNION	18.0%			8,000	1,440	
	overtime	20%			4,000	800	$10,240
755-03	ASSISTANT WARDROBE						
	PREP	4	Weeks		600	2,400	
	SHOOT	5	WEEKS		600	3,000	
	WRAP	0.6	WEEKS		600	360	
	EXTRA WARDROBE ASSIS...	5	Weeks		600	3,000	
	NONUNION	18.0%			8,760	1,577	
	overtime	20%			6,000	1,200	$11,537
755-06	COSTUME ALTERATION						
	ALTER		ALLOW		300	300	
	sales tax	8.25%			300	25	$325
755-07	COSTUME CLEANING						
	CLEANING		ALLOW		250	250	
	sales tax	8.25%			250	21	$271
755-08	COSTUME RENTAL						
	All Rental	5	Weeks		2,000	10,000	$10,000
755-09	COSTUME PURCHASE						
	WARDROBE PURCHASES		Allow		5,000	5,000	
	sales tax	8.25%			5,000	413	$5,413
755-10	KIT RENTAL						
	KIT RENTAL	5	Weeks		50	250	$250
755-20	LOSS & DAMAGE						
	L&D		ALLOW		1,000	1,000	$1,000
						Total For 755-00	**$39,035**
760-00	**MAKEUP & HAIRSTYLISTS**						
760-01	KEY MAKE-UP ARTIST						
	PREP	1	Week		800	800	
	SHOOT	5	Weeks		800	4,000	
	NONUNION	18.0%			4,800	864	
	overtime	20%			4,000	800	$6,464

Figure 6–6   Sample budget 3 ($1.5 million) (continued)

Acct#	Description	Amount	Units	X	Rate	Subtotal	Total
760-00	**MAKEUP & HAIRSTYLISTS (CONT'D)**						
760-02	ASST. MAKE-UP ARTISTS						
	SHOOT	5	Weeks		600	3,000	
	NONUNION	18.0%			3,000	540	
	overtime	20%			3,000	600	$4,140
760-04	KEY HAIR STYLIST						
	KEY HAIR - PREP	1	Week		800	800	
	SHOOT	5	WEEKS		800	4,000	
	NONUNION	18.0%			4,800	864	
	overtime	20%			4,000	800	$6,464
760-05	ASST. HAIR						
	ASST. HAIR	5	Weeks		600	3,000	
	NONUNION	18.0%			3,000	540	
	overtime	20%			3,000	600	$4,140
760-06	HAIR SUPPLY						
	HAIR SUPPLY	5	Weeks		1,000	5,000	
	sales tax	8.25%			5,000	413	$5,413
760-09	MAKE-UP SUPPLIES/APPL...						
	MAKE-UP SUPPLIES	5	Weeks		750	3,750	
	sales tax	8.25%			3,750	309	$4,059
760-10	KIT RENTAL						
	KIT RENTAL	5	Weeks	2	50	500	$500
						Total For 760-00	**$31,180**
765-00	**PRODUCTION SOUND**						
765-01	SOUND MIXER						
	SHOOT	5	WEEKS		800	4,000	
	NONUNION	18.0%			4,000	720	
	overtime	20%			4,000	800	$5,520
765-02	BOOM MAN						
	SHOOT	5	WEEKS		600	3,000	
	NONUNION	18.0%			3,000	540	
	overtime	20%			3,000	600	$4,140
765-04	CABLE MAN						
	CABLEMAN	4	Weeks		600	2,400	
	NONUNION	18.0%			2,400	432	
	overtime	20%			2,400	480	$3,312
765-05	PLAYBACK OPERATOR (A...						$0
765-06	SOUND EQUIP RENTALS						
	All Equipment Rental	5	WEEKS		1,300	6,500	$6,500
765-11	MISC.						
	PURCHASES & EXPENDAB...	5	Weeks		250	1,250	
	sales tax	8.25%			1,250	103	$1,353
765-10	KIT RENTALS						
	KIT RENTAL	5	Weeks		50	250	$250
765-20	LOSS & DAMAGE						

(continued)

Figure 6–6   Sample budget 3 ($1.5 million) (continued)

Acct#	Description	Amount	Units	X	Rate	Subtotal	Total
765-00	**PRODUCTION SOUND (CONT'D)**						
765-20	LOSS & DAMAGE (CONT'D)						
	All L&D	1			1,000	1,000	$1,000
						Total For 765-00	**$22,075**
770-00	**TRANSPORTATION**						
770-01	MESSENGER SERVICE/FE...						
	MESSENGER & FEDEX	12	Weeks		150	1,800	$1,800
770-02	DRIVER CAPTAIN						$0
770-05	MILEAGE ALLOWANCE						
	MILEAGE	5,000	MILES		0.31	1,550	$1,550
770-06	FUEL						
	FUEL - CARS/TRUCKS	8	Weeks		700	5,600	
	sales tax	8.25%			5,600	462	$6,062
770-10	LOC. VEHICLES/TRUCKS						
	PRODUCTION MOTORHOME	2	Weeks		1,500	3,000	
	TENTING	1	Week		500	500	
	CAMERA TRUCK W/ GUTS	5	Weeks		600	3,000	
	ART/PROP TRUCK	8	Weeks		400	3,200	
	15 PASS. VAN	5	Weeks	2	350	3,500	
	CUBE	7	Weeks		400	2,800	
	WARDROBE DEPT. CUBE	7	Weeks		400	2,800	
	GRIP/ELEC TRUCK	5	Weeks		400	2,000	
	RENTAL CARS	3	Weeks	4	350	4,200	
	city tax	6.0%			3,000	180	
	sales tax	8.25%			24,500	2,021	$27,201
770-20	LOSS, DAMAGE, & REPAIRS						
	L&D		Allow		1,000	1,000	$1,000
						Total For 770-00	**$37,613**
775-00	**LOCATION EXPENSE**						
775-01	SURVEY EXPENSE						
	FOOD	22	Days		15	330	
	FILM	5	Weeks		75	375	
	GAS	5	Weeks		75	375	
	PHONE/TIPS		Allow		200	200	
	SCOUT #1-DESERT						
	FOOD	3	DAYS	4	20	240	
	FILM	1	Flat		150	150	
	RENTAL CAR	3	Days		50	150	
	GAS	1	Flat		100	100	
	PHONES/CELLULAR/TIPS		ALLOW		150	150	
	SCOUT #2-DESERT						
	FOOD	2	Days	9	20	360	
	RENTAL CAR	2	Days	3	60	360	

Figure 6–6   Sample budget 3 ($1.5 million) (continued)

Acct#	Description	Amount	Units	X	Rate	Subtotal	Total
775-00	**LOCATION EXPENSE (CONT'D)**						
775-01	SURVEY EXPENSE (CONT'D)						
	GAS	2	Days	3	20	120	
	PHONES/CELLULAR/TIPS		ALLOW		250	250	
	city tax	6.0%			510	31	
	sales tax	8.25%			2,560	211	$3,402
775-02	LOCATION STAFF						
	LOCATION MANAGER-PREP	5	Weeks		800	4,000	
	SHOOT	5	WEEKS		800	4,000	
	LOCATION PA - PREP	3	Weeks		600	1,800	
	LOCATION PA-SHOOT	4	Weeks		600	2,400	
	NONUNION	18.0%			12,200	2,196	
	overtime	20%			6,400	1,280	$15,676
775-03	SITE RENTALS/PERMITS						
	BRECKENSTEIN'S ARCO	2	DAYS		750	1,500	
	DESERT DAHLIA	3	DAYS		1,000	3,000	
	KOUNTRY KITCHEN	2	DAYS		1,000	2,000	
	SITE/PERMIT FEES		ALLOW		5,000	5,000	
	TRAILER	2	Days		1,000	2,000	
	CASINO(ALL ROOMS, GAR...	2	Weeks		10,000	20,000	
	SUITES,VALET ST.,ELEV.,...						
	SLOTS,TABLES)						$33,500
775-04	HOTEL & LODGING						
	DP HOTEL	14	Days		40	560	
	DP PER DIEM	14	DAYS		30	420	
	1ST AC-HOTEL	12	Days		40	480	
	1ST AC PER DIEM	10	DAYS		30	300	
	2ND AC/LOADER - HOTEL	12	Days		40	480	
	2ND AC/LOADER-PER DIEM	10	DAYS		30	300	
	1ST AD HOTEL	14	Days		40	560	
	1ST AD PER DIEM	14	DAYS		30	420	
	2ND AD HOTEL	12	Days		40	480	
	2ND AD PER DIEM	12	Days		30	360	
	WARDROBE HOTEL	10	Days	2	40	800	
	WARDROBE PER DIEM	10	DAYS	2	30	600	
	MAKEUP HOTEL	10	Days	2	40	800	
	MAKEUP PER DIEM	10	DAYS	2	30	600	
	SOUND HOTEL	10	Days	2	40	800	
	SOUND PER DIEM	10	DAYS	2	30	600	
	GAFFER HOTEL	10	Days	2	40	800	
	GAFFER PER DIEM	10	DAYS	2	30	600	
	GRIP HOTEL	10	Days	2	40	800	
	GRIP DEPT. PER DIEM	10	Days	2	30	600	
	PROD.'S ASST. HOTEL	14	Weeks		40	560	
	PROD.'S ASST. PER DIEM	14	DAYS		30	420	
	SCRIPT SUPERVISOR HOT...	10	Days		40	400	
	PER DIEM	10	DAYS		30	300	

(continued)

Figure 6–6   Sample budget 3 ($1.5 million) (continued)

Acct#	Description	Amount	Units	X	Rate	Subtotal	Total
775-00	**LOCATION EXPENSE (CONT'D)**						
775-04	HOTEL & LODGING (CONT'D)						
	PROD. DESIGN HOTEL	14	Days		40	560	
	PROD. DESIGN PER DIEM	14	DAYS		30	420	
	ART. DIR. HOTEL	10	Days	2	40	800	
	ART. DIR. PER DIEM	10	DAYS	2	30	600	
	PROP. HOTEL	10	Days	2	40	800	
	PROP. PER DIEM	10	Days	2	30	600	
	LOCATION HOTEL	14	Days		40	560	
	LOCATION PER DIEM	14	Days		30	420	
	PA HOTEL	14	Days	2	40	1,120	
	PA PER DIEM	14	Days	3	30	1,260	
	sales tax	8.25%			11,360	937	$21,117
775-05	CATERING SERVICES						
	BREAKFAST @ $5/HEAD	25	Days	60	5	7,500	
	LUNCH $11/HEAD	25	Days	60	11	16,500	
	sales tax	8.25%			24,000	1,980	$25,980
775-06	EXTRA MEALS/SECOND M...						
	2ND MEAL	10	Days	60	10	6,000	
	EXTRA MEALS	10	Days		300	3,000	
	sales tax	8.25%			9,000	743	$9,743
775-07	PRODUCTION EXPENDABL...						
	PRODUCTION EXPENDABL...	5	Weeks		400	2,000	
	sales tax	8.25%			2,000	165	$2,165
775-08	CARTAGE						
	TRASH FEES		ALLOW		500	500	$500
775-11	FIREMAN/POLICE						
	FIREMAN	10	Hours	20	52	10,400	
	POLICE	8	Hours	15	52	6,240	
	TEAMSTERS	30%			16,640	4,992	$21,632
775-12	PARKING LOTS						
	PARKING LOTS	2	Weeks		700	1,400	$1,400
775-13	A/C/HEAT FEES						
	A/C HEAT FEES		ALLOW		500	500	$500
775-17	GRATUITIES						
	GRATUITIES - TIPS		ALLOW		300	300	$300
775-18	OFFICE						
	Office Rental & Furniture	20	Weeks		500	10,000	
	OFFICE SUPPLIES		Allow		3,000	3,000	
	PHOTOCOPY/FAX RENTAL	20	Weeks		200	4,000	
	sales tax	8.25%			7,000	578	$17,578
775-19	LOCATION MEDICAL EXPE...						
	ALLOCATION		ALLOW		500	500	$500
775-20	SHIPPING						
	FILM SHIPPING		ALLOW		1,000	1,000	
	sales tax	8.25%			1,000	83	$1,083
775-21	LOCATION SECURITY						

Figure 6–6   Sample budget 3 ($1.5 million) (continued)

Acct#	Description	Amount	Units	X	Rate	Subtotal	Total
775-00	**LOCATION EXPENSE (CONT'D)**						
775-21	LOCATION SECURITY (CONT'D)						
	LOCATION SECURITY	15	Days		300	4,500	
	NIGHT WATCHMAN	5	NIGHTS		300	1,500	
	NONUNION	18.0%			6,000	1,080	$7,080
						Total For 775-00	**$162,155**
785-00	**PRODUCTION DAILIES**						
785-01	NEGATIVE RAW STOCK						
	RAW STOCK (5298 - UNOP...	35,000	FEET		0.52	18,200	
	RAW STOCK (5298 - RECAN	25,000	FEET		0.3	7,500	
	RAWSTOCK (5248 - RECAN))	20,000	FEET		0.20	4,000	
	sales tax	8.25%			29,700	2,450	$32,150
785-02	DEVELOPING						
	80,000 FT DEVELOP	80,000	FEET		0.12	9,600	
	PREP @ 80,000 FEET	80,000	FEET		0.07	5,600	$15,200
785-03	TRANSFER DAILIES						
	TRANSFER TO VIDEO - 3/4"	80,000	FEET		0.24	19,200	$19,200
785-04	TAPE STOCK						
	TAPE STOCK - BETA 3/4"	25	TAPES		24	600	
	BETA SP TAPES	25	TAPES		41	1,025	
	VHS TAPES	50	TAPES		13	650	
	sales tax	8.25%			2,275	188	$2,463
785-05	TRANSFER SOUND DAILIES						
	TRANSFER SOUND DAILIES		ALLOW		5,000	5,000	$5,000
785-08	SCREEN DAILIES						
	SCREEN DAILIES		Allow		500	500	$500
						Total For 785-00	**$74,513**
797-00	**TESTS**						
797-02	TEST #1/FILM STOCK/CAM...						
	TEST		ALLOW		500	500	$500
						Total For 797-00	**$500**
	Total Production						**$783,931**
800-00	**EDITING**						
800-01	FILM EDITOR						
	Editor	20	Weeks		800	16,000	
	NONUNION	18.0%			16,000	2,880	$18,880
800-02	SOUND EFFECTS EDITING						
	SOUND EFFECTS EDITING		ALLOW		3,000	3,000	$3,000
800-03	MUSIC EDITING						
	Allocation		ALLOW		3,000	3,000	$3,000
800-04	NEGATIVE CUTTING						
	Allocation		ALLOW		5,000	5,000	$5,000
800-05	DIALOGUE EDITING						

(continued)

Figure 6–6 Sample budget 3 ($1.5 million) (continued)

Acct#	Description	Amount	Units	X	Rate	Subtotal	Total
800-00	**EDITING (CONT'D)**						
800-05	DIALOGUE EDITING (CONT'D)						
	DIALOGUE EDITING		ALLOW		5,000	5,000	$5,000
800-06	PROJECTION						
	PROJECTION		Allow		500	500	$500
800-07	CONTINUITY SCRIPTS						
	Continuity Scripts		ALLOW		500	500	$500
800-11	EDITORIAL FACILITIES						
	EDIT SUITE (INCL. PARKING)	20	Weeks		1,000	20,000	
	AVID SYSTEM	20	Weeks		1,200	24,000	
	HARD DRIVES/DECKS	20	Weeks		300	6,000	$50,000
800-12	EDITORIAL SUPPLIES/FOOD						
	SUPPLIES	20	Weeks		150	3,000	
	FOOD	20	Weeks		200	4,000	
	sales tax	8.25%			7,000	578	$7,578
800-14	POST PROD. SUPERVISION						
	POSTPRO SUPERVISION	10	WEEKS		800	8,000	
	NONUNION	18.0%			8,000	1,440	$9,440
800-17	OTHER COSTS						
	MISCELLANEOUS ITEMS		ALLOW		1,000	1,000	$1,000
800-18	ASSISTANT EDITOR						
	ASSISTANT EDITOR	16	Weeks		600	9,600	
	NONUNION	18.0%			9,600	1,728	$11,328
800-19	APPRENTICE EDITOR (INT...						
	APPRENTICE EDITOR (INT...						$0
						Total For 800-00	**$115,226**
810-00	**MUSIC**						
810-08	COMPOSER						
	COMPOSER	1	Flat		7,500	7,500	
	NONUNION	18.0%			7,500	1,350	$8,850
810-10	SONGWRITER						$0
810-21	RECORDING MUSICIANS						$0
810-22	SINGERS & VOCAL COAC...						$0
810-25	MUSIC SUPERVISOR						
	MUSIC SUPERVISOR	1	FLAT		7,500	7,500	
	NONUNION	18.0%			7,500	1,350	$8,850
810-26	MUSIC CLEARANCE SALA...						$0
810-27	MUSIC CLERICAL						$0
810-28	MASTER USE LICENSES						
	FESTIVAL LICENSES		ALLOW		2,500	2,500	$2,500
810-29	MUSIC PUBLISHING LICEN...						
	MUSIC PUBLISHING LICEN...		Allow		10,000	10,000	$10,000
810-33	SCORE (FACILITIES)						
	score facilities		ALLOW		5,000	5,000	$5,000
810-34	STUDIO EQUIPMENT RENT...						$0
810-35	MUSIC INSTRUMENT RENT...						$0

Figure 6–6   Sample budget 3 ($1.5 million) (continued)

Acct#	Description	Amount	Units	X	Rate	Subtotal	Total
810-00	**MUSIC (CONT'D)**						
810-36	MUSIC INSTRUMENT CART...						$0
810-41	PAYROLL TAXES/FRINGES						$0
810-42	PHONO						$0
810-43	MUSIC RESEARCH REPOR...						$0
						Total For 810-00	$35,200
820-00	**POSTPRODUCTION SOUND**						
820-01	DIALOGUE RECORDING (A...						
	ADR FACILITY		ALLOW		5,000	5,000	$5,000
820-03	SOUND EFFECTS (FOLEY)						
	SOUND EFFECTS/FOLEY		Allow		5,000	5,000	$5,000
820-06	DUBBINGV SESSION						
	SOUND MIX-TEMP AND FI...		ALLOW		15,000	15,000	$15,000
820-07	SOUND TRANSFERS						
	SOUND TRANSFERS		ALLOW		5,000	5,000	$5,000
820-09	PURCHASED SOUND EFFE...						
	PURCHASED SOUND EFFE...		Allow		1,500	1,500	$1,500
820-12	MAGNETIC TAPE FOR EDIT						
	Mag Tape		ALLOW		1,000	1,000	
	sales tax	8.25%			1,000	83	$1,083
820-13	OPTICAL NEG 35 & 35/32						
	DEVELOP OPTICAL NEG. ...	80,000	FEET		0.11	8,800	$8,800
						Total For 820-00	$41,383
840-00	**TITLES**						
840-01	TITLES (MAIN & END)						
	MAIN TITLE CARDS		Allow		3,000	3,000	
	END CREDIT CARDS/CRAWL		Allow		2,000	2,000	$5,000
840-02	MAIN TITLES						$0
840-03	END TITLES						$0
840-04	MISCELLANEOUS TITLES						$0
840-05	LABORATORY PROCESSING						
	LAB PROCESS FEE FOR TI...		Allow		2,000	2,000	$2,000
						Total For 840-00	$7,000
850-00	**OPTICALS, MATTES, INSERTS**						
850-01	OPTICAL EFFECTS/DUPE ...						
	OPTICAL EFFECTS		ALLOW		10,000	10,000	$10,000
850-02	MASTER POSITIVES						$0
850-03	LABORATORY PROCESSING						$0
850-04	SPECIAL PHOTO EFFECTS						$0
850-05	INSERTS						$0
850-11	PURCHASES						$0
						Total For 850-00	$10,000

(continued)

Figure 6–6   Sample budget 3 ($1.5 million) (continued)

Acct#	Description	Amount	Units	X	Rate	Subtotal	Total
860-00	**LABORATORY PROCESSING**						
860-01	REPRINTING & DEVELOPING						
	RE-PRINT & DEVELOP	5,000	FEET		0.22	1,100	$1,100
860-02	1ST TRIAL COMPOSITE P...						
	1ST TRIAL PRINT	9,000	FEET		0.20	1,800	$1,800
860-07	ANSWER PRINT/COLOR TI...						
	ANSWER PRINT	9,000	FEET		0.86	7,740	$7,740
860-08	SYNC REEL CHARGE						
	SYNC REEL CHARGE	10	REELS		38	380	$380
860-09	TELECINE						
	TELECINE	40	Hours		200	8,000	$8,000
860-17	LEADER & MISCELLANEOUS						
	LEADER & TAPE		Allow		1,000	1,000	
	sales tax	8.25%			1,000	83	$1,083
						Total For 860-00	$20,103
	Total Postproduction						$228,911
910-OO	**ADMINISTRATIVE EXPENSES**						
910-01	ACCOUNTING & TERMINAL...						
	SUPPLIES		ALLOW		500	500	$500
910-02	MPAA CERTIFICATE						
	MPAA CERTIFICATE		ALLOW		1,500	1,500	$1,500
910-03	POSTAGE & STATIONERY						
	Allocation		ALLOW		1,000	1,000	$1,000
910-05	LEGAL EXPENSE & FEES						
	LEGAL FEES		Allow		5,000	5,000	
	CORP. REGISTER/FILES/F...		Allow		1,000	1,000	$6,000
910-06	TELEPHONE/FACSIMILE						
	PHONE/FAX	20	Weeks		500	10,000	
	CELLULARS	20	Weeks	3	200	12,000	
	sales tax	8.25%			22,000	1,815	$23,815
910-12	DISTRIBUTION SCREENING						
	DISTRIBUTION SCREENING		Allow		2,000	2,000	$2,000
910-14	PARKING LOT EXPENSES						$0
910-16	FESTIVAL EXPENSES						
	FESTIVAL EXPENSES		ALLOW		500	500	$500
910-18	TITLE/CLEARANCE RPT.						
	TITLE & CLEARANCE REP...		ALLOW		1,000	1,000	$1,000
910-21	POLAROID/STILL FILM						
	POLAROID FILM		ALLOW		500	500	
	STILL FILM/DEVELOP		Allow		1,000	1,000	
	sales tax	8.25%			1,500	124	$1,624
910-22	PAYROLL CO.						
	PAYROLL CO.		ALLOW		3,000	3,000	$3,000
910-23	STORAGE						
	STORAGE FACILITY		ALLOW		500	500	$500

Figure 6–6   Sample budget 3 ($1.5 million) (continued)

Acct#	Description	Amount	Units	X	Rate	Subtotal	Total
910-00	**ADMINISTRATIVE EXPENSES (CONT'D)**						
910-35	WRAP PARTY						
	WRAP PARTY		ALLOW		2,000	2,000	$2,000
						Total For 910-00	**$43,439**
920-00	**PUBLICITY**						
920-01	UNIT PUBLICIST						
	PUBLICIST	1	MONTH		3,000	3,000	$3,000
920-02	STILL PHOTOGRAPHER						
	STILL PHOTOGRAPHER	1	Flat		2,000	2,000	$2,000
920-03	STILL FILM & PROCESSING						
	Still supplies & expendables		ALLOW		1,000	1,000	$1,000
						Total For 920-00	**$6,000**
	Total Other						**$49,439**
	Completion Bond: 3.00%						$39,187
	Contingency: 10.00%						$130,624
	Overhead: 1.00%						$13,062
	Insurance: 2.00%						$26,125
	TOTAL ABOVE-THE-LINE						**$243,957**
	TOTAL BELOW-THE-LINE						**$1,062,280**
	TOTAL ABOVE & BELOW-THE-LINE						**$1,306,237**
	GRAND TOTAL						**$1,515,235**

Figure 6–6   Sample budget 3 ($1.5 million) (continued)

$62,000 Budget Production	
SCRIPT DEVELOPMENT	
Printing/photocopying	$500
Mailing	$250
Application fees (writing workshops, etc.)	$100
Phone	$250
TOTAL SCRIPT DEVELOPMENT	**$1,100**
PREPRODUCTION	
Graphics	$100
Script copies (x90)	$750
Audition space	$150
Rehearsal space	$300
Set construction	$1,000
Costumes	$1,000
Props	$500
Food	$200
TOTAL PREPRODUCTION	**$4,000**
PRODUCTION	
EQUIPMENT -	
Camera (@ 1000/day x 6 days, based on a 2-day week)	$6,000
Lights (@ 250/day X 6, based on a 2-day week)	$1,500
Sound (@ 100/day x 6, based on a 2-day week)	$600
Incidentals (tape, gels, bulbs, cleaners, etc.)	$400
Generator rental/tie-ins	$300
Truck rental	$900
Equipment Insurance	$1,100
TOTAL EQUIPMENT	$10,800
STOCK & PROCESSING -	
Film (400 mins=16,000 ft=40 cans	$3,360
Processing (16,000 ft @ .15/ft)	$2,400
Nagra tape (14 30-min tapes @ $20 each)	$280
Videotape	$100
TOTAL STOCK & PROCESSING	**$6,140**
CREW	
Camera special	$600
Food	$2,100
TOTAL CREW	**$2,700**
LOCATIONS	
Permits	$50

Figure 6–7 $62,000 budget

Rental cafe	$150
Rental 110 Capp	$400
Reparation S. Van Ness	$300
Reparation Davis	$25
TOTAL LOCATIONS	**$925**
Administrative	
Phone	$250
Gas	$250
Photocopies (log sheets, etc.)	$50
TOTAL ADMINISTRATIVE	**$550**
TOTAL PRODUCTION	**$26,215**

Figure 6–7 $62,000 budget (continued)

$62,000 Budget Postproduction	
ADMINISTRATIVE	**COST**
Office supplies	$250
Phone/fax	$500
Photocopies	$200
Stills	$200
Mailing	$100
Gas	$250
Videotape	$50
Videocassettes	$30
TOTAL ADMINISTRATIVE	**$1,580**
ROUGH CUT	
Shipping	$100
Nagra transfer (16,000 ft @ .75 less 10%)	$1,080
Sync sound	$0
Edge coating (32,000 ft @ .02/ft)	$576
Flatbed rental ($700/mo)	$2,100
Editing expendables and equipment (bench etc)	$2,400
Editing room rental	$600
Editing special 1	$2,050
Editing special 2	$600
Tape/DAT to mag transfer	$500
Sound design	$250
Pickups shoot	$1,000
Rough cut screening room rental	$300
Hospitality/stewardship	$150
TOTAL ROUGH CUT	**$11,706**
FINE CUT	
Shipping	$300
Sound design/score expenses	$250
Conforming	$2,000
Answer print from AB roll (3,600 ft @ 1.05/ft)	$3,402
Mix Sound (incl Foley)	$10,000
Optical track negative (3,600 ft @ .20/ft)	$648
Release prints (3,600 ft @ .32/ft X 2) $1,037 x 2	$2,074
Titles	$1,000
Hospitality/stewardship	$150
TOTAL FINE CUT	**$19,824**
FESTIVALS	**COST**
Transfer to video (once, workprint/once, release print)	$1,200
Video copies	$150

Figure 6–7 $62,000 budget (continued)

Shipping	$200
Submission fees (6 festivals @ $50/ea)	$300
Publicist	$500
Press kits	$250
Press mailing	$250
Stills	$300
Hospitality/Stewardship	$150
TOTAL FESTIVAL PHASE	**$3,300**
Total Postproduction	**$36,410**
Total Production	**$26,215**
Grand Total Production & Postproduction	**$62,625**

Figure 6–7 $62,000 budget (continued)

7 PREPRODUCTION

Well, if preproduction goes well, I am pretty much not very busy during production, and that is the ideal. Preproduction periods tend to be intensely geared toward organizing every single day as much as possible, all with an eye toward figuring if our days are that organized, we'll be able to have a little time left.
—Christine Vachon, Killer Films

For the line producer, the bulk of the work is during preproduction. Staying focused, organized, on schedule, and in constant communication with the crew (while trying to remain calm) will ensure a smooth run into production. There is a saying about producers: "If you've done your job right in preproduction, you'll have nothing to do during production." That, of course, is not exactly true. There will be plenty to do during production, but it will be less hectic if all goes smoothly during preproduction. Make sure that the crew is on track and able to move forward. If you find that you are idle for a time during any part of the day, help someone else. There's not enough time or money for oversights or inefficiency.

When you're ready for preproduction you might say to yourself, "Where do I begin?" From our experience with productions (and that same feeling), we've compiled a master list (the preproduction checklists) of everything we've needed to prepare, set up, organize, and account for when beginning each show. Following these checklists has helped ensure that our shows run smoothly and efficiently.

Remember, each film is different and will have specific needs, but you will probably have to deal with each item on each checklist while prepping for almost any film. There may be additional items to add to your checklists depending on your film's needs. Use the checklists that follow as a guideline.

GETTING THE BEST DEAL

Getting the best deal doesn't necessarily mean compromising the film or skimping on locations, crew, or equipment. Being creative and honest are the keys to making deals that are affordable. Be honest with vendors, location owners, and others about your budget, and explain the type of film you're making. You'd be surprised how supportive and agreeable people can be.

Try to make flat-rate deals or weekly flat-rate deals rather than paying for equipment and expendables by the day. Whenever possible, secure equipment based on a three-day week; this means that if a vendor quotes you a price per day, you will only be charged for three days over the course of one week. This is an important negotiating point. Sometimes, you can even negotiate a two-day week.

When calling vendors to discuss your equipment needs, availability, and prices, you will often put equipment you need to rent on hold. A hold ensures that the equipment you want will not be rented to another production during the dates you specify. Ask the vendor how long equipment can be held and what the hold guarantees. If you put equipment on hold at a particular rental house but find a better deal at a second place or find that you no longer need the equipment, you should notify the first vendor. This courtesy is important in establishing a relationship with vendors; it also ensures that you aren't tying up equipment unnecessarily and won't ultimately be charged for it. You might also ask the first rental house if they can match the best price you have been quoted.

Making the best deal may save you money for any unanticipated costs that may arise. Take another look at the equipment, supplies, locations, crew, catering services, and vehicles that your film needs. Will a creative approach to any of these areas save money without compromising your film, cast, or the crew? (See "When Your Budget Is Way Too High" in Chapter 6.)

THE FUNCTIONAL OFFICE

Before you enter the war zone of preproduction, equip and organize your office with the basic essentials. This may sound ridiculous, but if you don't properly set up and organize your office beforehand, a huge mess will ensue; during each day of preproduction you will amass papers, contracts, purchase orders, and notes that you will need to refer to later but won't be able to find. (See Figure 7–1.)

Choose the space you will be working in carefully. Keep in mind that you'll need bathrooms, air-conditioning or heat as the weather dictates, ample space, and windows. You will be keeping long hours, so be considerate of neighbors who will be disturbed by traffic.

Office furniture can be costly; look for good deals on used furniture in the classified ads and at swap meets. Borrow furniture from sympathetic outsiders. Do anything necessary to set up your office so that it is functional, comfortable, and spacious enough for crew.

You'll need ample desk space and a good light for each person working in the office. Ideally, you'll have extra desks for various department people who roam in and out of the office and need to do paperwork or make calls. Each workstation should be equipped with a decent chair, pens, notepads, and a phone.

Filing cabinets are essential to the functional office. Set up your filing system before you amass a pile of daunting paperwork. *Go through the preproduction and production checklists, and create files for every item listed.* Let the files hang there empty. When the need arises, you'll be able to find or file each piece of paper.

Go to the office supply store and load up on pens, paper, paper clips, a stapler, staples, sticky notes, an address card file, corkboards, tacks, and other essentials. Purchase what you need to do your job correctly. Don't forget petty cash booklets, purchase order books, and other forms from the office supply or stationery store. You will thank yourself for having the necessary supplies handy when you've got three phone lines holding and several department heads waiting for petty cash. You don't want your efficiency to be hindered by not having set up your office properly.

In addition to office supplies, you'll need to consider such capital items as phones, a fax machine, computers, a copy machine, a refrigerator, and a microwave. These should be one-time expenses. Phone lines are the production office's lifeline. Install enough phone lines to sustain the office.

It will be money well spent. A fax machine and e-mail are other office musts. Install a designated fax line.

Most key production personnel will have their own computers. If not, consider renting a few computers for key personnel or securing a product placement agreement with a computer manufacturer if there is a way to work it into your film. It is essential that you have one computer that functions as the brain of the production. It must have ample memory and the necessary software loaded, including word-processing software, a spreadsheet program, and perhaps Movie Magic Scheduling and Budgeting. Finally, if you can buy, rent, or borrow a copy machine, do so. If not, befriend the proprietor of the local copy shop and set up an account there; you will need to make many copies each day. Having a small refrigerator and possibly a microwave is also important. It will increase the chances of healthy eating by production office staff.

Resource guides, maps, telephone books, production books (such as *LA 411* or *NYPG*), and street atlases should be available on the production office bookshelf. You may need more than one copy of some of these books. Check if crew members own these before you spend the cash on multiple copies.

A functional office, set up and organized before the crew comes on and preproduction officially begins, will be a sturdy leg to stand on when things get nuts—and they will.

PREPRODUCTION CHECKLISTS

Some of the tasks included in the preproduction checklists will carry over into the production period. The week in which you deal with many of these items will vary according to the needs of your film and how much preproduction time you have. The checklists that follow are based on a four- to six-week preproduction period (see also CD-ROM).

Legal, Financial, and Accounts Checklist

The following items should be taken care of during the first two weeks of preproduction.

- File the necessary paperwork to incorporate the production company.
- Hire an accountant.
- Engage a lawyer.
- Set up a bank account; order checks.
- Secure production insurance and certificates (week 2).

"TITLE"
PROCEDURES

PRODUCTION OFFICE

Production Company, Inc.
Address

Phone and Fax

OFFICE HOURS

During preproduction, office hours are *Monday thru Saturday*, ___ am to ___ pm. The last week of preproduction which is "dates", the office will stay open later, and on Saturday "date", if your department needs to be working. If it is an emergency, and you need to reach "Name", feel free to call at anytime. If you need to come to the office after hours, make arrangements with "Name" first, or call before coming. Please do not just show up. During shooting, the office will have the same call time as the set if not earlier. Please keep in mind that if you will be coming to the office and it is late at night or in the early morning hours, please be very quiet and respectful of the neighbors. You may park _____.

TIMECARDS

All time crew cards must be turned in by the first lunch/dinner break on Wednesdays. Payday is every Thursday.

PETTY CASH

All petty cash must be submitted on a weekly basis (if possible) in the envelope provided from the production office. Each receipt must be affixed to an 8 1/2″ by 11″ piece of paper, and must be numbered according to the number on the envelope. All receipts must be originals, not photocopies. This includes messenger charges, bills for photocopying, gas charges, or any other receipt which is to be reimbursed. "Name" is the only one who can distribute petty cash.

DEAL MEMOS

Please make sure you have completed a deal memo, W4, an I-9 form, and a start form. All payroll related forms must be returned to "Names" *as soon as possible*.

HOUSE ACCOUNTS/VENDORS

All applications and/or inquiries for house accounts must be processed and approved by "Name". The name, address, telephone number, and tax ID number for each vendor must appear on the application. We will need to know who is authorized to sign on the account. We will notify you when the account has been opened.

PURCHASE ORDERS

Purchase orders or numbers and forms are available in the production office. Each time you rent or purchase an item(s) from a vendor, you must give them an official purchase order, and a copy to the production office. When placing an order, you are required to obtain the actual or estimated rental cost of the items. All purchase orders should be submitted to the production office for approval prior to placing an order or purchasing goods. However, purchase orders should never be held waiting for an amount or an invoice to match. The production office will handle those functions. No invoices will be paid without pre-approved purchase orders to back them up.

CHECK REQUESTS

Check requests are available in the production office. If you need a rush check, please mark it rush and indicate the date the check is needed clearly on the request and to whom it should be returned. Put all check requests in the check request box for approval.

Use a check request form if you have not received an invoice. However, we do need a paid invoice <u>and</u> a purchase order to backup any request when the check is distributed.

*If there is anything you need in way of forms, supplies, or vendor information, ask the office staff. Also, we may already have an account with certain vendors, have done business with them before, or want to use a specific vendor. Please inquire within the office first.

CHECK CASHING AND BANK INFORMATION

Bank Address and Phone Number
Contact: "Name"

Figure 7–1 Office procedures sample

- Fill out and file SAG paperwork; post bond (week 1).
- Engage a payroll company.
- Set up a computerized accounting system/check register.
- File contact information, driver's licenses, Social Security numbers, and credit card information for the producer, line producer, and director.
- Create a chart of accounts based on the budget.
- Always have petty cash on hand.
- Set up vendor accounts (week 2 and as department heads are hired).
- Start a list of deposits paid that you'll need to recover from vendors.
- Negotiate a deal with a lab (week 2).
- Make product placement inquiries and prepare letters (weeks 2 and 3).
- Have a research/title report done; clear usages in script for legal purposes (weeks 2 and 3).

About the Legal, Financial, and Accounts Checklist

Incorporation. The production company making the movie must be incorporated. File for your company's corporate status in the state in which it will conduct business. An accountant or an attorney can help you with this, or you can incorporate the company yourself over the Internet. You will need to pay filing fees and state corporation fees.

Accountant. If you plan to hire an accountant who will cut checks to vendors, oversee the accounting of the show, and pay cast and crew payroll, he or she should start at the outset.

Hiring a Lawyer. If you can afford to do so, hire a lawyer to prepare your above-the-line contracts and set up the corporate structure of the production entity making the film. A lawyer will ensure that your contracts and paperwork are in order and can advise you with any legal issues pertaining to the script. If you can't afford a lawyer, seek some advice from organizations that provide free legal advice, colleagues, and contract books.

Bank Account. Set up a bank account immediately so you can issue deposit or rent checks for your office space, purchase office supplies, retain an attorney, and establish credit with vendors. Set up the bank account in the name of the production company, and order checks for that account. (Ideally, this should be an interest-bearing account.) The bank will require documents of incorporation. The line producer should be able to sign these checks.

Production Insurance. Secure production insurance for the course of the show; you'll need it to rent equipment, se-

cure locations, hire the cast, and more. Your show must be insured against any loss, injury, or damage. Do this in week 1 of preproduction so that insurance certificates can be issued to vendors and locations. The standard liability limit on production insurance policies is $1 million. Check film guides, or contact local film organizations, an attorney, or the film commission in the city in which you are filming if you need assistance finding a production insurance company.

SAG Paperwork. To employ SAG actors, your production company must become a signatory of the guild. Contact SAG, let them know your budget level, and they will forward you the required paperwork. The guild usually requires financial assurances in the form of a bond, a cash deposit, or a security agreement. Bonds are posted on a film for the protection of the performers employed by the production company. The bond amount is a percent of the total wages for actors in your budget, not to exceed 40%. When you have paid the actors and filed the necessary payroll and completion paperwork, SAG will return the bond.

Request and begin filling out the SAG paperwork package immediately! You should request the SAG paperwork from the guild at least 30 days before production is scheduled to begin. The package is dense and will take some time to fill out. Much of the paperwork must be filed with the guild early on; you will file other items at the end of the show. Instructions are included in the package. (See "Cast Checklist" below for more on SAG paperwork.)

Payroll Company. Call around and compare the rates of payroll companies before you engage one. It is advisable to have a payroll company pay both cast and crew paychecks, especially if yours is a SAG show. Payroll companies usually require a set-up fee and charge per check issued. It is well worth the money to hire a payroll company to account for deductions and fringes, which can be time-consuming. Upon securing a payroll company, send copies of all cast and crew contracts, W4 forms, I-9 forms, and weekly time cards.

Check Register/Accounting System. Set up a check register on your computer in order to account for all checks issued, deposits, transfers, and withdrawals. It is extremely important that you account for every transaction made within the production account, whether it be a payment or a deposit. This check register should indicate the date any transaction was made, the check number of each check issued, and the budget account code and item for which the purchase was made. This way, when you actualize your budget, you have accounted for all checks and are able to know whether you are over- or underbudget.

Important Information to Keep on File. Often, you'll need a credit card or other form of identification (such as a driver's license or Social Security number) to set up accounts or to make purchases. A credit card may be required as a deposit when renting equipment or in case an emergency comes up. It is advisable to have the producer's or line producer's credit card information, Social Security number, and driver's license on file, just in case. Try to avoid using credit cards for purchases. Whenever possible purchase items and make deposits with checks instead. Have the bank account information and the film's employee identification number on file where they will be easy to find. (When you file to incorporate your production company, the state in which you file will assign the corporation an employee identification number.) This information may be required on credit applications and purchase orders.

Chart of Accounts. Create a chart of accounts (account codes that correspond to each line item in the budget). If you are using Movie Magic Budgeting, you have the option of printing out a chart of accounts based on the budget. Use these codes when actualizing the budget, writing checks, and coding petty cash envelopes. This will allow you to determine how much money was spent in each category and line item, helping you remain on budget. (See the *Swingers* chart of accounts reproduced in Figure 7–2.)

Petty Cash. Petty cash is used for small purchases, such as gas, tolls, tips, parking, office supplies, inexpensive props, and food. Always have petty cash on hand and have crew members properly account for the petty cash they receive and spend. Keep track of all petty cash given to crew members. Code each purchase listed on the completed petty cash envelopes according to the chart of accounts. You will need to account for petty cash purchases when actualizing the budget.

Vendor Accounts. Whenever possible, set up credit accounts with vendors to avoid having to pay for equipment and supplies upon receipt (unless, of course, you can make a better deal by paying up front). Often department heads will have relationships with equipment houses allowing you to secure the best possible deal from those vendors. Start organizing your needs and setting up accounts early on.

Deposits. Vendors often will require a deposit for equipment or materials that you will be renting for the production. Keeping track of deposits made to vendors will help you to remember who you will need to get money back from when the show has wrapped. You will need to be sure to account for any deposits that will be returned when actualizing your budget. Remember that until a deposit is returned, it is money that is unavailable during production.

Lab. Call around to determine which lab will accommodate the needs of your film for the best rates. Do this during week 2 of preproduction or when the editor is hired so that the producer, director, and editor can discuss the film's needs. If possible, secure a package deal at a reduced rate with the lab. Many labs offer reduced rates for student films and non-profit films. Be prepared to write the lab a deposit check. Discuss the turnaround time on dailies, and coordinate drop-off and pickup times. Establish a contact person at the lab in case a problem arises.

Product Placement/Legal Clearance. Go through the script to identify any brand-name products that you plan to use in the film. Contact the manufacturer of each to request clearance and a donation (see Figure 7–3). For example, if there is a particular brand of beverage that you want to have in a shot, contact the manufacturer to obtain a signed letter clearing the use of the beverage in the film and to request that the manufacturer donate beverages to the production. The company may want to see the script and how you plan to use or refer to the product in the film. If you don't get permission to use specific brand-name items in the film, don't use them. You'll run the risk of being sued, and the unauthorized use of brand names could hinder your ability to set up a distribution deal later.

Product placement means free advertising for the manufacturer, and it can also be a way to raise money toward the production budget. It may be worth your while to ask the beverage company for a financial donation since you will be promoting and advertising its product. If you have the means, you can hire a company to approach potential product sponsors for you. Product placement arrangements can save you money, and you may be surprised how many companies are willing to donate their products.

Research/Title Report. Research reports are done on a script in order to ensure any usages or references made in the script. They are prepared to avoid illegal usages. For instance, if references are made to actual persons or places, the research report will indicate if and why a change to a particular reference is necessary. This is a safeguard against any lawsuits made against the production company or a distributor if and when the film secures distribution. A title report is done on the title of a film to alert you when and if other films, books, television shows, articles, etc. have been released under the same title, and whether it is necessary to make a title change. If the film secures distribution, these reports will be delivery items required by the distributor.

SWINGERS

Chart Of Accounts

Acct#	Description	Acct#	Description	Acct#	Description
		600-00	**STORY**		
600-01	RIGHTS PURCHASED	600-03	WRITERS	600-04	SCREENPLAY PURCHASE
		610-00	**PRODUCER**		
610-01	EXECUTIVE PRODUCER	610-02	PRODUCER	610-03	ASSOCIATE PRODUCER
610-07	PRODUCER'S ENT.	610-08	PRE-PRODUCTION EXPENSES		
		620-00	**DIRECTOR**		
620-01	DIRECTOR	620-05	CASTING DIRECTOR	620-08	CASTING EXPENSES
		630-00	**CAST**		
630-01	PRINCIPAL PLAYERS	630-02	DAY PLAYERS	630-06	LOOPING/ADR (INCL. 1 DA...
630-08	OVERTIME	630-09	MEDICAL EXAMS	630-20	SIDE DEALS
		650-00	**TRAVEL & LIVING**		
650-03	WRITER'S TRAVEL	650-03	WRITER'S LIVING	650-01	PRODUCER'S TRAVEL
650-01	PRODUCER'S LIVING	650-02	DIRECTOR'S TRAVEL	650-02	DIRECTOR'S LIVING
650-06	CAST TRAVEL	650-06	CAST LIVING		
		700-00	**EXTRA TALENT**		
700-02	EXTRAS AND STAND-INS	700-05	EXTRAS CASTING		
		705-00	**PRODUCTION STAFF**		
705-01	LINE PRODUCER	705-02	PROD. MGR.	705-03	FIRST ASSISTANT DIRECT...
705-04	SECOND ASSISTANT DIREC...	705-06	SCRIPT SUPERVISOR	705-08	ESTIMATOR/PROD. ACCOU...
705-10	PRODUCTION ASSISTANTS				
		710-00	**CAMERA**		
710-01	DIRECTOR OF PHOTOGRAPHY	710-03	1ST ASST CAMERAMAN	710-04	2ND ASST CAMERAMAN /...
710-06	STILL CAMERAMAN	710-08	CAMERA RENTALS	710-09	CAMERA SUPPLIES
710-11	CAM ACCESSORIES/VIDEO...	710-20	LOSS, DAMAGE & REPAIR		
		715-00	**ART/SET DESIGN(MATERIALS IN PROPS)**		
715-01	PRODUCTION DESIGNER	715-02	ART/SET DIRECTOR	715-03	SET DESIGNERS
		725-00	**SET OPERATIONS**		
725-01	1ST COMPANY GRIP/KEY ...	725-02	BEST BOY GRIP	725-03	CRANE/DOLLY GRIPS
725-04	EXTRA GRIPS	725-05	CAMERA DOLLIES	725-06	CAMERA CRANES
725-08	GRIP EQUIPMENT RENTALS	725-09	GRIP PURCHASES	725-10	GRIP BOX RENTALS
725-11	CRAFT SERVICE/SERVICE...	725-12	SET CLEANUP & TRASH DI...	725-19	FIRST AID
725-20	LOSS & DAMAGE	725-24	DRESSING ROOM RENTALS	725-30	LOCATION LOAD AND UNLO...
		730-00	**ELECTRICAL**		
730-01	GAFFER	730-02	BEST BOY	730-05	GLOBES/CARBONS/SUPPL...
730-07	GENERATOR RENTAL	730-08	ELECTRICAL EQUIP RENTALS	730-09	ELECTRICAL EQUIP PURCH...
730-10	BOX RENTAL	730-20	LOSS, DAMAGE, & REPAIR		
		745-00	**SET DRESSING**		
		750-00	**PROPERTIES**		
750-01	PROPERTY MASTER(SEE S...	750-04	PICTURE VEHICLES LABOR...	750-05	PICTURE VEHICLE RENTALS
750-08	PROP RENTALS	750-09	PROP PURCHASES	750-10	PROP BOX RENTALS
750-20	LOSS & DAMAGE				
		755-00	**WARDROBE**		
755-04	COSTUME DESIGNER	755-03	ASST. WARDROBE	755-06	ALTERATIONS - L&M
755-07	CLEANING & DYEING	755-08	WARDROBE RENTALS	755-09	WARDROBE PURCHASES
755-10	HAND BOX RENTALS	755-20	LOSS, DAMAGE & REPAIRS		
		760-00	**MAKEUP & HAIRSTYLISTS**		
760-01	MAKE-UPARTIST(AND HAI...	760-02	EXTRA MAKEUP ARTIST(A...	760-06	WIG & HAIR PURCHASE
760-09	MAKE-UP SUPPLIES/APPL...	760-10	KIT RENTALS		

Figure 7–2 Swingers *chart of accounts*

Chart Of Accounts

Acct#	Description	Acct#	Description	Acct#	Description
		765-00	PRODUCTION SOUND		
765-01	SOUND MIXER	765-02	BOOMMAN	756-05	PLAYBACK OPERATOR
765-06	SOUND EQUIP RENTALS	765-11	SUPPLIES AND EXPENDAB...	765-20	LOSS & DAMAGE
		770-00	TRANSPORTATION		
770-01	MESSENGER SERVICE	770-02	TRANSPORTATION COORD.	770-05	MILEAGE ALLOWANCE
770-06	FUEL	770-10	LOC. VEHICLES/PRODUCTI...	770-11	CAMERA DEPARTMENT
770-20	LOSS, DAMAGE, REPAIRS				
		775-00	LOCATION EXPENSE		
775-01	SURVEY EXPENSE	775-02	LOCATION STAFF	775-03	SITE RENTALS/PERMITS/...
775-04	HOTEL & LODGING	775-05	CATERING SERVICES	775-06	2ND MEALS/EXTRA MEALS
775-07	PRODUCTION EXPENDABLES	775-11	FIRE/POLICE	775-14	AIRPORT PICKUP/DELIVERY
775-15	LOCATION LOCK & UNLOAD	775-17	GRATUITIES	775-18	OFFICE RENT/FURNITURE/...
775-20	LOSS & DAMAGE	775-21	LOCATION SECURITY	775-22	PARKING LOTS(FOR CREW ...
		785-00	PRODUCTION DAILIES		
785-01	NEGATIVE RAW STOCK	785-04	SOUND RECORDING TAPE	785-09	VIDEO TAPE TRANSFERS
		800-00	EDITING		
800-01	FILM EDITOR	800-02	SOUND EFFECTS EDITING	800-03	MUSIC EDITING
800-04	NEGATIVE CUTTING	800-06	PROJECTION	800-11	EDITORIAL FACILITIES
800-12	EDITORIAL SUPPLIES/FOOD	800-14	POST PROD. SUPERVISION	800-18	ASSISTANT EDITOR
800-19	APPRENTICE EDITOR (INTE...				
		810-00	MUSIC		
810-08	COMPOSER	810-25	MUSIC SUPERVISOR	810-26	MUSIC CLEARANCE SALAR...
810-27	MUSIC CLERICAL	810-28	MASTER USE LICENSES	810-29	MUSIC PUBLISHING LICENS...
810-30	PRESCORE	810-31	REHEARSAL MUSICIANS	810-32	DEMO COSTS
810-33	SCORE (FACILITIES)	810-34	STUDIO EQUIPMENT RENT...	810-35	MUSIC INSTRUMENT RENT...
810-37	MUSIC TRANSFERS				
		820-00	POST PRODUCTION SOUND		
820-01	DIALOGUE RECORDING/ADR	820-02	NARRATION RECORDING/V...	820-03	SOUND EFFECTS (FOLEY)
820-06	DUBBING SESSION	820-07	SOUND TRANSFERS	820-13	OPTICAL NEG 35 & 35/32
		840-00	TITLES		
840-01	TITLES (MAIN & END)	840-02	MAIN TITLES	840-03	END TITLES
840-04	MISCELLANEOUS TITLES	840-05	LABORATORY PROCESSING		
		850-00	OPTICALS, MATTES, INSERTS		
850-01	OPTICAL EFFECTS/DUPE N...	850-02	MASTER POSITIVES	850-03	LABORATORY PROCESSING
850-04	SPECIAL PHOTO EFFECTS	850-11	PURCHASES		
		860-00	LABORATORY PROCESSING		
860-01	REPRINTING & DEVELOPING	860-02	1ST TRIAL COMPOSITE PR...	860-03	MASTER POSITIVE PRINT
860-06	DEVELOP SOUND NEGATIVE	860-07	ANSWER PRINT		
		910-00	ADMINISTRATIVE EXPENSES		
910-01	ACCOUNTING & TERMINAL...	910-02	MPAA CERTIFICATE	910-03	POSTAGE & SHIPPING & F...
910-04	XEROX & MIMEO (NO SCRI...	910-05	LEGAL EXPENSES & FEES	910-06	TELEPHONE/FACSIMILE
910-12	PREVIEW EXPENSE/DIST. S...	910-18	RESEARCH REPORT/TITLE ...	910-19	PRODUCTION EXPENDABLES
910-20	CORPORATE FILING	910-21	POLAROID & B/W STILL FI...	910-22	PAYROLL CO.
		920-00	PUBLICITY		
920-01	PUBLICITY - ALL COSTS	920-02	SPEC. STILL PHOTOGRAPH...	920-03	STILL FILM & PROCESSING
920-05	PUBLICITY STAFF - T&E	920-09	SPACE MEDIA	920-11	OUTSIDE SERVICES

Figure 7–2 Swingers *chart of accounts (continued)*

PRODUCT PLACEMENT RELEASE

PRODUCTION COMPANY, Inc.
ADDRESS

The undersigned agrees to provide the following product to PRODUCTION COMPANY, Inc. for use in the motion picture/movie now entitled *"TITLE"* (the "Picture"):

_____

_____

The company grants to you, your successors, licensees and assigns, the nonexclusive right, but not the obligation to use and include all or part of the trademark and/or logo associated with the above listed product in the Picture, without limitation as to time or number of runs, for reproduction, exhibition and exploitation, in any and all manner, methods, and media, whether now known or hereafter known or devised, and in the advertising, publicizing, promotion, trailers, and exploitation thereof.

The company warrants and represents that it is the owner of the product or direct provider of the services listed above or a representative of such and has the right to enter this agreement and grant the rights granted to PRODUCTION COMPANY, Inc. hereunder, with the understanding that PRODUCTION COMPANY, Inc. will not discredit the aforementioned product.

In full consideration of the Company providing the product to PRODUCTION COMPANY, Inc., PRODUCTION COMPANY, INC. agrees to accord "Company" screen credit in the end titles of the positive prints of the Picture in the following form:
"_____furnished by _____."

The Company understands that any broadcast identification of its products, trademarks, trade names or the like which PRODUCTION COMPANY, Inc. may furnish, shall, in no event, be beyond that which is reasonably related to the program content.

I further represent that neither I nor the Company which I represent will directly or indirectly publicize, or otherwise exploit the use, exhibition or demonstration of the above product and/or services in the picture without the express written consent of PRODUCTION COMPANY.

Sincerely yours,

Agreed and Accepted by

By_____

_____
(Authorized Signatory)

_____
(Please Print Name)

_____
(Producer)

_____
(Production Company
Address and Phone Number)

Figure 7–3   Product placement release

Office Setup Checklist

These items should be taken care of during the first week of preproduction:

- Post the production office's rules and procedures; hand them out to crew members when hired.
- Purchase office supplies.
- Set up the production office.
- Rent or purchase furniture.
- Organize the filing system; create files for each item in the preproduction and production checklists.
- Purchase, rent, or borrow a computer; install software programs.
- Purchase local film guides, phone books, street atlases, form books, and other reference materials.
- Purchase petty cash sign-out books and purchase order books.
- Have extra keys made for the office.
- Hang a calendar or whiteboard and a bulletin board for notes, memos, and dates.
- Set up a computerized check log; create a check log/ purchase order notebook.
- Set up check request and petty cash request systems.
- Organize a contract book with divisions for the production company, writer, partnership, director, crew, cast, and so on.
- Organize your personal production binder with labeled dividers.
- Prepare two production notebooks.
- Enter phone numbers and other contact information into the address database or card file.
- Post the address, phone and fax numbers, name of contact person, hours of operation, and night drop times for the lab that you will be using to process film each day.
- Prepare and gather production forms, SAG forms, and contracts.

About the Office Setup Checklist

Just as important as a comfortable and functional office is the internal setup of that office. It is worthwhile to spend time preparing forms, contracts, notebooks, and so on, to ensure the efficient operation of your office.

Check Log/Purchase Order Notebook. Organize a check log/purchase order notebook so that all accounts and paid checks are filed with the corresponding paperwork. If there is ever a dispute about payment, you can refer to your canceled checks. Refer to this notebook when actualizing your budget and preparing a daily cost overview. A check log is similar to the check register that you keep for your own checking account, except that attached to each printed-out check entry is the purchase order or invoice that belongs to it.

Check Request System. A check request system will keep you organized. Create a check request box for filled-out check request forms so that each day you or the accountant can prepare the necessary checks.

Personal Production Binder. Get a large three-ring binder with labeled dividers to keep as your personal production notebook during the course of the show. The following list is an example of what you may want to have in your personal notebook. (Some of the forms listed here are defined in "About the Legal, Financial, and Accounts Checklist." Other forms are explained later in this section.)

Bank account information

Beeper and cell phone numbers

Budget

Calendar

Cast list

Chart of accounts

Crew list

Copies of Exhibit G forms, Taft-Hartley forms, call sheets, and production reports

Copy of the script and any page changes

Daily cost overview sheets

Daily raw stock log

Emergency numbers, equipment maintenance numbers, and other phone numbers

Insurance certificates

Lab information

List of locations and location contracts

Petty cash tracking sheet for petty cash issued

Permits issued by film commissions

Schedules, day-out-of-days sheets, strip boards, and break-downs

Small SAG rule booklet

Vendor list

Production Notebooks. Compile two production notebooks. Divide each of these large notebooks into numbered sections for each day of filming. For example, if you will be shooting for 30 days, you will need 30 dividers. File the call sheet, production report, Exhibit G forms, Taft-Hartley forms, script notes, camera reports, and sound reports for each shoot day in the numbered section for that day. The producer will keep one of the notebooks, and the other will remain with the production company after the show has been wrapped.

Production Forms, SAG Forms, and Contracts.   Gather and prepare the production forms, SAG forms, and contracts you'll need for preproduction and production. Create a file for each. You may want to store some forms in manila envelopes on the wall or on a table in the office so that they are easily accessible to the crew; check requests, vendor/cast/crew packs, petty cash envelopes, and mileage sheets, for example, should be easily accessible. Following is a list of the forms you should have on hand.

Call sheets (Figure 7–4). Call sheets, which provide vital information for each shoot day, are issued to the cast and crew daily during production. The front of the call sheet lists the director, producer, location, weather, interior or exterior scene, cast, and special equipment information; the back of the call sheet lists each cast and crew member and his or her call time for that day. A map or directions to the location should be attached to the call sheet. A copy of each day's call sheet should be filed in the appropriate notebooks and office files.

Production reports (Figure 7–5). During production, the assistant director will fill out a production report each day and turn it in to the office the next day. The reports should be filed in the appropriate office file, your production binder, and the production notebook with that day's call sheet, Exhibit G forms, and other paperwork. The production report will indicate when each cast member reported to and was released from makeup, what time he or she began filming, when he or she was released from the set, and what time he or she broke for meals. Crew call times, crew meal times, camera call times, first shot, the amount of footage shot, which scenes were shot that day, and which shots were retakes are also recorded on the production report. The back of the production report is the same as the back of the call sheet. Production reports also list information about faulty equipment, meal penalties, and on-set injuries. Copies are sent to SAG and the payroll company each week and the original is filed in the production notebook.

Exhibit G forms (Figure 7–6). The Exhibit G form is provided and required by SAG. The AD will fill it out each day on the set. The call time, makeup time, and meal break times for each cast member who worked that day are reported on the form, which the cast member must sign. The Exhibit G must be sent to the payroll company and to SAG each week and should be filed in the office notebooks and files each day.

Taft-Hartley forms (Figures 7–7 and 7–8). The Taft-Hartley is another SAG form that the AD will fill out on the set if necessary. Under the provisions of the Taft-Hartley agreement, a nonguild member is permitted to work on a SAG show for a 30-day period. After the initial 30 days, the actor must join the guild to continue working on the SAG set. The production company must fill out and submit a Taft-Hartley form to SAG within 15 days of the actor's first day of work, or the production company will be fined. There is a cost involved when you "Taft-Hartley" an actor, and it is typically paid by the production company. Taft-Hartley forms are also sent to the payroll company and should be kept in the office files.

Mileage sheets (Figure 7–9). Mileage sheets should be available to all crew members who use their personal vehicles to run errands for the production. If you are paying mileage rather than gas, the driver must fill out a mileage sheet. Submit these forms to your production accountant or payroll company.

Check requests (Figure 7–10). A check request is exactly what it sounds like—a request for a check. Any item or piece of equipment that has to be paid for up front requires a check request. (Remember to keep a list of all checks issued as deposits so that you can get them back at the end of the show.) The check request should indicate what the check is for (you will need to account for it by account code later when you actualize the budget), to whom it should be made out, and the amount. If the check must be mailed, the request should also indicate to whom the check should be sent, the address, and the date it is needed. If the check is issued to a vendor or another company, make sure that the crew member filling out the request fills in the vendor's employee identification number in the space provided.

Petty cash requests. The same information found on a check request should be indicated on a petty cash request. Set up the same system for petty cash requests as you do for check requests.

Petty cash envelopes (Figure 7–11). When crew members are given petty cash, they must take a petty cash envelope and record each item purchased and its cost on the envelope. Petty cash envelopes can be turned in each week or when the crew member has spent all of the petty cash. He or she should take a new envelope when more petty cash is doled out. When petty cash envelopes are turned in to the office, code each purchase on the envelope according to your chart of accounts. Use these envelopes when actualizing the budget and when preparing your daily cost overview.

Daily raw stock logs (Figures 7–12 A,B). Daily raw stock logs are forms you either purchase or create to keep track of the amount of film shot, wasted, and unused each day.

CALL SHEET

DATE _____ 7/2/95 _____

PRODUCTION COMPANY _____ Double Down _____   DIRECTOR _____ Doug Liman _____
SHOW _____ SWINGERS _____   PRODUCER _____ Simpkins/LaLoggia _____
SERIES EPISODE _____   LOCATION _____ Mike's Apartment 5870 Franklin _____
PROD# _____ DAY # __3__ OUT OF __20__   SUNRISE __6:27 am__ SUNSET __7:15 pm__

ANTICIPATED WEATHER __Hot & sun 70/101__

IS TODAY A DESIGNATED DAY OFF? ☐ YES ☐ NO

CREW CALL _____ 4:30 pm _____   ☐ Weather Permitting   ☒ See Attached Map

LEAVING CALL _____   ☒ Report to Location   ☐ Bus to Location

SHOOTING CALL _____ 5:30 pm _____

Set Description	Scene Nos.	Cast	D/N	Pages	Location
INT. Mike's Apartment DAY	pu 53	1	D		Mike's Apt.
-Mike against wall					
INT. Mike's Apartment NIGHT	3	1	N	4	
-answering machine/Trent on phone					
INT. Mike's Apartment NIGHT	64	1	N	3/8	
-Mike considers calling Lorraine					

Cast	Part Of	Leave	Makeup	Set Call	Remarks
Jon Favreau	MIKE	5:00 pm		5:30 pm	
Atmosphere & Stand-ins					

NOTE: No forced calls without previous approval of unit production manager or assistant director.   All calls subject to change.

Advance Schedule Or Changes

7/5/95 Set #3

CHRISTY'S TRAILER
Valley Village Mobile Home Park 8250 Lankershim, N. Hollywood
Scene #19-25

Assistant Director _____   Production Manager _____

(continued)

Figure 7–4   Call sheet (front) (Reprinted with permission)

PRODUCTION REQUIREMENTS

PICTURE:				NO.			DATE	
NO.	ITEM	TIME	NO.	ITEM	TIME	NO.	ITEM	TIME
	PRODUCTION			SOUND			MEALS	
	DIRECTOR			MIXER			BREAKFASTS	
	UNIT MANAGER			RECORDER			BOX LUNCHES	
	ASST. DIRECTORS			MIKE BOOM			HOT LUNCHES	
	SCRIPT SUPERVISOR			CABLE UTIL.			DINNERS	
	DIALOGUE COACH							
	STUDIO TEACHER			PLAYBACK OPERATOR			TRANSPORTATION	
	CHILD WELFARE WORKER			PLAYBACK MACHINE			DRIVER CAPTAIN	
							DRIVERS	
	CAMERA			PROPERTY				
	DIRECTOR OF PHOTO.			PROPERTY MASTER			CAMERA INSERT CAR	
	CAMERA OPERATOR			ASST. PROP. MASTER			CAMERA TRUCK	
	1ST. ASSISTANT						PICTURE CARS	
	2ND. ASSISTANT							
	EXTRA OPERATOR			SET DECORATOR				
	STEADICAM			LEADMAN				
	ASST.			SWING GANG			MISC CARS	
	EXTRA OPERATOR							
	EXTRA ASSISTANT							
	STILL CAMERA						STANDBY CARS	
	OPERATIONS			MAKE-UP				
	ART DIRECTOR			MAKEUP ARTIST				
	CONST. COORD.						STRETCHOUT	
	KEY GRIP							
	2ND. CO. GRIP			HAIR STYLIST			BUSSES	
	DOLLY GRIP							
	EXTRA GRIPS							
				BODY MAKEUP WOMAN			GOOSE WITH SOUND	
	CRAB DOLLY						SOUND TRUCK	
	CRANE						ELECTRICAL TRUCK	
	HYSTER FOR HIGH SPOT			BODY MAKEUP MAN			PROP TRUCK	
							WARD. TRUCK	
				COSTUME			GRIP TRUCK	
	CRAFT SERVICE			COSTUMER (MEN)			HORSE WAGON TRUCK	
							WATER TRUCK	
	GREENSMAN						HONEY WAGON	
				COSTUMER (WOMEN)			DRESSING ROOM TRAIL.	
	PAINTER							
	SPECIAL EFFECTS							
				MUSIC				
				MUSIC REP.				
	PORT. DRESSING RMS.			SIDELINE MUSCIANS			ANIMAL TRAINER	
				SINGERS			ANIMAL HANDLER	
							DOGS	
	SCHOOL ROOMS			PROCESS			CATS	
				PROCESS PROJECT.			HORSES	
	ELECTRICAL			PROCESS GRIPS				
	GAFFER			PROCESS EQUIP.				
	BEST BOY						OTHER ANIMALS	
	GENERATOR OPERATOR							
	LAMP OPERATORS			POLICE/FIRE/MED.			ANIMAL WELFARE (A.H.S.)	
				STUDIO POLICE				
				WHISTLEMAN				
	GENERATOR			MOTORCYCLE POLICE				
	WIND MACHINE			FIRE WARDEN				
				FIREMAN				
				FLAGMAN				
				WATCHMAN				
				FIRST AID				

DEPARTMENT	SPECIAL INSTRUCTIONS

ASST. DIR. _____   UNIT PROD. MGR. _____

Figure 7–4   Call sheet (back) (continued)

DAILY PRODUCTION REPORT

No. of Days on Picture Including Today

REH.	TRAVEL	HOLIDAYS	IDLE	RETAKES & ADDED SCENES	WORK	TOTAL	AHEAD	
							BEHIND	

DIRECTOR _____

WORKING TITLE _____

PRODUCTION NO. _____

DATE _____

DATE STARTED _____

ESTIMATED FINISH DATE _____

SET

SET NO.   LOCATION

CALL   LEAVE   ARR. LOCATION   1st SHOT   AM   PM   WRAP   ARR. STUDIO/HOTELS

CREW LUNCH   TO   CREW SUPPER   TO   1st SHOT

CAMERA CALL   CAMERA WHIP   SOUND CALL   SOUND WRAP

SCRIPT	SCENES	PAGES	MINUTES	SETUPS	ADDED SCENES	RETAKES	Scenes Completed Today
Scenes in Script							
Taken Previously							
Taken Today							
Yet to be Taken							
FILM USE/STOCK							
Good							
Waste							
N.G.							
Total Today							
Total-to-Date							

CAST	WHSFR TR	MAKEUP WDBE.	WORKTIME ON SET	WORKTIME DIS. STUDIO	MEALS 1ST MEAL IN	MEALS 1ST MEAL OUT	TRAVEL TIME LEAVE FOR LOCATION	TRAVEL TIME ARRIVE LOCATION	DIS. LOC.	ARRIVE STUDIO

EXTRA TALENT-MUSICIANS, ETC.

NO.	RATE	ADJ. TO	O.T.	T.T.	WARD.	MPV	NO.	RATE	ADJ. TO	O.T.	T.T.	WARD.	MPV

Figure 7–5 Daily production report

SCREEN ACTORS GUILD PERFORMERS PRODUCTION TIME REPORT

Picture Title __SWINGERS__

Shooting Location __CHRISTY'S TRAILER__

Prod. No. __1__ Date __9-5-95__ Contact __NICOLE LALEGGIA__ Phone No. __(213) 555-1234__

Is Today a Designated Day Off? * Yes ___ No __✓__

Please Complete in Ink Using 24 Hour Clock (ex. 4:00 pm = 16:00):

CAST	CHARACTER	W S R T / MINOR	Report Makeup Wdbe.	Report on set	Dismiss on set	Dismiss Makeup Wdrbe	ND Meal	1st Meal Start	1st Meal Finish	2nd Meal Start	2nd Meal Finish	Leave for Location	Arrive on Location	Leave Location	Arrive at Studio	Start Adj.	Minors Tutoring Time	No. of Outfits Provided	MPVs	Forced Call	PERFORMER'S SIGNATURE
JON FAVREAU	MIKE	W	6⁰⁰A	8⁰⁰A	2⁰⁰P	2³⁰P		12⁰⁰P	12³⁰P												(signature)
VINCE VAUGHN	TRENT	SW	7¹⁵A	9³⁰A	3⁴⁵P	4⁰⁰P		12²⁰P	12³⁰P												(signature)
DEENA MARTIN	CHRISTY	SW	7³⁰A	9³⁰A	3³⁰P	4⁰⁰P		12²⁵P	12³⁵P												(signature)
KATHLEEN KENDA	LISA	SW	10¹⁵A	8³⁰A	2⁴⁵P	3³⁰P		12⁰⁰P	12³⁰P												(signature)

Figure 7–6 Exhibit G form

196

SCREEN ACTORS GUILD
TAFT/HARTLEY REPORT

ATTENTION: _____ ATTACHED ?: ☐ RESUME* ☐ PHOTO

EMPLOYEE INFORMATION

NAME _____ SS# _____

ADDRESS _____ AGE (IF MINOR) _____

CITY/STATE _____ ZIP _____ PHONE (_____) _____

EMPLOYER INFORMATION

NAME _____ Check one: ☐ AD AGENCY
                                                          ☐ STUDIO
ADDRESS _____   ☐ PRODUCTION COMPANY

CITY/STATE _____ ZIP _____ PHONE (_____) _____

EMPLOYMENT INFORMATION

Check one: CONTRACT: ☐ DAILY   CATEGORY: ☐ ACTOR
                       ☐ 3-DAY   ☐ SINGER   ☐ OTHER
                       ☐ WEEKLY   ☐ STUNT

WORK DATE(S) _____ SALARY _____

PRODUCTION TITLE _____ PROD'N/COM'L # _____

SHOOTING LOCATION (City & State) _____

REASON FOR HIRE (be specific) _____

_____

_____

_____

_____

_____

Employer is aware of General Provision, Section 14 of the Basic Agreement that applies to Theatrical and Television production, and Schedule B of the Commercials Contract, wherein Preference of Employment shall be given to qualified professional actors (except as otherwise stated). Employer will pay to the Guild as liquidated damages, the sums indicated for each breach by the Employer of any provision of those sections.

SIGNATURE _____ DATE _____
           Producer or Casting Director – Indicate which

PRINT NAME _____ PHONE (_____) _____

*PLEASE BE CERTAIN RESUME LISTS ALL TRAINING AND/OR EXPERIENCE IN THE ENTERTAINMENT INDUSTRY.

Figure 7–7   SAG Taft-Hartley report

SAG EXTRA

TAFT/HARTLEY REPORT

ATTENTION: _____ ATTACHED?: ☐ RESUME ☐ PHOTO

EMPLOYEE INFORMATION

NAME _____ SS# _____

ADDRESS _____ AGE (IF MINOR) _____

CITY/STATE _____ ZIP _____ PHONE (_____)_____

EMPLOYER INFORMATION

NAME _____ Check one: ☐ CASTING OFFICE
                                           ☐ STUDIO
ADDRESS _____   ☐ PRODUCTION COMPANY

CITY/STATE _____ ZIP _____ PHONE (_____)_____

EMPLOYMENT INFORMATION

CHECK ONE: General Extra ☐   Special Ability Extra ☐   Dancer ☐

WORK DATE(S) _____ SALARY _____

PRODUCTION TITLE _____

SHOOTING LOCATION (City & State) _____

REASON FOR HIRE (be specific) _____

_____

_____

_____

_____

Employer is aware of General Provision, Section 14.G of the Screen Actors Guild Codified Basic Agreement of 1989 for Independent Producers as amended that applies to Theatrical and Television production, wherein Preference of Employment shall be given to qualified professional extras (except as otherwise stated). Employer will pay to the Guild as liquidated damages, a sum which shall be determined by binding arbitration for each breach by the Employer of any provision of those sections.

SIGNATURE _____ DATE _____
        Producer or Casting Director (indicate which)

PRINT NAME _____ PHONE (_____)_____

Figure 7–8   SAG extra Taft-Hartley report

MILEAGE LOG

NAME: _____   WEEK ENDING _____

SHOW: _____   PROD # _____

DATE	LOCATION		PURPOSE	MILEAGE
	FROM	TO		

TOTAL MILES: _____

_____ MILES @ _____ ¢ Per Mile = $ _____

Approved By: _____   Date: _____

Pd. By Check # _____   Date _____

Figure 7–9   Mileage log (Reprinted with permission)

CHECK REQUEST

DATE: _____

DATE NEEDED: _____

AMOUNT: _____

TO:_____

ADDRESS and PHONE: _____

_____

_____

SSN OR FED-ID #: _____

DESCRIPTION: _____

REQUESTED BY: _____

APPROVED BY: _____

ACCOUNT: _____

CHECK# AND DATE: _____

PO#: _____

Figure 7–10   Check request form

PETTY CASH ENVELOPE

Date: _____

Name: _____

Position: _____

Picture: _____

Check No: _____ Check/Cash Received: _____

RECEIVED BY:

	DATE	TO WHOM PAID	PURPOSE	ACCOUNTING USE ONLY	AMOUNT	
1						
2						
3						
4						
5						
6						
7						
8						
9						
10						
11						
12						
13						
14						
15						
16						
17						
18						
19						
20						
21						
22						
23						
24						

UPM: _____ Prod'n: _____

Audit: _____ Dept: _____

Show # _____

TOTAL RECEIPTS		
PETTY CASH ADVANCED		
CHECK/CASH ENCLOSED		
CHECK/CASH DUE		

TRANS. # _____

VENDOR # _____

VOUCHER # _____

Figure 7–11 Petty cash envelope

RAW STOCK INVENTORY

SHOW _____ PROD # _____

WEEK ENDING _____

	52_____	52_____	52_____	52_____

EPISODE/WEEKLY TOTALS

Print _____ _____ _____ _____
No Good _____ _____ _____ _____
Waste _____ _____ _____ _____

Total ** _____ _____ _____ _____

PURCHASED

Previously Purchased _____ _____ _____ _____
Purchased This Episode/Week + _____ _____ _____ _____

Total Stock Purchased _____ _____ _____ _____

USED

Stock Used To Date _____ _____ _____ _____
Used This Episode/Week** + _____ _____ _____ _____

Total Stock Used _____ _____ _____ _____

Total Purchased _____ _____ _____ _____
Total Used – _____ _____ _____ _____

Estimated Remaining Stock _____ _____ _____ _____

(Remaining Stock As Per
 Assistant Cameraman) _____ _____ _____ _____

RAW STOCK PURCHASES MADE DURING
THIS EPISODE/WEEK:

P.O. #_____ _____ _____ _____ _____
P.O. #_____ _____ _____ _____ _____
P.O. #_____ _____ _____ _____ _____
P.O. #_____ _____ _____ _____ _____
TOTAL _____ _____ _____ _____

NOTES:

Figure 7–12 (A) Raw stock inventory form (Reprinted with permission)

DAILY RAW STOCK LOG

SHOW _____   PROD #_____

DATE _____   DAY #_____

CAMERA	ROLL #	GOOD	N.G.	WASTE	TOTAL

	DRAWN	GOOD	N.G.	WASTE	TOTAL
PREVIOUS					
TODAY					
TOTAL					

UNEXPOSED ON HAND	TOTAL EXPOSED

Figure 7–12   (B) Daily raw stock log (Reprinted with permission)

Walkie-talkie sign-out sheets (Figure 7–13). Have walkie-talkie sign-out sheets available on the set daily. Borrowed walkie-talkies should be returned at the end of each day. In the event that one is missing, the sign-out sheet will be of use in tracking it down.

Stationery and fax cover sheets. Create letterhead and fax cover sheets for the production company. Make copies, and keep them in the office for all outgoing correspondence.

Location, cast, and crew contracts (Figures 7–14, 7–15, 7–16, 7–17, and 7–18). You can purchase standard contract forms from a production supply house or create them yourself. Keep enough copies of each on hand. The film's needs may be such that special paragraphs have to be included in the standard contracts; having them on a computer makes them easy to amend.

Purchase orders (Figure 7–19). Use a purchase order (PO) when renting vehicles or equipment or purchasing materials or expendables. File purchase orders in the check log with the corresponding invoices and checks. Even if you're not reporting to the accounting office of a production company (which would require POs), filling out a purchase order each time you put equipment or materials on hold will be helpful in keeping track of what has been ordered from which rental house and the cost and date. The rental house may refer to your order by the PO number rather than by item or production company name.

Petty cash sign-out books. When crew members receive petty cash, they should sign the petty cash book or sign-out sheet. This system will help you keep track of who was issued petty cash and how much.

Location/filming notices (Figure 7–20). Filming notices are posted at a location to alert patrons or passersby that filming is taking place on the premises. The AD should have notices available on the set, and the location manager will post them at the appropriate locations. If you plan to shoot in a residential neighborhood after designated filming hours (as established by the local film commission), you will need permission from both the film commission and surrounding neighbors.

Personal releases (Figure 7–21). If you are filming or will have a still photographer at a location while it is open to the public, you must secure a signed personal release from anyone who appears in a shot.

Vendor lists (Figure 7–22). Compile a list of vendors and rental houses as you rent or buy equipment and materials. The vendor list should include contact names, addresses, telephone and fax numbers, cellular and beeper numbers, and any other pertinent information. It is appropriate to list

banks, labs, copy shops, caterers, emergency numbers, hospitals, parking lot information, weather forecast phone numbers, and similar information on the vendor list. On the first page of the list, be sure to include the production office's address and telephone and fax numbers, the film's title, and the date. Have updated lists printed out and available for crew members.

Daily Office Responsibilities Checklist

- Review to-do lists; update with office staff.
- Have petty cash on hand.
- Issue checks per check requests.
- Compile pickup and return lists for preproduction needs.
- Check in with the director regarding schedule and equipment needs.
- Check in with each department head regarding schedule and budget.
- File all paperwork in office files at day's end.
- Prepare a daily cost overview sheet.
- Actualize the budget for prepro costs when quotes for equipment, vehicles, locations, lab, food, etc. come in.
- Remember to eat and sleep.
- Thank the crew.

About the Daily Office Responsibilities Checklist

To Do Lists. To stay on top of everything you'll need to do each day (and each week), compile a daily to do list for yourself. To do lists will help ensure that you remain on schedule, on budget, and on top of everything that needs to be accomplished. Compile your to do list from the preproduction checklists. Go through each checklist, identify items that must be dealt with that day, and put them on your list. Each person working in the office should have his or her own personal to do list. Check the lists with your colleagues to be certain that there is no overlap and that all the bases are covered. It is extremely important to review the to do lists at the end of each day with each office member so that everyone is prepared and ready to go the next day. Cross off only the items that have been completed. Transfer the items that must still be addressed to the next day's to do list.

Petty Cash. It will save everyone time if you have enough petty cash on hand to issue to crew members. Check petty cash requests so you know how much you should have on hand and when.

Check Requests. Empty the check request box at the end of each day, and prepare any checks that will be needed for the next day. Write the check number and the date of the check on the check request, and file it in the appropriate file. Occasionally, a check must be cut right away. When this hap-

WALKIE-TALKIE SIGN-OUT

Date	Walkie-Talkie #	Signed out by:	Time Out	Time Returned

Figure 7–13   Walkie-talkie sign-out sheet

pens, fill out a check request so that you have a record of the check number, amount, and date issued. File it.

Pickup Lists. As preproduction heats up, equipment, expendables, vehicles, and supplies will have to be picked up and made ready for production (Figure 7–23). Have a separate pickup list for each day that pickups are scheduled and for each person who is making a pickup. Do the same for when returns need to be made; indicate the date and time of return on the return list and be sure the proper paperwork is received. Check with rental houses to find out what time equipment can be picked up. Put pickup times down on the list next to each destination. Don't pick up anything too soon! Wait until you need it because many rental houses charge by the day. Review each person's pickup list each day to see where he or she will need to be and when. Make sure he or she has a beeper or a mobile phone during pickups in case you have to send him or her on another run or

add something to the pickup list. Gather any checks, cash, purchase orders, and insurance certificates needed for a given set of pickups and issue them to the person facilitating the pickup. The person making the pickup must get paperwork from each vendor that indicates whether the pickup has been paid for or a deposit has been made. All paperwork should be handed in to the office at the end of each day and filed accordingly.

Director Check-in. It is important that you remain in constant communication with the director. Make sure that his or her needs are attended to. During preproduction, the director must meet with department heads, the casting director, and the cast, and he or she must also scout potential locations. Know the director's schedule. Discuss with him or her all equipment needs, location setups or concerns, changes to the shooting schedule, casting decisions, and other issues.

LOCATION AGREEMENT

Dear

You have advised the undersigned that you are producing a _____ tentatively entitled
_____ (the "Picture"). In consideration of your payment to the
undersigned for the sum of $_____,_____ you and the undersigned hereby agree as follows:

1. The undersigned hereby irrevocably grants you and your agents, employees, licensees, successors and assigns:

    (a) The right to enter and remain upon the property, which shall include not only real property but any fixtures, equipment or other personal property thereat or thereon, located at: _____
    _____ (the "Property"), with personnel and
    equipment (including without limitations, props, temporary sets, lighting, camera and special effects equipment) for the purpose of photographing scenes and making recordings of said Property in connection with the production of the Picture on the following date(s): Prep: _____ ; Shoot:
    _____ ; Strike: _____. If the weather or other conditions are not favorable for such purpose on such date(s), the date(s) shall be postponed to _____ .

    (b) The right to take motion pictures, videotapes, still photographs and/or sound recordings on and of any and all portions of the Property and all names associated there with or which appear in, on or about the Property.

    (c) All rights of every nature whatsoever in and to all films and photographs taken and recordings made hereunder, including without limitation of all copyrights therein and renewals and extensions thereof, and the exclusive right to reproduce, exhibit, distribute, and otherwise exploit in perpetuity throughout the universe (in whole or in part) such films, photographs and recordings in any and all media, whether now known or hereafter devised, including without limitation in and in connection with the Picture and the advertising and other exploitation thereof.

2. You agree to indemnify and to hold the undersigned harmless from and against all liability or loss which the undersigned may suffer or incur by reason of any injury to or death of any person, or damage to any property (ordinary wear and tear excepted), directly caused by any of your agents or employees when present on the Property or by reason of the use by any of your agents or employees or any equipment brought by them on to the property.

3. The undersigned warrants and represents (as a condition to the payment of the compensation referred to above), that the undersigned has the full right and authority to enter into this agreement and grant the rights herein granted, and that the consent or permission of no other person, firm, or entity is necessary in order to enable you to exercise or enjoy the rights herein granted.

4. The undersigned hereby releases you from, and covenants not to sue you for, any claim or cause of action, whether known or unknown, for defamation, invasion of his privacy, right of publicity or any similar matter, or any other claim or cause of action, based upon or relating to the exercise of any of the rights referred to in Paragraph 1 hereof; provided, however, that the foregoing shall not affect your obligations to indemnify the undersigned pursuant to Paragraph 2 hereof.

5. The undersigned further warrants neither he/she or anyone acting for him/her, gave or agreed to give anything of value, except for use of the Property, to anyone at _____
or anyone associated with the production for using the Property as a shooting location.

Figure 7–14   Location agreement

6. This agreement shall inure to benefit of and shall be binding upon your and our respective successors, licensees, assigns, heirs and personal representatives. You shall not be obligated actually to exercise any of the rights granted to you hereunder; it being understood that your obligations shall be fully satisfied hereunder by payment of the compensation referred to above. The agreement constitutes the entire agreement between the parties with respect to the subject matter hereof and cannot be amended except by a written instrument signed by the parties.

Very truly yours,

ACCEPTED & AGREED TO:

_____
(Signature)

By _____

_____
(Please print name)

_____
(Title)

_____
(Address)

_____

_____
(Phone Number)

_____
(Business Phone)

_____
(Fed. ID # or Soc. Sec. #)

Figure 7–14   Location agreement (continued)

Neighboring Location Agreement

I understand that PRODUCTION COMPANY, Inc., its employees, assigns, or other representatives will be using a nearby location in the production of their upcoming film "TITLE." I also understand that this project may involve crew members and their accompanying equipment. I understand that this crew may create some noise, both during the day or night, and agree not to hold PRODUCTION COMPANY, Inc. responsible for any discomfort, physical or otherwise, that they, their employees, assigns, other representatives, or equipment may cause me between the dates of _____ and _____.

I have read the foregoing and fully understand the meaning and effect thereof and, intending to be legally bound, I have signed this release.

_____
RESIDENT

_____
PRODUCTION COMPANY, INC.

_____
DATE

_____
DATE

_____
ADDRESS

Figure 7–15   Neighboring Location agreement

"PRODUCTION COMPANY", INC./LLC
CREW DEAL MEMO
"TITLE"

NAME: _____

ADDRESS: _____

CITY: _____ STATE: _____ ZIP: _____

PHONE: (___)_____ FAX: (___)_____

SS# _____ FED. I.D.# _____

LOAN OUT CORP.: _____

POSITION: _____

START DATE: _____ EST. FINISH DATE: _____

WEEKLY RATE: _____

ADDT'L TERMS:_____

SCREEN CREDIT: [End Credits] _____

Subject to the terms and conditions of this agreement, PRODUCTION COMPANY, INC., ("Producer") hereby engages you and you accept such engagement in the position stated above, in connection with the production of the feature film tentatively entitled "TITLE," (the "picture"). You agree to perform any and all services required by the Producer in your position to the best of your abilities as such services are commonly performed in the motion picture industry. You shall supply all the necessary tools, equipment and supplies commonly used in the industry to perform such services. Producer shall have the right to request, and you agree to provide to Producer or Producer's representative a written, catalogued inventory of all tools, equipment and supplies you supply, if any. Producer is not liable for loss or damage of such tools, equipment, or supplies as you provide.

If you shall provide your own transportation to and from the locations at which your services are to be rendered in connection with the Picture, and/or if you use your own vehicle in connection with the production of the Picture, then you further agree that any personal vehicle used will be adequately insured for collision damage, liability damage and property damage belonging to third parties, all in such amounts as are reasonably necessary. You agree to provide Producer with proof of insurance and valid driver's license. You hereby indemnify Producer and Producer's representatives against any and all liability and claims whatsoever in connection with your automobile or transportation during the term of this agreement.

All items purchased for the Picture, whether directly or indirectly, by the Producer, shall remain Producer's property. You warrant that you have not entered into and shall not enter into any agreements to perform work during the term of this agreement which could in any way interfere with the rendering of your services hereunder. Producer or Producer's representative retains the right to terminate this agreement at any time for any reason.

All out of pocket expenses incurred in connection with the Picture will be reimbursed only to the extent that they are pre-approved by the department head, line producer and verified by original receipt. There will be no exceptions. Also, all purchases and rentals must be by Purchase Orders. Purchase Orders must be approved by department heads.

In full consideration of your fully performing your obligations under this agreement, Producer agrees to pay you and you agree to accept a combination of cash compensation and deferred compensation (if any) as per the sum(s) listed above. Deferred compensation (if any) shall be paid at the same time as and on a pari passu basis with all other crew deferrals. You accept that said compensation is based on a _____ work week. The _____day work week may be working days or working nights or a combination of the two. Compensation for any work week consisting of less than _____ days shall be based on a daily rate equal to _____ the weekly compensation rate paid for each day actually worked.

Figure 7–16   Crew deal memo

The screen credit, accorded to you hereunder shall be positioned at Producer's discretion. No casual or inadvertent failure to accord such credit, nor any breach of any third party contract with Producer concerning such credit shall be a breach hereof by Producer.

Your services will be performed as a specifically ordered or commissioned work made-for-hire, and Producer shall own all results and proceeds of your services rendered hereunder in perpetuity to use for all purposes, including without limitation to the exploitation of the Picture or otherwise. This agreement may be assigned to any entity by Producer provided such entity assumes all executory obligations. You may not assign this agreement. You agree to maintain the secrecy of all Producer's confidential information which comes into your possession by virtue of your participation in the Picture.

A waiver of any breach provision shall not be deemed a waiver of any preceding or subsequent breach of the same or any other provision. This agreement contains the full and complete understanding between Producer and yourself with reference to the within subject matter, supersedes all prior agreements and understandings, written or oral, and cannot be modified except by the written instrument signed by both parties. This agreement is governed by the laws of the State of California. This agreement is not valid until signed by Producer.

FOR PRODUCTION COMPANY, INC.:

_____

Producer

_____

Date

AGREED TO AND ACCEPTED BY:

_____

Employee

_____

Date

Figure 7–16   Crew deal memo (continued)

CREW DEAL MEMO

PRODUCTION CO. _____ DATE _____

SHOW _____ PROD # _____

NAME _____ SOC. SEC. # _____

ADDRESS _____ PHONE (Home) _____

_____ (Beeper) _____

START DATE _____ (Fax) _____

JOB TITLE _____ ACCOUNT # _____

UNION/GUILD _____ GUARANTEE _____ weeks

RATE (In Town) _____ Per [Hour] [Day] [Week] for a [5] [6] _____-day week

(Distant Loc.) _____ Per [Hour] [Day] [Week] for a [5] [6] _____-day week

ADDITIONAL DAY(S) PRO-RATED @ _____ (th) Of a week

OVERTIME _____ After _____ hours _____ After _____ hours

BOX RENTAL _____ Per Day/Week

EQUIPMENT/VEHICLE RENTAL _____ Per Day/Week

MILEAGE ALLOWANCE _____ Per Day/Week

NOTE: Box & Equipment rental & mileage allowance are subject to 1099 reporting. Any equipment rented by the Production Co. from the employee must be listed or inventoried before rental can be paid.

TRAVEL/ACCOMMODATIONS _____

EXPENSES/PER DIEM _____

OTHER _____

□ LOAN OUT

CORP. NAME _____ FED. ID # _____

ADDRESS (If Different From Above) _____

AGENT _____ AGENCY _____

ADDRESS _____ PHONE # _____

_____ FAX # _____

EMPLOYER OF RECORD _____

ADDRESS _____ PHONE # _____

_____ FAX # _____

IF AWARDED SCREEN CREDIT, HOW WOULD YOU LIKE YOUR NAME TO READ _____

APPROVED BY _____ TITLE _____

ACCEPTED _____ DATE _____

Form **W-4** — Employee's Withholding Allowance Certificate — OMB No. 1545-0010

Department of the Treasury Internal Revenue Service ▶For Privacy Act and Paperwork Reduction Act Notice, see reverse. **19**

1 Type or print your first name and middle initial / Last name / 2 Your social security number

Home address (number and street or rural route)

3 □ Single □ Married □ Married, but withhold at higher Single rate. Note: If married, but legally separated, or spouse is a nonresident alien, check the Single box.

City or town, state, and ZIP code

4 If your last name differs from that on your social security card, check here and call 1-800-772-1213 for more information . . . ▶□

5 Total number of allowances you are claiming (from line G above or from the worksheets on page 2 if they apply) . 5

6 Additional amount, if any, you want withheld from each paycheck . . . . 6 $

7 I claim exemption from withholding and I certify that I meet BOTH of the following conditions for exemption:
• Last year I had a right to a refund of ALL Federal income tax withheld because I had NO tax liability; AND
• This year I expect a refund of ALL Federal income tax withheld because I expect to have NO tax liability.
If you meet both conditions, enter "EXEMPT" here . . . . . . ▶ 7

Under penalties of perjury, I certify that I am entitled to the number of withholding allowances claimed on this certificate or entitled to claim exempt status.

Employee's signature ▶ / Date ▶ , 19

8 Employer's name and address (Employer: Complete 8 and 10 only if sending to the IRS) / 9 Office code (optional) / 10 Employer identification number

Figure 7–17   Crew deal memo and W-4 form

STATION 12:   DEAL START:

BY: DEAL SET:

CAST DEAL MEMO

SHOW TITLE:

DIRECTOR: PRODUCERS:

ARTIST NAME: ROLE:

ADDRESS: AGENT:

CITY, ZIP:

          AGENCY:

ARTIST PH#:

SS#:   FAX:

CORP. NAME: MANAGER:

FED ID#:

START DATE:

LOCATION:

COMPENSATION: $ + 10% PER WEEK FOR _____ WEEKS. ANY ADDITIONAL DAYS WILL BE PRORATED BASED ON A SIX (6) DAY WEEK.

$ + 10% PER DAY FOR _____3___ DAYS.

LOOPING:

BILLING/CREDIT:

TRANSPORTATION:

ADDITIONAL NOTES:

          APPROVED:

_____

_____
PRODUCTION COMPANY, INC.

_____
AGENT

Figure 7–18   Cast deal memo

PURCHASE ORDER

DATE _____   P.O. # _____

SHOW _____   PROD # _____

COMPANY _____

ADDRESS _____   PHONE # _____

_____   FAX # _____

VENDOR _____   PHONE # _____

ADDRESS _____   FAX # _____

_____

CONTACT _____

VENDOR SS # OR FED. I.D. # _____

☐ PURCHASE   ☐ RENTAL   ☐ SERVICE

DESCRIPTION	CODING	AMOUNT

INCL. TAX IF APPLICABLE: _____

SET #(s) _____   TOTAL COST: $ _____   Per Show ☐
                                                                       Day ☐
IF TOTAL COST CANNOT BE DETERMINED   Week ☐
AT THIS DATE, ESTIMATE OF COSTS WILL   Month ☐
NOT EXCEED $ _____

IF P.O. IS FOR A RENTAL, PLEASE ESTIMATE DATE OF RETURN _____

ORDER PLACED BY _____   DEPT. _____

APPROVED BY _____   DATE _____

cc: Vendor (Orig.)   Accounting Dept.
        Production Manager   Department Head

Figure 7–19   Purchase order (Reprinted with permission)

ATTENTION:

Please be aware that by entering this establishment and/or its environs, you are granting "PRODUCTION COMPANY Inc.", its employees, agents, and assigns, the right to photograph you and use your picture, silhouette, and other reproductions of your physical likeness (as the same may appear in any still camera photograph and/or motion picture film), in and in connection with the exhibition, theatrically, on television or otherwise, of any motion pictures in which the same may be used or incorporated, and also in the advertising, exploiting, and/or publicizing of any such motion picture, but not limited to television motion pictures without any compensation, monetary or otherwise. You further give the said company the right to reproduce in any manner whatsoever, any recordation made by said company of your voice and all instrumental, musical, or other sound effects produced by you.

By entering this establishment and/or environs you hereby certify and represent that you have read the foregoing and fully understand the meaning and effect thereof and accept this agreement as legally binding.

Figure 7–20   Location/filming notice

RELEASE

AUTHORIZATION TO REPRODUCE PHYSICAL LIKENESS

For good and valuable consideration, the receipt of which from _____ is acknowledged, I hereby expressly grant to said _____ and its employees, agents, and assigns, the right to photograph me and use my picture, silhouette, and other reproductions of my physical likeness (as the same may appear in any still camera photograph and/or motion picture film), in and in connection with the exhibition, theatrically, on television or otherwise, of any motion pictures in which the same may be used or incorporated, and also in the advertising, exploiting, and/or publicizing of any such motion picture, but not limited to television motion pictures. I further give the said company the right to reproduce in any manner whatsoever any recordation made by said company of my voice and all instrumental, musical, or other sound effects produced by me.

I hereby certify and represent that I have read the foregoing and fully understand the meaning and effect thereof and, intending to be legally bound, I have hereunto set my hand this _____ day of _____, _____.

WITNESS:

_____

_____   _____

Figure 7–21   Personal release statement

SWINGERS

Double Down Productions
4692 Olympic Blvd. Los Angeles, Ca. 93628
phone: 213-555-6767 213-555-4676 fax

VENDOR CONTACT LIST
9/5/95   white

AIRPORT	LOS ANGELES AIRPORT	310-555-4765
ANIMALS	AMERICAN HUMANE 1534 Higgins St. Sherman Oaks, CA 91234 Contact: Bobbi Berns	818-555-9878
BAKERY	FLUFFIN' MUFFINS 234 Oakwood Dr. San Simente, CA 98987	323-555-5654
BANK	CENTURY FIRST 4545 American St. Holsby Heights, CA 95676	310-555-7879
CAMERA EQUIP.	VISIONQUEST USA 167 Willowbrook Ave. Century City, CA 98456	213-555-9084
CATERING	BIG FAT DADDY-O'S Stephenson Alley Inglwood, CA 95656	323-555-4453
COPIERS	DOUBLE DITTO 3298 Ninth Street Beverly Hills, CA 95612	310-555-3987
DRUG STORE	THE BIG FIX 345 Alamo Station Complex Hollywood, CA 99567	323-555-0978
EXTRAS	BABES -R- US 1314 La Tunera St. Silverlake, CA 99678	310-555-7698
FILM STOCK	EXPOSURE 9845 Wilson Drive Beverly Hills, 90213	213-555-0989
FLORIST	POCKET FULL OF POSIES 657 Emilie Ave. Los Feliz, CA 94875	323-555-3456

Figure 7–22   Vendor list

PICKUP & RETURN LIST

VENDORS	PICKUP	RETURN	DEPOSIT
ART RENTALS Art Supply USA 112 Fullerton, L.A.	4/15 After 9:00 am Table	5/9 Before 8:00 AM	$1,000
CAMERA EQUIP Hollywood Camera 324 Cahuenga, H'wood	4/12 After 10:30 am Camera, accessories	5/8 Before 9:00 AM	$25,000
DOLLY/TRACK Chapman Rentals 657 Arlington St. S. Pedro	4/12 After 9:00 am Dolly, track, jib arm	5/8 Before 9:00 AM	$8,000
ELECTRIC EQUIP Dan's Electric 3912 Eden Ln. H'wood	4/15 After 10:00 am 5-ton truck, loaded	5/9 Before 5:30 PM	$5,300
CRANE Panacrane West 16 E. Nicole, Bev Hills	Delivery	Pickup at wrap	$2,300
DAILIES FROM LAB Monochromatic 87 E. Burbank, Van Nuys	4/17-5/8 8:30 PM SHARP!	At wrap daily	*
GRIP EQUIP Adolf Gassme 42 Market St. Alameda	4/15 After 11:15 am (see electric)	5/9 Before 8:00 PM	$5,000
CAMERA SUPPLIES Kim's Cam 341 Columbus, Azusa	4/15 After 2:30 PM Air, chamois, sharpies	5/9 Before 12:30 PM	$1,000
WARDROBE JC Penney 413 MCA Ave, How'd	4/12 After 3:00 PM Costumes	5/10 anytime after 12 noon	$1,500
SOUND EQUIPMENT Free Quency 989 Allstar Lane, L.A.	4/15 After 9:30 am Walkies, nagra, slate	5/9 Before 9:00 AM	$2,000

Figure 7–23 Pickup and return list

Department Check-ins. Checking that each department is on schedule and on budget is extremely important as preproduction heats up. Meet with all department heads each week. Make sure that they are successfully securing the materials and equipment they need, that they have updated schedules and recent script changes, and that their departments are on budget. All department heads should meet with the director and discuss the needs of the film during their first week of work. Checking in with department heads lets them know that you are there if they need any help and allows you to stay on top of the budget for each department and know that everything will be ready for production. Having a weekly meeting with key staff members is also useful for informing them of any demands particular to a location (see the Locations Checklist) or any other issues that arise that relate to their work. When discussing the budget with department heads, reduce the figure of their departmental budgets by about 25% because odds are, they will go overbudget; this way, you are covered.

Filing Paperwork. Each day you will accumulate myriad pieces of paper, including purchase orders, invoices, pickup paperwork, contracts, and letters. It is essential that you file all paperwork at the end of each day. Allowing paperwork to pile up on your desk will ultimately result in a big mess. You will need to refer again to much of this paperwork, and if you secure a distributor for the film, you may be required to deliver paperwork such as cast and crew contracts to the distribution company.

Daily Cost Overview Sheet. Track your costs for budget purposes. A daily cost overview sheet will help you actualize your budget and track money that you've spent and money that is available. It is essential that you know where you are over- and underbudget. A typical cost overview sheet has designated spaces for certain common costs that might arise (Figure 7–24). There is also space on the sheet to account for any unanticipated costs incurred, such as electric or grip equipment costs or fringes. Once you have prepared your cost overview sheet, file it with the other daily cost sheets.

Actualizing Your Budget. When actualizing your budget, track original costs against current costs (see Figure 6–3 at the end of Chapter 6). This is how you will account for over- and underspending. Figure into your current costs any completed petty cash envelopes. (Be sure you code them according to your chart of accounts to ensure that you account for them properly.) Don't close out any budget accounts if costs will still be incurred in that category. Actualize the budget when all of the above- and below-the-line accounts have been closed and the final costs have come in. If you used Movie Magic Budgeting to compile your budget, you can easily actualize it by going into the Tools menu and choosing the Compare command. Enter your current costs in the box provided, and the program will calculate the variance.

Schedules and Lists Checklist

You will have to compile, organize, and arrange schedules, lists, and meetings as you hire cast and crew members, secure locations, negotiate with vendors, and hold department meetings. Attend to each of the following items daily, as necessary.

- Update, color-code, and distribute schedules, day-out-of-days sheets, strip boards, and script changes.
- Prepare office memos; distribute them to the crew or put in crew boxes.
- Compile crew, cast, and vendor packs.
- Compile production expendables list; place orders with vendors. (Include expendables for makeup, prop/art department needs, wardrobe, craft service, and catering.)
- Start compiling a thank-you list; write thank-you notes or buy gifts.
- Start compiling main and end title credits.
- Compile a list of days on which only a skeleton crew will be needed.
- Compile a list of days on which a second-unit crew will be used.
- Once you have made a lab deal, compile a schedule for picking up dailies from the lab and delivering them to the editor.

About the Schedules and Lists Checklist

Schedule Updates. Any schedule, list, or script page that is changed or updated (such as the day-out-of-days sheets, shooting schedule, strip, and script board) must be redistributed to all cast and crew members. Changes to the script and schedules are reflected by color-coding the updated pages (printing them on paper of different colors). The white copy (of a script, schedule, day-out-of-days sheet, and so on) is the first shooting version. The industry-standard color code for subsequent changes is blue, pink, yellow, green, goldenrod, gray, buff, and salmon. Put the date in a header at the top of each page.

Changes to the script or schedule may prove necessary for a variety of reasons, including falling behind schedule, not being able to secure a location for the time you originally anticipated, actor availability, and weather problems. It is imperative that there be communication regarding any change in schedule between the AD and the production manager or line producer and the cast and crew. If anyone is unaware of the schedule change, it will cause mishaps that can cost time

DAILY COST OVERVIEW

SHOW _____   PROD # _____

DATE _____   DAY # _____

                  START DATE _____

SCHEDULED FINISH DATE _____

    REVISED FINISH DATE _____

	PER CALL SHEET	SHOT	AHEAD/BEHIND
# OF SCENES			
# OF PAGES			

	AS BUDGETED AND/OR SCHEDULED	ACTUAL	COST (OVER)/UNDER
CAST OVERTIME	_____	_____	_____
COMPANY SHOOTING HOURS	_____	_____	_____
MEAL PENALTY	_____	_____	_____
EXTRAS & STAND-INS	_____	_____	_____
CATERING	_____	_____	_____
RAW STOCK	_____	_____	_____
UNANTICIPATED EXPENSES:			
_____	_____	_____	_____
_____	_____	_____	_____
_____	_____	_____	_____
_____	_____	_____	_____

                              TOTAL FOR TODAY _____

                              PREVIOUS TOTAL _____

                              GRAND TOTAL _____

PREPARED BY _____   APPROVED BY _____

Figure 7–24 Daily cost overview (Reprinted with permission)

and money. The production office is responsible for making sure that the schedule changes are printed according to color code and immediately distributed among all crew members and all affected cast members.

Office Memos. It is essential that all crew be alerted to any changes, delays, meetings, and so on, so that the show can remain on schedule and everyone will be on the same page. During preproduction the crew is not usually in the office all day. Putting memos in each crew member's box or hanging manila folder will ensure that crew will be advised of anything that comes up. Often, one member of each department will check in to the office each day to pick up any memos, script and schedule updates, petty cash or checks, and will alert their department to any memos.

Crew and Vendor Packs. Crew and vendor packs help ensure that all goes well during preproduction and production. Crew and vendor lists contain addresses, phone numbers, and contact information. A master vendor and crew list, updated as new information comes in, should be kept on the production manager's or coordinator's computer. These packs should be distributed among crew. Date them so that when you print new ones, the old ones can be thrown away. You can also print updates on colored paper. This is important so that everyone remains on the same page and can do his or her job properly. For example, you don't want the DP trying to contact a lab you once planned to use when you've made a better deal at a different lab and have forgotten to replace the new lab information with the old lab information.

Production Expendables. Expendables are items that can either be purchased or rented depending on what they are and what they will be used for, and are usually items other than heavy equipment. For instance, craft service and catering will need tables, chairs, coolers, extension cords, and urns. The makeup and hair department will need chairs and a makeup mirror and table with lights. The wardrobe department may need a rolling rack and a steamer. These items are considered expendables, and can most often be rented from the same facility and often are inexpensive. They should be picked up prior to production, and either the production department or the member of the department the expendable is rented for can facilitate the pickup. Compile an expendables list for each department. Many of your departments will need items that can be rented from the same vendor. Make sure all production expendables rented from the same facility are referenced on the same purchase order, and they are all accounted for at the end of each filming day.

Thank-You List. Start compiling a thank-you list at the beginning of preproduction. Include individuals and businesses that have made in-kind donations or have somehow been a "friend" of the production (contributed time, money, materials, services, and so on). Determine whether each person or business should receive a thank-you note, a small gift, or a thank-you credit at the end of the film. Don't take anyone's goodwill for granted. Creating an ongoing thank-you list with a brief note of what each person contributed and where he or she works will greatly assist you. If you send a thank-you note or a gift to someone who has helped out, note that on your list. Silly as all this may sound, it is unlikely that you would be able to retain this information in your head—someone inevitably would be forgotten.

Crew and Cast Credits. On crew and cast contracts, include a line that indicates how the person's name will appear in the film's credits, or create a simple form on which each cast and crew member prints out this information (Figure 7–25). File these forms and have your coordinator put the list in the computer. This is not an urgent task; if the pace slows during production, do it then.

Skeleton Crew List. Low-budget shows often have several days when only a skeleton crew is needed. Determine which days may be skeleton crew days based on the schedule. If you are paying your crew daily rates, using a skeleton crew on some days will save you money. Don't do this with your key department heads, however, and be fair about limiting crew members' days, especially if you are paying them little to begin with. If you are paying your crew on a weekly basis, it may not be worth scheduling skeleton crew days unless the location dictates it. The best way to organize skeleton crew days, while still being fair to crew members, is to schedule them at the end of the shoot so that the crew does not have to come on and off the job.

Second-Unit Filming List. During filming, there may be days when no actors are required and a limited crew, called a second-unit crew, can be used. Often, second-unit filming days are scheduled at the end of the shoot. Make sure that you have budgeted for the costs involved by accounting for equipment, raw stock, locations, and crew you will need for each second-unit filming day.

Dailies Pick-Up. It is important that dailies be picked up from the lab each day so that the director, the editor, and the producer(s) can view the footage from the previous day and the editor can begin assembling the film. If possible, one person should oversee picking up of dailies. This way, you are sure that dailies will be picked up and delivered to the editor. Find out what time dailies are ready each day, and notify the editor as to when to expect them. Secure a contact name at the lab for the person handling dailies in case there is a problem.

"TITLE"
Credit List

Please confirm that your name and credit are as you would like them to appear on screen. If your name is as you wish it to appear (i.e., spelling, nicknames, etc.), please initial. Thank you. We love you.—Production Office

1st AD   "NAME OF CREW MEMBER"

_____

Production Manager

_____

2nd Assistant Director

_____

Production Coordinator

_____

Editor

_____

Assistant Editor

_____

Figure 7–25   Credit list

Crew Checklist

Crewing should begin in week 1 of preproduction. The hiring order indicated in the following checklist is based on a four- to six-week preproduction period.

- Hire a production manager or production coordinator (week 1).
- Schedule meetings with key crew members and the director.
- Hire an office production assistant (week 1).
- Hire a director of photography and members of the camera department (weeks 1 and 2).
- Hire members of the locations department (week 1).
- Hire an assistant director and other members of the department (week 2); start scheduling and filling out paperwork two or three weeks before production begins and as locations are secured.
- Hire crew for the art, prop, and production design departments (week 1 or 2).
- Hire crew for the wardrobe department (week 2); get cast sizes and set up fittings.
- Hire other office and set production assistants (weeks 1 to 4).
- Hire electricians and grips (weeks 2 and 3).
- Hire members of the makeup and hair department (week 3); schedule meetings with cast and makeup and hair artists.
- Hire sound department crew (week 3).
- Hire transportation department crew (week 3).
- Hire editing department crew (week 3); discuss lab and editing facility needs.
- Hire a script supervisor (week 3).
- Secure crew deal memos as the crew is hired; send copies to the payroll company.
- Have crew members fill out W4 forms, I-9 forms, and start forms as they are hired; file forms and send copies to the payroll company.
- Have the department heads fill out kit rental forms as needed.
- Have the heads of the prop/art, makeup, and wardrobe departments and the script supervisor start their continuity notebooks.
- Set up mailboxes or hang manila folders for each crew member as he or she is hired.
- Compile a list of extra crew members (day players) for larger shoot days.
- Make petty cash available to all departments with sign-out slips and petty-cash envelopes.
- Ascertain any special meal needs or dietary requirements of crew members.
- Schedule a preproduction meeting with all crew members the week before production; arrange for a place to hold the meeting.

About the Crew Checklist

Hiring. Crewing should begin in week 1. (See Chapter 6 for a description of each crew member's responsibilities.)

If you don't have contacts or leads for every department you need to crew, there are many ways to locate gifted crew members:

Post signs at local film schools.

Post signs at local film support organizations (such as the IFP), and look through the classified ads in their monthly newsletters.

Ask people you know in the business or people you have already hired for recommendations.

Post signs at equipment rental houses.

Contact the local film commission. This is a great way to locate competent crew, but they will most likely be quite experienced and therefore somewhat expensive.

Contact the producer of a film in your budget range and ask for recommendations and résumés.

Post signs at art schools for the art and props departments.

Post signs at cosmetology schools for the hair and makeup departments.

Look in the classified section of the trades.

Post a notice in the classified section of the trades.

Hiring Process and Interviews. It is essential that the director be involved in hiring crew members, especially department heads. Gather sample reels of people's work, portfolios that display work they've done, and references of people with whom they've worked in the past. This is particularly important for hiring department heads. You may want to conduct an initial round of interviews and then submit a smaller group of select individuals to the director. How you involve the director in the hiring process will depend on the relationship you have with the director and the extent to which he or she is available to participate in the process. The following are the most important things to establish when interviewing potential crew members:

The crew member knows what is expected of him or her and is qualified for the job.

He or she is a team player who will get along with other crew members.

You have made clear to the crew member the long hours required and the pay being offered.

The philosophy of the shoot is clear.

The crew member is responsible and punctual.

The crew member has a vehicle or transportation to and from work each day.

Crew Deal Memos. Have each crew member fill out a crew deal memo (see Figure 7–16). Make sure that the deal memo is completed in full and that the crew member's rate is clearly indicated. Start and finish dates and any deferral arrangements should also be included. Give the crew member a copy, file the original in the contract book, and place another copy in the production files. Create your own deal memos, or purchase a standard form from any production supply and form store. If you are using a payroll company to prepare crew payroll, send a copy of each crew member's deal memo.

Department Head Meetings. It is essential that each department head meet with the director to discuss the vision, look, feel, and equipment needs of the film. Schedule the initial meeting; thereafter, department heads can check in with the director on their own. The DP, the production designer or art director, the gaffer, the AD, the location manager, the key grip, and the electrician will need to scout locations with the director as they are secured.

W4 Forms and I-9 Forms/Start Forms. When hired, each crew member must fill out a W4 form with important information including name, address, social security number, and the number of deductions for tax withholding purposes. Crew must also fill out start/I-9 paperwork that indicates the dates for which they will be employed by the company, social security number, and the number of deductions they are claiming (Figure 7–26). In order for the payroll company to process and pay the employee, all of these forms will need to be completed; this information will be reported to the government. Make copies for the office files, and attach them to the crew member's deal memo. Send the originals to the payroll company.

Kit Rental Forms. If you are paying kit rental fees to crew members who rent their own supplies or equipment to the production, have them fill out a kit rental form (Figure 7–27). Kit rental fees are nontaxable and are usually paid on a weekly basis or as a one-time flat fee. File each kit rental form in the office files, and attach a copy to the crew member's deal memo. Send another copy to the payroll company with the crew member's time card. (See Chapter 6 for more on kit rentals.)

Continuity Notebooks. It is essential to have some record of how actors and sets look for a given scene to reference for continuity. The continuity notebooks will allow you to recreate how an actor was dressed and made up so when script days need to be recreated, they will match. The costume designer, set designer or prop master, production designer, script supervisor, and makeup and hair artists will need instant or still film and notebooks to catalog wardrobe, makeup and hair, and the props and set design. The notebooks belong to the production when the show wraps. The editor will be given the script supervisor's notes each day and will receive the notebook he or she has compiled, which includes all script notes, at the end of production. The editor will refer to the notes while assembling the film.

Crew Mailboxes. Set up a box or hang a large manila envelope for each crew member on one of the office walls. Put any paperwork (such as schedules and updates, memos, script pages or changes, and contracts) and any messages in crew members' boxes or folders. This system is efficient and helps ensure that the office remains neat and organized and that crew members receive the necessary paperwork.

Extra Crew. Often there are days during production when departments may need extra help due to lighting needs particular to a location, heavy lifting or operating of equipment, time constraints at a given location, if there will be a lot of extras or cast on set, and so on. You will want to have a list ready of crew members you may be able to hire by the day (often referred to as *day players*). Keep résumés of those who you didn't hire because they were unavailable at the time, or ask department heads for recommendations of crew they have worked with before and like. You don't want to be scrambling at the last minute to find crew.

Petty Cash. As crew members are hired, explain how petty cash is handled and discuss their needs and responsibilities. Whenever petty cash is distributed, have the crew member sign a petty cash receipt. Issue a petty cash envelope. Generally, petty cash envelopes should be filled out in pencil by the crew member spending the money so changes can be made if there are any mistakes. Ask your crew to tape receipts to an 8 1/2-by-11-inch sheet of paper, number each receipt, and highlight the total on each. Your job will be infinitely easier if the numbers on the receipts match the numbers on the outside of the envelope. It is customary to retally the numbers on the front of the petty cash envelope on a calculator that has a paper feed and to tape the paper feed to the envelope and highlight the matching totals. Check the math whenever a petty cash envelope is handed in. Encourage crew members to submit check requests whenever possible rather than paying for anything expensive with cash. The only

I01349969

U.S. Department of Justice
Immigration and Naturalization Service

OMB No. 1115-0136
Employment Eligibility Verification

Please read instructions carefully before completing this form. The instructions must be available during completion of this form. **ANTI-DISCRIMINATION NOTICE.** It is illegal to discriminate against work eligible individuals. Employers **CANNOT** specify which document(s) they will accept from an employee. The refusal to hire an individual because of a future expiration date may also constitute illegal discrimination.

Section 1. Employee Information and Verification. To be completed and signed by employee at the time employment begins

Print Name: Last	First	Middle Initial	Maiden Name
Address (Street Name and Number)		Apt. #	Date of Birth (month/day/year)
City	State	Zip Code	Social Security #

I am aware that federal law provides for imprisonment and/or fines for false statements or use of false documents in connection with the completion of this form.	I attest, under penalty of perjury, that I am (check one of the following): ☐ A citizen or national of the United States ☐ A Lawful Permanent Resident (Alien # A _____) ☐ An alien authorized to work until ___/___/___ (Alien # or Admission # _____)

Employee's Signature	Date (month/day/year)

Preparer and/or Translator Certification. (To be completed and signed if Section 1 is prepared by a person other than the employee.) I attest, under penalty of perjury, that I have assisted in the completion of this form and that to the best of my knowledge the information is true and correct.

Preparer's/Translator's Signature	Print Name
Address (Street Name and Number, City, State, Zip Code)	Date (month/day/year)

Section 2. Employer Review and Verification. To be completed and signed by employer. Examine one document from List A OR examine one document from List B **and** one from List C as listed on the reverse of this form and record the title, number and expiration date, if any, of the document(s)

List A	OR	List B	AND	List C
Document title: _____		_____		_____
Issuing authority: _____		_____		_____
Document #: _____		_____		_____
Expiration Date (if any): ___/___/___		___/___/___		___/___/___
Document #: _____				
Expiration Date (if any): ___/___/___				

CERTIFICATION - I attest, under penalty of perjury, that I have examined the document(s) presented by the above-named employee, that the above-listed document(s) appear to be genuine and to relate to the employee named, that the employee began employment on (month/day/year) ___/___/___ and that to the best of my knowledge the employee is eligible to work in the United States. (State employment agencies may omit the date the employee began employment).

Signature of Employer or Authorized Representative	Print Name	Title
Business or Organization Name	Address (Street Name and Number, City, State, Zip Code)	Date (month/day/year)

Section 3. Updating and Reverification. To be completed and signed by employer

A. New Name (if applicable)	B. Date of rehire (month/day/year) (if applicable)

C. If employee's previous grant of work authorization has expired, provide the information below for the document that establishes current employment eligibility.

Document Title: _____ Document #: _____ Expiration Date (if any): ___/___/___

I attest, under penalty of perjury, that to the best of my knowledge, this employee is eligible to work in the United States, and if the employee presented document(s), the document(s) I have examined appear to be genuine and to relate to the individual.

Signature of Employer or Authorized Representative	Date (month/day/year)

Form I-9 (Rev. 11-21-91) N

Figure 7–26   Employee start form

BOX RENTAL INFORMATION

PRODUCTION COMPANY _____

EMPLOYEE _____ S.S.# _____

LOAN OUT COMPANY _____

FEDERAL ID# _____

RENTAL RATE: $ _____ PER WEEK/DAY
(Must be recorded on employee time card each week)

RENTAL COMMENCES ON: _____

INVENTORY (Attach additional pages if necessary):

_____
_____
_____
_____
_____
_____

Employee/Loanout agree that the equipment listed herein is rented to Production Company for use under Employee/Loanout's direction and control. Employee/Loanout are solely responsible for any damage to or loss of such equipment and hereby waive any claims against Entertainment Partners for any loss or damage of any kind and agree to look solely to Production Company to resolve any such claims. Entertainment Partners shall have no obligation to indemnify Employee/Loanout against any losses or damage, or to provide any insurance coverage for the benefit of Employee/Loanout covering the equipment herein described.

I attest that the above-described equipment represents a valid rental for this production.

EMPLOYEE SIGNATURE _____ DATE

APPROVAL SIGNATURE _____ DATE

Figure 7–27 Box rental information sheet

time cash is preferable is when the vendor or merchant is cutting you a major deal on a cash-only basis. If you're uncertain how the petty cash situation is going to work with your crew or if you've never worked with someone before, dole out only a small amount of money at a time.

Special Meal Needs. Members of your crew may have dietary needs that can be easily accommodated. Make arrange-

ments with craft service and catering for any special meals, beverages, or snacks that crew members have (within reason).

All-Crew Preproduction Check-in Meeting. Schedule an all-crew check-in meeting for the last week of preproduction either at the office or in a space large enough to accommodate the entire crew. (See "The Last Week of Preproduction" later in this chapter.)

Cast Checklist

- Hire a casting agent (week 1 or before).
- Fill out and file SAG paperwork; post bond (weeks 1 and 2).
- Prepare for auditions: secure a casting space, arrange for beverages and food, prepare sides, make copies of the sign-in sheet, and forward head shots to the casting director (weeks 1 and 2).
- Have the casting director fill out cast contracts and deal memos; file them and send them to SAG as the cast is hired.
- Have cast members fill out W4 forms, I-9 forms, and start forms as they are hired; forward copies to SAG and the payroll company.
- Have the casting director "station-12" cast members as they are hired.
- Ask the insurance carrier about required medical exams; schedule medical exams for four or five principal players as they attach and before production begins; schedule a medical exam for the director if required.
- Ensure that wardrobe fittings and makeup tests are scheduled (weeks 3 and 4).
- Compile the cast list as cast members are hired.
- Secure rehearsal space; schedule rehearsal time with the actors and the director.
- Arrange for extras, or hire an extras casting agent; determine how many location extras will be needed and when.
- Give the assistant director the SAG paperwork and forms that will be filled out on the set.
- Have the SAG payroll time cards on hand to be filled out weekly and forwarded to SAG and the payroll company.
- Make travel arrangements for out-of-town actors if necessary and determine how they will be transported to and from the set.
- Ascertain special meal needs or dietary requirements of any actors.

About the Cast Checklist

Casting Agent. If your film is largely cast already, you may not need a casting agent until the second week of preproduction. On the other hand, if you have to attach name talent or any talents to secure your financing, you may have to bring a casting director on board earlier. The time frame will depend on the project, but it may be as much as 12 months before your film is given the green light.

SAG Paperwork. Request and begin filling out the SAG paperwork package immediately! (See the Legal, Financial, and Accounts Checklist.) SAG guidelines and the rule hand-book are provided in the package. It's not a bad idea to enlarge the pages of the SAG agreement that outline the daily responsibilities of the signatory and post them in the production office for quick reference. The guild requires that you include the film's budget and shooting schedule with your signatory paperwork. (The package specifies what to include and when.) Your casting director, if you have one, can be helpful with much of the SAG paperwork. SAG production forms are also included in the package and should be copied for use during production (Exhibit G forms, Taft-Hartley forms, casting data reports, and so on). Give copies to your AD to fill out each day on the set. These forms may be purchased in bulk at a production form supply house.

Auditions. Before you begin casting sessions, secure a space to hold auditions. Beverages should be provided at all casting sessions. What you can or want to do beyond providing drinks will be based on your budget.

Sides are the pages of dialogue that are read by actors auditioning for a part. Choose scenes from the script that give the actors a fair amount to work with and will allow you to see their potential. Sides should be copied before auditions are held and should be made available to actors before their auditions.

If yours is a SAG show, each actor is required to sign a SAG sign-in sheet, which must be sent to SAG (Figure 7–28). Even if yours is not a SAG production, a sign-in sheet will be useful for recording who has read, for what part, and how he or she can be reached.

The casting director, the director, and the production office all refer to head shots. The casting agent will likely forward a large number of head shots to the director or producer for approval on whom to call in to read. You can solicit head shots by running a breakdown through breakdown services. A breakdown in this instance refers to a list of each of the principal characters you seek to cast and a description of what they're like, such as personality, age, ethnicity, etc. Expect to receive many unsolicited head shots from actors responding to the listing. Forward them to the casting director if you have one.

Cast Contracts and Deal Memos. Each cast member must fill out a SAG weekly or daily contract and a deal memo with the production company (Figures 7–29 and 7–30). Copies of each must be given to SAG, the payroll company, the actor, and the actor's agent and filed in the contract notebook and office files. The deal memo should include the actor's name, contact information, start and finish dates, pay rate, deferred compensation (if any), transportation and accommodations to be provided, looping dates, and station 12

SCREEN ACTORS GUILD THEATRICAL & TELEVISION SIGN-IN SHEET

PRODUCER: _____
PROD'N CO: _____
PROD'N OFFICE _____
PHONE # _____

CASTING REP: _____
CASTING REP. PHONE: _____
PRODUCTION TITLE: _____
EPISODE: _____

AUDITION DATE: _____

Casting Director's Signature

CASTING REP:
Please fill in time seen for each actor

(1) NAME	(2) SOCIAL SECURITY OR SAG MEMBER NUMBER	(3) ROLE	(4) AGENT	(5) PROVIDED?		(6) ARRIVAL TIME	(7) APPT. TIME	(8) TIME SEEN (Cast. rep.)	(9) TIME OUT	(10) TAPED?	(11) ACT. INI.
				PARK	SCRIPT						

Figure 7–28   SAG sign-in sheet

information. The contracts are standard employment agreements that can be purchased from a production supply house or obtained frrom SAG. If you have a casting director, he or she will help with filling out and securing contracts and deal memos from performers as they are hired.

W4 Forms and Start/I-9 Forms. Cast members must also fill out W4 forms and Start/I-9 forms. Attach these forms to each cast member's contract and forward copies to the payroll company and SAG (see Figures 7–17 and 7–26).

Station-12. SAG requires that an actor's status be cleared with the guild before beginning work on any production. The production must "station-12" an actor within 15 days of hiring him or her. SAG requires that members of the guild pay yearly dues. If they have not paid their dues, they must do so before working on your set. The production company will pay a fine for any actor working on a set whose status has not been cleared with the guild. The SAG package outlines how to station-12 an actor. If you have a casting agent, he or she will usually handle this task. Fill out the station-12 status on the production company deal memo you have with the actor.

Cast Medical Exams. To secure production insurance, medical exams for a few of your principal players and the director are often required. As you attach your principal cast members, schedule physical exams. Physical exams must be concluded before production begins. Have the physician send the examination records to the production office, and then forward the records to your insurance carrier. Make sure you budget properly for this expense.

Wardrobe Fittings and Hair and Makeup Tests. Wardrobe fittings and makeup tests are important and must be scheduled prior to production. Leave ample time to replace, make, or alter any items of wardrobe; to cut, dye, and fit wigs; to test prosthetics or masks; and to determine the makeup needs for each cast member. Ideally, the costume designer and makeup and hair artists will facilitate these meetings. The degree of support required from the production office will vary. Make sure a space for fittings and tests is arranged for. The line producer should ensure that these meetings occur, and that all wardrobe will be ready and any hair and makeup needs have been tended to and will be ready when filming begins.

Cast List. As cast members come on board, start compiling a cast list similar to the list you've compiled for the crew. Include each actor's name; address; telephone, beeper, and cell phone numbers; and agent information. This list will be useful for myriad reasons, including securing cast members for rehearsal time, wardrobe fittings, and makeup and hair tests.

Rehearsals. The AD, in conjunction with the director, is often responsible for scheduling rehearsal time and pairing actors who need to rehearse with each other. The production office is responsible for securing the rehearsal space.

Extras. Compile a list of the locations where extras are needed and calculate approximately how many you will need to create the desired atmosphere. If you will need to hire a number of extras for many of your locations, it is advisable that you hire an extras casting agent. If many of your locations will be open to the public while you are filming, or there are a limited number of days for which a limited number of extras are needed, it may be more cost efficient to hire extras a few days before through an extras casting company. Remember to have all extras fill out W4 forms (see Figure 7–17), start/I-9 forms (see Figure 7–26), and an extras voucher. Forward these forms to both SAG and the payroll company.

SAG Paperwork for the AD. There are some forms included within the SAG package that will need to be given to the AD and filled out on the set either daily or when necessary. Forms, such as the Exhibit G (the actor's daily time report), Taft-Hartley forms, extras contracts (if there will be extras on a particular day), day players contracts if they have not yet been signed for any reason or there is a last-minute hire, and accident forms in case there are any cast injuries, will need to be completed. These forms when completed should be turned in to the office each day and forwarded to SAG every week. Make sure that the necessary SAG paperwork is in the AD's kit just before production begins.

Time Cards. Cast members' time cards must be forwarded to SAG and to the payroll company each week (Figure 7–31). The guild requires that actors be compensated for rehearsal time, just as they are paid for shoot days, travel days, and looping days.

Travel and Transportation for Actors. If you have hired actors that will need to travel from out-of-town to the production, you will need to make the necessary travel arrangements. Make flight reservations early on for any out-of-town actors, and compile a master list of each actor who will be flying. On low-budget shows try to make the same arrangements for each actor. However, depending on who the actor is, first-class flight accommodations may need to be booked if stipulated in the actor's contract. Make sure that arrangements have been made to have them picked up and returned to the airport.

You will also need to make transportation arrangements to and from the set for any out-of-town actors. If possible,

**THE PERFORMER MAY NOT WAIVE ANY PROVISION OF THIS CONTRACT
WITHOUT THE WRITTEN CONSENT OF SCREEN ACTORS GUILD, INC.**

**SCREEN ACTORS GUILD
MINIMUM FREE LANCE CONTRACT
FOR THEATRICAL MOTION PICTURES**

Continuous Employment—Weekly Basis—Weekly Salary
One Week Minimum Employment

THIS AGREEMENT, made this_____ day of _____, 19_____, between_____
_____, hereafter called "Producer", and
_____, hereafter called "Performer".

W I T N E S S E T H :

1. PHOTOPLAY, ROLE, SALARY AND GUARANTEE. Producer hereby engages Performer to render services as such
   in the role of _____, in a photoplay, the working title of which is now
   _____, at the salary of $_____ per "studio week" (Schedule B Performers must
   receive an additional overtime payment of four (4) hours at straight time rate for each overnight location Saturday).
   Performer accepts such engagement upon the terms herein specified. Producer guarantees that it will furnish Performer not less than _____ week's employment (if this blank is not filled in, the guarantee shall be
   one week). Performer shall be paid pro rata for each additional day beyond guarantee until dismissal.

2. TERM: The term of employment hereunder shall begin on

   on _____

   on or about* _____
   and shall continue therafter until the completion of the photography and recordation of said role.

3. BASIC CONTRACT. All provisions of the collective bargaining agreement between Screen Actors Guild, Inc. and Producer, relating to theatrical motion pictures, which are applicable to the employment of the Performer hereunder,
   shall be deemed incorporated herein.

4. PERFORMER'S ADDRESS. All notices which the Producer is required or may desire to give to the Performer may
   be given either by mailing the same addressed to the Performer at_____
   or such notice may be given to the Performer personally, either orally or in writing.

5. PERFORMER'S TELEPHONE. The Performer must keep the Producer's casting office or the assistant director of
   said photoplay advised as to where the Performer may be reached by telephone without unreasonable delay. The
   current telephone number of the Performer is _____.

6. MOTION PICTURE AND TELEVISION RELIEF FUND. The Performer (does) (does not) hereby authorize the Producer to deduct from the compensation hereinabove specified an amount equal to _____ per cent
   of each installment of compensation due the Performer hereunder, and to pay the amount so deducted to the Motion
   Picture and Television Relief Fund of America, Inc.

7. FURNISHING OF WARDROBE. The (Producer) (Performer) agrees to furnish all modern wardrobe and wearing ap-
   parel reasonably necessary for the portrayal of said role; it being agreed, however, that should so-called "character"
   or "period" costumes be required, the Producer shall supply the same. When Performer furnishes any wardrobe,
   Performer shall receive the cleaning allowance and reimbursement, if any, specified in the basic contract.

   Number of outfits furnished by Performer _____ @ $_____
                                  (formal) _____ @ $_____

8. ARBITRATION OF DISPUTES. Should any dispute or controversy arise between the parties hereto with reference
   to this contract, or the employment herein provided for, such dispute or controversy shall be settled and determined
   by conciliation and arbitration in accordance with the conciliation and arbitration provisions of the collective bargaining agreement between the Producer and Screen Actors Guild relating to theatrical motion pictures, and such provisions are hereby referred to and by such reference incorporated herein and made a part of this Agreement with the
   same effect as though the same were set forth herein in detail.

9. NEXT STARTING DATE. The starting date of Performer's next engagement is_____.

10. The Performer may not waive any provision of this contract without the written consent of Screen Actors Guild, Inc.

11. Producer makes the material representation that either it is presently a signatory to the Screen Actors Guild collective
    bargaining agreement covering the employment contracted for herein, or that the above-referred-to photoplay is covered
    by such collective bargaining agreement under the Independent Production provisions of the General Provisions of
    the Screen Actors Guild Codified Basic Agreement as the same may be supplemented and/or amended.

    IN WITNESS WHEREOF, the parties have executed this agreement on the day and year first above written.

PRODUCER_____PERFORMER_____

BY_____Social Security No._____

*The "on or about" clause may only be used when the contract is delivered to the Performer at least seven days before
 the starting date. See Codified Basic Agreement, Schedule B, Schedule C, otherwise a specific starting date must be stated.

Production time reports are available on the set at the end of each day, which reports shall be signed or initialed by the
Performer.

Attached hereto for your use are the following: (1) Declaration Regarding Income Tax Withholding ("Part Year Employment Method of Withholding") and (2) Declaration Regarding Income Tax Withholding. You may utilize the applicable
form by delivering same to Producer. Only one of such forms may be used.

NOTICE TO PERFORMER: IT IS IMPORTANT THAT YOU RETAIN A COPY OF THIS CONTRACT FOR YOUR PERMA-
                      NENT RECORDS.

Figure 7–29   SAG freelance contract

THE PERFORMER MAY NOT WAIVE ANY PROVISION OF THIS CONTRACT WITHOUT THE WRITTEN CONSENT OF SCREEN ACTORS GUILD. INC.

SCREEN ACTORS GUILD

DAILY CONTRACT
(DAY PERFORMER)
FOR THEATRICAL MOTION PICTURES

Company _____   Date _____

Date Employment Starts _____   Performer Name _____

Production Title _____   Address _____

Production Number _____   Telephone No.: (____) _____

Role _____   Social Security No. _____

Daily Rate $ _____   Legal Resident of (State) _____

Weekly Conversion Rate $ _____   Citizen of U.S. ☐ Yes ☐ No

COMPLETE FOR "DROP-AND-PICK-UP" DEALS ONLY:

Firm recall date on _____

or on or after * _____

("On or after" recall only applies to pick-up as Weekly Performer)

As ☐ Day Performer   ☐ Weekly Performer

*Means date specified or within 24 hours thereafter.

Wardrobe supplied by Performer   Yes ☐   No ☐

If so, number of outfits _____ @ $_____

(formal) _____ @ $_____

Date of Stunt Performer's next engagement: _____

The employment is subject to all of the provisions and conditions applicable to the employment of DAY PERFORMER contained or provided for in the Producer-Screen Actors Guild Codified Basic Agreement as the same may be supplemented and/or amended.

The performer does hereby authorize the Producer to deduct from the compensation hereinabove specified an amount equal to _____ percent of each installment of compensation due the Performer hereunder, and to pay the amount so deducted to the Motion Picture and Television Relief Fund of America, Inc.

Special Provisions:

PRODUCER _____   PERFORMER _____

BY _____

Production time reports are available on the set at the end of each day. Such reports shall be signed or initialed by the Performer.

Attached hereto for your use is Declaration Regarding Income Tax Withholding.

NOTICE TO PERFORMER: IT IS IMPORTANT THAT YOU RETAIN A COPY OF THIS CONTRACT FOR YOUR PERMANENT RECORDS.

Figure 7–30   SAG daily contract

PRODUCTION COMPANY: _____

PRODUCTION TITLE: _____

NAME: _____

EMPLOYEE #: _____

WEEK ENDING: _____

G/L CODE	DATE	DAY	WORK STATUS SW R W WF H SWF TR	LEAVE MOTEL	ARRIVE MAKE-UP/ WARDROBE	ARRIVE ON SET	NDB	FIRST MEAL From To	SECOND MEAL From To	DISMISS on SET	DISMISS Make-up Wardrobe	ARRIVE at MOTEL	STUNT ADJUSTMENT	ACTUAL HOURS	TRAVEL TIME 1 1/2X	OT 1 1/2X	OT 2 X	6th DAY PREMIUM	MEAL PENALTY	FORCE CALL
		SUN																		
		MON																		
		TUE																		
		WED																		
		THU																		
		FRI																		
		SAT																		
														TOTAL HOURS						

G/L CODE	PAY CODE#	SAG PENSIONABLE	HOURS	TOTAL
	472	Base Salary		
	415	Daily OT (1.5x)		
	420	Daily OT(2x)		
	416	Travel (1.5x)		
	490	Weekly OT		
	474	6th Day Prem.		
	437	Holiday Prem.		
	476	Stunt Adj.		
	473	Guarantee		
	447	Location Allow.		
		Other / Misc.		

G/L CODE	PAY CODE#	NON PENSIONABLE	TOTAL
	449	Meal Penalty	
	430	Forced Call	
	488	Wardrobe	
	452	Drive - to	
	464	Per Diem NT	
	465	Per Diem TX	
	464	Per Diem NT	
	465	Per Diem TX	
		Other / Misc.	

Schedule: _____

Daily Rate: _____

Weekly Rate: _____

Days / Weeks Guaranteed: _____

Days Paid: _____

Last Day Worked: _____

Theatrical / Motion Picture ☐

Division ☐

TOTAL DUE: _____

SAG P&W DUE: _____

Figure 7-31   Talent worksheet

230

designate a production assistant or "talent liaison" who is responsible for getting the necessary actors to and from the set on the days that they are needed. Often, actors may request that the production rent them a car while they are working on location, if the budget can afford it, and may want to drive themselves to and from the set.

Locations Checklist

- Have the location manager begin scouting and photographing locations (weeks 1–2).
- Compile a list of possible locations and assemble folders for location photos; show them to the director and the producer.
- Arrange and schedule location scouts with the necessary crew.
- Secure permits as locations are locked; notify the film commission.
- Secure signed location contracts and releases as the locations are locked.
- Arrange to have insurance certificates sent to each secured location.
- Determine whether a generator will be necessary or whether you will tie in for power at each location.
- Arrange through the film commission for police officers and fire fighters as necessary.
- Arrange for security as needed.
- Prepare filming notices, personal and still releases, neighbor sign-off releases, and notice of filming; add to the AD kit.
- Determine the setup of each location; make necessary arrangements for crew parking and cartage, bathrooms, dressing rooms, holding areas, production office, and craft service and catering areas.
- Compile a list of expendables needed for each location, and place other items on hold (layout board, cones, rope, bullhorn, chairs, tables, tents, and so on).
- Have extra keys made for the locations if necessary.
- Draw a map to each location.
- Secure a stage if needed; organize strike, rig, and prelight days.
- Update the shooting schedule and strip board as locations are locked.

About the Locations Checklist
Scouting for Locations. If you have a four-, five-, or six-week preproduction period, the location manager should begin work in week 1 or 2 of preproduction, depending on how many locations have to be secured, whether you will be filming at any out-of-town locations, and the budgets limitations. After an initial meeting with the director and producer

to discuss the look of the locations, the dates when the locations will be needed, the budget, and any other concerns, the location manager will compile a list of all scripted locations. If there are multiple locations, you may have to hire an assistant location manager for a few weeks to assist with paperwork, notices that have to be posted, and permits that have to be secured and filed.

Finding appropriate locations that are affordable and available when you need them isn't always easy, and you may need an extra week or several days to scout for locations, especially if they are out-of-town. If there is little time to lock locations and the location manager is having trouble finding suitable options, inquire at a location rental office, which will have listings and photos of locations that are regularly used and available for filming for a fee. Check local film guides, or contact the film commission in your area.

If the locations that have been scripted actually exist, it is ideal to lock those locations if possible since they are likely to best serve the film's look. However, make sure that the scripted locations are convenient for the production in terms of access and travel; as with any other location, they must be affordable and available to you when you need them. If necessary, find a substitute location that will better serve the needs of the film, or build the location on a stage. *Swingers* was set in Los Angeles, and we filmed in most of the actual bars and other locations that Jon Favreau scripted. We were fortunate to secure those locations at an affordable price when we needed them. Other bars that we shot in were not the actual bars scripted. We shot in these substitute bars because of budget limitations, availability, or other production-related concerns. For example, the Treasure Island Casino was scripted, but it was completely out of our budget range. We locked another casino that was available and that we could afford.

Location Files. As the location manager scouts for potential locations, he or she will photograph them (interiors, exteriors, and specific areas of the location that will be used for filming). Create a file for each potential location, and include such pertinent information as the address, cost, how power will be provided (generator or tie-in), names of contacts, and the dates the location is available. The director and producer will go through the files to determine the suitability of potential locations and to decide which locations the director should scout. The production office is responsible for housing the files. Be sure your location manager has ample instant or still film and enough petty cash for gas, phone calls, and food while scouting.

Location Scouting with Crew. Try to keep scouting to a minimum. It is best that the location manager narrow down the location choices based on what would best serve the film's needs (proximity, dates available, and cost) before bringing options to the director. Once the majority of your locations have been locked (some may not be locked until production if they are difficult to find or secure), the location manager and line producer will schedule scouts of each location. The director, producer, first AD, DP, gaffer, key grip, and location manager will scout locations for setups, equipment needs, power issues, lighting needs, and other concerns. Schedule locations that are within the same vicinity on the same day. Be sure to have enough instant film on hand. Be prepared to pay crew members for the days they scout and to reimburse them for meals and mileage or gas.

On *Swingers,* we were able to scout several of our locations on the same day because they were located near one another. We did not have an overwhelming number of locations to secure, and most of the locations scripted were actual places, so the location manager was able to lock many of them quickly, with minimal scouting. We scouted several potential locations just to be sure that there wasn't a location that would better serve the look of the film. For instance, although the Derby was the scripted location, we scouted several other possibilities because we were concerned about the high ceilings, the cost, the lighting, and the power issues in the Derby. We also weren't sure if we would be able to film on the days we needed to. Ultimately, we made the right deal and the majority of the footage was shot while the Derby was open to the public, which saved us money on extras and the site rental itself.

Permits.   Once your locations have been determined, you will have to obtain permits for each one. The location manager should obtain the contact information for the local film commission. The city or state film commission will often issue all of the permits for the production. You may be able to secure a blanket permit if your locations are all within the same city and near one another. (See Chapter 6.) The production can be shut down if you fail to have the proper paperwork and permits on hand. The location manager will contact the city permit office to determine which locations require permits and the fees involved, which will be determined by such factors as where on the premises you will be shooting, whether a location will be open to the public, and whether a location is also used as a public thoroughfare. The permit office will issue the production permits once the permit fees have been paid and will tell you whether a fire fighter or police officer will be required at any of your locations. It takes time to secure permits and to fill out the necessary paperwork, so the location manager should contact the permit office as locations are locked. Be sure that the

production office has copies of each permit issued and that the AD has a copy of each permit on the set.

Location Contracts and Releases.   Once your locations have been locked, your location manager must secure location contracts (see Figures 7–14 and 7–15). Whether you are filming in a bar, a restaurant, a private home, a car dealership, or a park, you must have the owner, the manager, or another representative sign a contract with the production company agreeing to the terms set forth. Fill in the dates of filming, the production company's name, the film's title, the address of the location, the site rental fee to be paid, any screen credit that has been promised, and the name of the location contact. The contract protects the production in case of a dispute as to whether a fee was paid or permission was given to film at the location. The permit office may want to see your signed location contracts before issuing a permit. If you are scheduled to film at a location in a residential area, you must abide by certain rules. For instance, there are specific filming hours for residential neighborhoods, and if you intend to film after the city's filming hours, an extended-hours filming release from the permit office will be required (Figure 7–32). Contact the permit office for the filming rules and guidelines in your area. Signatures must be gathered from local residents to acknowledge that they have been notified that filming will take place in their neighborhood on certain days and during certain hours. You will need a minimum number of signatures before permission can be granted. Copy all permits, releases, and contracts in triplicate: one for the office file, one for the AD kit, and one for your personal notebook.

Insurance Certificates.   Each location must be covered under the production insurance policy, and the representative of each location must receive an insurance certificate. Ask your insurance carrier to send a certificate to each location as it is locked. The certificate indicates that the production is covered for any loss or damage that may occur at the location during filming. Proof of insurance for each location must be on hand during filming; make sure it is filed in the AD kit. The permit office may want to verify that you have insured each location before it issues permits.

Generator and Tie-ins.   The location manager, together with the gaffer, will identify the locations for which a generator must be rented. Ideally, a generator should be rented for the entire show, if you can afford it, to provide ample power for running lights, charging the walkie-talkies and batteries, and plugging in coffee urns, hot plates, microwaves, irons, and the wardrobe steamer. Your locations may allow you to tie in for power, which means that you can run your

COUNTY & CITY OF LOS ANGELES - FILM PERMIT
SIGNATURE SURVEY FOR EXTENDED HOUR,
WEEKEND AND/OR LONG TERM FILMING

Dear Resident/Merchant/Business Representative,

We are planning to film scenes of _____ at _____ .

Proposed date(s): _____ hours: from _____ a.m./p.m. to _____ a.m./p.m.

Description of scenes & parking:

_____

_____

_____

_____

We have applied for the necessary permit and maintain all legally required liability insurance. If a permit is granted, all personnel required to ensure public safety will be on location. We agree to abide by all County or City filming rules and any specific guidelines applicable to your neighborhood.

We will make every effort not to disturb you and will not arrive earlier or vacate the neighborhood later than the specified time. Thank you, in advance, for your cooperation and hospitality while we are filming in your neighborhood.

If you have any questions or concerns regarding this request, please contact us at the production office or by pager. Please don't hesitate to call us.

_____
Production Company

_____
Production Office phone#

_____
Location Manager

_____
Production Manager

Or you may contact:

EIDC/Los Angeles Film Office
7083 Hollywood Blvd.
Los Angeles, CA 90028
213.957.1000
Office Hours: 8am - 6pm Mon. - Fri.

AFTER HOURS HOTLINE: (24 hours a day)
800.201.5982
Give the operator your name, phone no.
and a brief message.

I DO NOT OBJECT to the filming permit.
I DO OBJECT to the filming request. Reasons (optional)

_____

I DO NOT OBJECT but prefer not to sign my name.

_____
Signature

_____
Print Name

_____
Address

_____
Phone (optional-for verification purposes only)

In multiple unit buildings, managers may sign on behalf of tenants but must notify all tenants.

Total no. of units in building_____
Addresses signed for_____

I, as manager of the above building, have notified all of the tenants and know of no substantial objection to the proposed filming activity.

_____

Manager, Address

Figure 7–32   Film permit for extended hours

lights and other equipment without a generator from the location itself. Be prepared to pay electrical costs if they are above the norm for the location (a tie-in will typically drive up an electric bill). The gaffer will be able to determine if a tie-in is an option, and usually, if limited lights will be used, this may be preferable. (It may save you money in terms of gas purchases and generator rental, it will be less noisy, and you may not need a fire fighter present.) You will need to identify your power source so the permit office can instruct you about fire personnel requirements in order to make the necessary rental arrangements.

Police Officers and Fire Fighters. Depending on the location at which you are filming, whether you have a generator or special equipment on the set, whether you are using equipment that will be set up on the sidewalk at a location, whether you are filming any type of special effect or stunt (fire, car chase, gun fight, etc.), and whether your locations are open to the public while filming, the permit office may require a city official be present on your set. When your location manager is permitting each location, based on the information given to the permit office about each location, the permit office will determine for which locations and for how long you will need a police officer and/or a fire fighter present. These officers are on set to ensure the safety of the cast, crew, extras, passersby, and anyone who is affected by the production. They will also help keep the public off your set and will block off parking and traffic lanes if necessary. The rate they are paid is determined by the union.

Security. You may find it necessary or preferable on certain days to hire private security personnel when filming large party scenes, outdoors, or at night. On *Swingers,* we hired two security guards while filming the party scene. We shot at a friend's house and knew there would be many people going in and out. Having hired security reduced the risk of damaging the house that we filmed in, of people being injured, and of equipment and materials being lost, broken, or stolen. The security guards helped us maintain order in what might otherwise have been an uncontrollable situation. If you will be filming in a dangerous neighborhood or will be leaving equipment overnight at a location, security is a must. As the line producer, you won't be able to oversee everything, but you are responsible for the location, equipment, and materials.

Filming Notices and Personal Releases. The location manager is responsible for posting filming notices at locations that will be open to the public while you are filming (see Figure 7–20). Filming notices alert patrons that you are filming on the premises and that they may be in a shot. The local film commission and the permit office require that you post notices. Check with each permit office for guidelines for each of your locations. Make sure that notices have been posted where they can be seen easily. You may want to post several. On *Swingers,* we posted notices in all of the bars we filmed in while they were open to the public. We also secured personal releases from patrons whom we specifically asked to be in the background of a shot. Have both types of notices and releases on the set and in the AD kit.

Setup. The location manager should determine the setup of each location before you are scheduled to film there. The location manager should photograph or sketch the layout of each location. After the AD and the location manager have discussed the needs of the scenes being shot at each location, they will determine how to best use the space. For example, will a trash receptacle have to be rented, and if so, where will it be placed? Will the location accommodate dressing areas for the actors and a makeup station? If not, you may have to rent a motor home to use as a bathroom, an office, a changing area, and a makeup station. Where will the motor home be parked? Determine where each department will keep its materials and where department personnel will work. Where will crew and production vehicles park? Will you have to rent a parking lot? You will need a designated craft service area and a place where tables, chairs, and catering can be set up. Determine where the restrooms are and where equipment can be stored. Figure out the best place to run the generator, keeping in mind both size and noise. Is there a place to house the production office? Will you view dailies at the location, and if so, where? All of these factors must be considered, and your location manager, together with the AD, should be prepared to direct crew members to the appropriate place when they arrive at the location so no time is wasted. A floor plan of the location will allow the necessary personnel to answer these questions beforehand and to direct the crew accordingly during production.

Expendables. You may need to purchase or rent certain items for your locations. Compile a list of expendables that may be needed at each location. (See the Schedules and Lists Checklist.) Consider the following:

Rope for sectioning off areas

Parking cones for directing cars to parking areas or for blocking off areas

Bullhorns if the location is large or if there are several actors, crew members, and extras on the set to direct

Butt cans for cigarettes (you can save empty coffee cans to use as butt cans), trash cans, and trash bags

Tables and chairs for catering and workstations

Director's chairs for cast, crew, and extras while on the set

Coffee urns, coolers, chafing dishes, tablecloths, thermoses, hot plates, and extension cords for craft services and catering

Portable fans or stationary heaters as the weather dictates

Wardrobe racks and a steamer for the wardrobe department

Flashlights, batteries, a fire extinguisher, and a first aid kit

Makeup mirrors, chairs, and tables for the makeup and hair department

Bungee cord for securing equipment in production vehicles

Hand carts or dollies for transporting heavy equipment

Tents for changing rooms or eating areas as the weather dictates

Layout board for the safety of the cast and crew and for the protection of the location floor

Keep a list of all rented expendables, or post the purchase orders for these rentals on a bulletin board in the office. Many of these items are small (and inexpensive) and could easily be lost or confused with other similar items owned by crew members. You will have to replace or purchase whatever items end up lost or damaged. Production expendables should be kept together if possible when they are collected at the end of each day, and it is safest to store them in one production vehicle. Designate a production assistant who will account for all expendables; he or she should keep a checklist of expendables and make sure that each item on the list is accounted for when wrapping each day.

Keys. The AD and the location manager should have a key to every location unless arrangements have explicitly been made for a manager or owner to let you in. The production office should have a key on file so that if your location manager won't be on the set at call or if your AD is stuck in traffic and running late, someone else will have a key to the location. Keys are often lost, so it is best to have copies. When filming is complete, return all copies of keys to the location, or destroy them.

Maps. Maps of each location and travel directions should be drawn by the location manager and attached to the call sheet for each location. The page number in the street atlas on which the location appears should also be indicated on the map, and the name of the nearest hospital, its phone number, and the address should be noted.

Update Shooting Schedules. As discussed in Chapter 5, the shooting schedule is always subject to change. The availability of locations and cast members are variables that will affect the schedule. Try to lock your locations based on your preliminary shooting schedule, which was compiled based on multiple factors (easy transition between day and night filming, actor availability, location proximity, and out-of-town filming). You may find, however, that locations are not available when you need them. Change your schedule based on location availability only when the location in question is the location that will best serve the needs of the film. Keep in mind that changing the schedule to accommodate locations will have repercussions, so be sure that actors and other locations are all available based on the updated shooting schedule. (See the Schedules and Lists Checklist.)

On *Swingers,* we updated the shooting and one-line schedules several times. We were unable to lock many of our locations for the time we had originally scheduled them for and therefore had to revise the schedule based on location availability. For instance, we originally scheduled filming in the Dresden Room for *two nights,* but the Dresden Room was only able to accommodate us for *one day,* which did not correspond with the date we had tentatively scheduled. We knew that it was important for the look of the film to shoot at the Dresden Room, so we figured out how to make it work based on the availability of other locations and actors. We wanted to do all of our out-of-town filming at the end of the shoot. We didn't want to put our actors on hold or break up the flow of shooting at the Los Angeles locations. We also knew it would be fun for the crew to have a change of pace, spend our last few production days in Vegas, and wrap the show there.

Camera Checklist

- Rent camera package (when the director of photography comes on, weeks 2 and 3).
- Schedule camera and film tests (week before production).
- Arrange to have an insurance certificate sent to the camera house.
- Rent monitors, VCR, video tap, special equipment, and so on.
- Rent a camera bag or camera van.
- Compile a camera supply list; give the second assistant camera operator petty cash to purchase supplies; pick up cores, bags, cans, and camera reports (week 4).
- Schedule camera prep day for the first assistant camera operator (week before production).
- Purchase film stock (week 3).

About the Camera Checklist

Camera Package. The camera package you choose should suit the needs of your shoot. When renting, keep the budget, the DP's shooting style, and the kinds of locations in which you will be filming in mind. It makes the most sense to wait until your DP comes on board before you cut a deal on the camera package. Get a list of the equipment that the DP would like included (with the caveat that the budget may not be able to sustain everything requested). Ask the DP if there is a camera house with which he or she has a relationship (that is, a rental house that will make you a deal if you mention the DP's name or the DP orders the package him- or herself). Secure multiple quotes before you make a final decision on a package.

Camera and Film Test. When you make the deal on your camera package, negotiate a day, about a week before production begins, to do some test shooting to ensure that the camera, lenses, and film stock are what is needed.

Insurance Certificate. Most likely, you will have to set up a vendor account with the camera house. This is also the appropriate time to arrange to have an insurance certificate, or "cert," sent to the rental house. Establish with the insurance company who will send the insurance certs to your vendors. If the insurance company will be sending off the certificates, compile a list of certs that need to be issued, and fax it to the insurance company toward the close of each workday.

Monitors and VCRs. You may want to rent a monitor and a VCR for screening dailies or a video tap for viewing scenes as you are shooting. It is usually most efficient to rent as much of your equipment as you can from as few rental houses as possible. This reduces the number of pickups and returns, purchase orders, and so on that you'll have to handle.

Camera Bag or Camera Van. Rent a camera bag or camera van, depending on the needs and budget of your shoot. A camera van is a convenience but is not essential. Remember that the camera department will require a changing bag and a sturdy table to work on, at the very least. On *Swingers,* we used a camera bag and a table, which was both cost- and time-efficient because our lightweight Aaton camera only took 400-foot loads, and the magazines had to be loaded frequently. Having the changing bag nearby helped us maintain our pace.

Camera Expendables. The second AC is usually responsible for purchasing expendables for the camera department. Sometimes, the production office will receive a detailed list of expendables from the camera department, and a production assistant will make the purchases.

The same is true for a production assistant picking up cans, cores, bags, and camera reports, all of which can be had, usually free of cost, from the laboratory that will be processing your film. Extra film cans are required for downloading film, short ends, recanning, and so on. Cores are what go in the center of the film roll and keep the film rolled properly, and bags are for storing the film as a precaution to keep the film from being exposed to light. Often, the lab will print information specific to your production on the camera reports. This should be arranged in advance. As a courtesy to the lab and to other productions, be sure to return the unused cans, bags, and cores to the lab, along with any unused, uncustomized camera reports, at the end of the shoot.

Camera Prep. The first AC will prep the camera package just before the shoot. This process can take up to eight hours. Ask the rental house what time your AC can start prepping the camera. Make sure that he or she has a vehicle large enough to transport the equipment when finished prepping and that he or she knows where the equipment should be stored to ensure its safety. If necessary, arrange for a production assistant to meet him or her with a production vehicle to transport the camera equipment when prepping is complete.

Film Stock. Refer to your budget to determine how many feet of stock have been budgeted for and whether it's 16mm or 35mm. Ask the DP and the director which stocks will be required for the shoot. Call the company that manufactures the stock (Kodak, Fuji, etc.) and several film stock houses to compare prices. If you are a student or a member of the IFP or a local independent film organization, you may be entitled to a discount. Ask the vendor. Be careful to store the film in a cool, dry place.

Purchasing film stock is simple if you have the money to buy factory unopened stock. If you're buying recans or short ends, your task is less straightforward. As soon as the DP and the director have determined which stocks will be required for the shoot, call film stock houses that deal in recans. (In Los Angeles, try Dr. Rawstock, Steadi-Systems, and Studio Film and Tape.) If you are shooting somewhere other than New York or Los Angeles, you will probably have to deal through these vendors. Plan to pay shipping. Let vendors know which film stocks you will need and how many feet you require. If they do not have the total footage you need for the shoot (and they probably won't), establishing a good working relationship with someone who works there is essential. On *Swingers,* we had to call several recan raw stock houses each day to find the film stock we needed. Another possibility is to purchase recanned film stock directly from another production that is wrapping. If you know of any such productions, contact the production manager or line producer and find out if the production will sell its recanned stock to you at a reduced rate. If you are accumulating film stock in this piecemeal manner, it will be necessary, and somewhat more difficult, to track all your footage. (Recans are usually not standard loads. For example, a recan may be a 380-foot load or a 750-foot load, as opposed to factory unopened stock, which is sold in loads of 100, 400, and 1,000 feet.)

Regardless of whether the film you purchase is factory unopened or recanned, keep a record of the raw stock purchased, the raw stock issued to the camera department, and the raw stock shot. (The latter will be calculated and recorded by the camera department on each day's camera report.) On *Swingers,* our raw stock purchase continued from the first week of preproduction through the final week of production. It was a constant quest for Kodak 5298 stock, most of which we managed to purchase at incredibly low prices from various vendors in Los Angeles. We also shot Kodak 5248 for exterior daytime shots, which was somewhat less expensive. If you have any questions about a particular film stocks, ask the manufacturer.

Grip and Lighting Checklist

During the second or third week of preproduction, discuss the film's grip and lighting needs with the director, DP, the key grip, and the gaffer.

- Rent a grip and electric package and a truck, or hire department keys with their own equipment and trucks.
- Rent a dolly and a crane, and hire operators as needed.
- Purchase grip and electric expendables.
- Schedule a scout for each location for the director, the key grip, and the gaffer.
- Discuss with the gaffer which generator to rent and at which locations you may be able to tie in.
- Arrange to have insurance certificates sent to the rental houses.
- Schedule prelight/prerig days for locations during production.
- Discuss special equipment needs.

About the Grip and Lighting Checklist

Grip and Electric Package.   Ideally, hire a key grip or a gaffer who owns his or her own equipment and has a truck that you can rent for the production. If not, you'll have to rent the equipment and vehicle from a rental house. After a discussion with the director, the gaffer, and the key grip and a scout of the locations that have been locked, secure the lighting and grip equipment lists from the respective department heads. Make sure that both department heads know that you may not be able to secure everything on their lists. Even if you're renting the bulk of your equipment from a crew member, you may still need to rent some items from a rental house. Considerations to bear in mind when deciding on a rental house or vendor are cost, quality, if they have the bulk of your needs, and accessibility from your location or production headquarters.

Dolly and Crane.   Among the items that you may need to rent are a dolly (don't forget the track) and a crane. You will want to have a dolly grip for those days when you're using the dolly. This can be someone who is already on the crew if he or she can be spared. Cranes often come with an operator. If not, make sure that someone in the department is familiar enough with the equipment that he or she can operate the crane efficiently and safely. If a crane operator must be hired, ask your department head for recommendations, and inquire with the rental house. Send an insurance certificate to all vendors.

On *Swingers,* we used a wheelchair as a dolly for most of the shots that required one because that was the least expensive option that still enabled us to secure the shots we wanted. This "doorway dolly" served us well because our locations were small and dolly track would have taken up too much space. We rented a dolly for one day, for the shot at the diner in which the boys are sitting at a large round table and a dolly with circular track was required to shoot the scene. Another less expensive option is a golf cart. Wheelchairs and golf carts both work great, depending on what shots you need.

Expendables.   As with the camera department, lighting and grip expendables can be purchased either by the production or by the lighting and grip departments themselves. Sometimes, department members include expendables as part of their kit; the production pays for the expendables either as part of the kit rental or through an invoice that the crew member submits. Otherwise, you'll need to secure a detailed list of supplies from the key grip and gaffer or make sure that the departments have ample petty cash to cover their needs. If the departments are responsible for purchasing these items, make sure that they know their total budget for expendables and that they submit their receipts to the production office.

Location Scout.   The scout is of extreme importance to ensure the feasibility of a location in terms of grip and electric concerns and to determine which equipment will be essential. If your locations are not locked by week 3, you'll need to consider which locations are available to scout. Have your grip and electric departments scout locations as they are locked, but do not ask them to inspect one location a day if they are not yet on the payroll. Instead, have them scout several locations at a time unless you are in a bind and need their input immediately to determine which location to secure.

Generator and Tie-ins. As discussed earlier, scouting will reveal which locations will require a generator, where you may tie in, and for which locations existing power is ample.

Prelight/Prerig Days. Depending on the lighting needs of the show and the rental arrangements for a given location, have your lighting and/or grip departments prelight/prerig a location before filming there if possible. This day of setup allows the shoot day at a given location to get off to a quicker start. At some locations, prelighting/prerigging will be mandatory to ensure that you don't waste everyone else's time on the production day. Try to assess on the scout which, if any, of the locations will require a prelight/prerig day. Make sure that both the location and the crew are available for prelight/prerig days. You may need to bring on extra crew members (day players; see the Schedules and Lists Checklist) for these days so that you maintain the necessary crew on the set and avoid overtime.

Sound Checklist

- Secure the sound package; arrange to have insurance certificates sent to the sound house or the sound mixer if you are renting equipment directly from your sound mixer (week 4).
- Purchase or rent sound supplies and expendables: slate, cellulars, walkie-talkies, microphones, batteries, cable, tapes, magnetic stock, and so on.
- Arrange for playback if needed.
- Arrange for bands, musicians, and live music if needed.
- Gather sound reports and sound tape.

About the Sound Checklist
Sound Package. Once the sound mixer has been hired, identify the film's sound package needs. Based on your locations (that is, large interior space or exterior highway), the setup of each scene, and the number of characters in each scene, your sound mixer will determine with the director the types of microphones and other equipment that will be needed. Because sound equipment can be costly, rent only the equipment that is essential, and keep the equipment only for the days you need it. You can always rent a piece of equipment again later if it turns out that you need it. Whether you rent your sound package from the sound mixer or a sound house, an insurance certificate must be provided.

If possible, hire a sound mixer who can provide his or her own equipment. On *Swingers,* our sound mixer had his own equipment and a van to transport it. We made a flat deal with him for both. His kit included all of the necessary mics, booms, cable, batteries, a slate, and a mixing board.

Sound Supplies and Expendables. The sound department will need a variety of supplies, such as DAT tapes, batteries, extra booms, magnetic stock for each day, and markers. Provide the sound mixer with blank sound reports. A copy of each sound report is submitted to the lab attached to the corresponding sound roll. Find out if the sound mixer has a relationship with a sound house that will make you a deal on supplies or equipment.

Playback. If you are filming a scene that requires sound or music playback, discuss the required equipment with the sound mixer and the director. Playback is the recording of a song that will be used in the final mix on DAT tape, with time code, a stereo, and speakers, on which to literally play the song back on the spot and a smart slate so that you can synchronize the recording. On *Swingers,* we needed to film a band live while shooting in a location that was open to the public, so we arranged for playback on the set, and later synchronized the band's lyrics of the recording to the picture.

Sound Reports and Sound Tape. At the end of each filming day, collect the sound rolls and their corresponding sound reports, and send them to the lab with the film and the camera reports. The lab will match the sound to the footage based on the information recorded on the sound reports. One copy of the sound report should stay with the sound mixer, one copy should be given to the editor the following day along with the script supervisor's notes and camera reports, and copies should be filed in the production notebooks.

Travel and Transportation Checklist

Arrange for the following as needed in accordance with your budget, cast, crew, locations, and equipment.

- Call the film commission in the city or state in which you are filming.
- Arrange travel to distant locations.
- Prepare per diems for nonlocal cast and crew.
- Rent motor homes, dressing rooms, and honey wagons as needed.
- Rent production vehicles as needed.
- Have extra keys made for truck locks and for each production vehicle.
- Arrange for drivers of production vehicles (weeks 3 and 4); file copies of the drivers' licenses.
- Have mileage sheets and petty cash on hand.

About the Travel and Transportation Checklist

Film Commission. The first thing you should do if you are filming on location is contact the local film commission. (See "Permits" in the Locations Checklist.) Determine the local guidelines, rules, permit requirements, and so on. Ask for a listing of local crew members, and establish a contact person at the film commission who can help you with your needs. If you will be on location for an extended period of time, a local bank account will facilitate many tasks, including renting equipment and securing locations.

Travel Arrangements. Start organizing travel arrangements early on if you will be filming out of town. Making reservations well in advance may save you money. Make flight reservations for the cast and crew, or rent passenger vans or cars. You may be able to make a package deal with an airline if a significant number of people will be traveling. Whenever possible, transport actors to distant locations via airplane rather than by car since it is a far more comfortable and faster means by which to travel, and the actors' needs can be catered to.

If you will be on location for several nights, make hotel or motel arrangements for the cast and crew. Determine lodging costs as early as you can to secure the best rate and to ensure availability. Accommodate your cast and crew according to the travel and lodging terms negotiated in their contracts. For instance, if a cast member was guaranteed a first-class flight and a suite in a hotel, you must honor those terms. On low-budget shows, try to establish a favored-nations policy that prohibits any elaborate arrangements for any one cast or crew member. If special arrangements have not been guaranteed, ask crew members to share rooms. If you have hired nonlocal cast or crew members, the production will need to accommodate their travel to the city in which you will be filming, and you may need to rent a vehicle for their use while working on the show. (You must also pay per diems for nonlocal cast and crew members.)

On *Swingers,* we traveled to Las Vegas for three days and three nights to film the casino scenes. We rented a passenger van for 14 members of the crew. Two crew members transported equipment and film stock in their own cars, which also provided us with smaller vehicles for getting around Las Vegas. Traveling by passenger van saved us gas, valet, and gratuity costs. We booked flights for the 4 cast members who were needed in Las Vegas and picked them up at the airport. Hotel rooms were provided for each cast member at a reasonable rate, and the crew, including the director and producers, shared ten hotel rooms (2 crew members to a room). We did not screen dailies while in Las Vegas, so it was not necessary to ship the film and sound tape back to Los Angeles for transfer. We brought ample raw stock with us so that we were able to get the coverage we

needed while we had the casino because we knew we could not afford to go back for reshoots. Arrangements were made to store both the footage and the camera equipment in a cool, secure place within the hotel.

Per Diems. If the production will be filming at a distant location, it will be necessary to pay per diems to the nonlocal cast and crew. (Try to hire local crew members if you will be filming at a distant location for some time.) Check with SAG for the current minimum per diem rate paid to cast members while on location. At the time this book went to press, the SAG per diem rates were $12 for breakfast, $18 for lunch, and $30 for dinner, totaling $60. The government per diem rate on location for crew is $32.50 (breakfast $6.50; lunch $9; dinner $17).

On *Swingers,* we paid per diems to the four cast members according to SAG rates. The crew received what the budget could sustain, which was $25 per day to cover miscellaneous expenses such as meals, tips, etc. The per diem is not meant to cover personal expenses like snacks or phone calls. If the crew is working for low money, the production company should consider picking up the hotel room charges in the interest of good working relations. We treated the crew to dinner with production funds on two nights in addition to the on-set meals provided during filming.

Motor Homes and Dressing Rooms/Honey Wagons. Based on your locations, budget, and cast contracts, you may need to rent motor homes or star trailers for the course of the show or for particular locations. If you will be at a given location for some time, production may need a designated workspace. If there is no space within the location itself and it is neither cost- nor time-efficient for crew members to drive back and forth between the office and the set with paperwork, film stock, messages, supplies, and so on, rent a motor home if it can easily be parked nearby. Motor homes usually come with a driver, an office setup, a makeup station, a wardrobe area, and a bathroom. They can be costly, but it may be worthwhile to rent one for a few of your locations for convenience sake.

Dressing rooms are often provided to cast members either because their contracts stipulate so or because suitable changing rooms are not available at the location. Renting tents is a cost-effective way to provide dressing rooms for your cast, a makeup station, and so on, if there is enough space at the location to set them up. Usually, on low-budget shows, the cast is hired on a favored-nations basis, and motor homes, star trailers, or honey wagons are provided only if required for the show to run smoothly.

On *Swingers,* we did not budget for any motor homes or star trailers. The cast and crew were hired on a favored-nations basis, and the budget could not sustain such accommodations. When we scouted our locations, we determined where the cast would change and where makeup would be applied. The production office was located at our house, so there was ample room for wardrobe and makeup to be done at the office if space was not available on location. Most of our locations were within 20 minutes of the production office, and it was convenient for both cast and crew to drive between the set and the office. When necessary, the cast dressed at the production office and then drove to the location, where the wardrobe and makeup departments were able to set up small workstations for any needs the cast had during filming. Production was able to deliver paperwork, call sheets, supplies, and so on, several times each day between the set and the office.

Department Vehicles. Refer to your budget to determine which departments will need production trucks or cube vans. Often, the grip and electric department heads have their own trucks, or you can rent your grip and electric equipment by truck size (that is, a 5- or 10-ton truck that comes loaded with grip and electric equipment). If possible, combine the materials rented by your set design department, prop department, and art department onto one production truck. (Be sure that pickups and drop-offs are coordinated carefully among the departments sharing a production vehicle.) See if the head of the wardrobe department can use his or her own vehicle or can fit the wardrobe racks on the production truck. The production vehicle will be used to store craft service and catering items, production expendables, and, if need be, sound equipment and makeup and hair expendables. The sound mixer should be able to fit the sound equipment in his or her own vehicle or in the production truck. On *Swingers,* the art director and the sound mixer had their own trucks or vans, which were used to pick up and transport most of their materials and equipment. Any expendables that they needed were picked up and returned by production.

When a vehicle must be rented will depend on which department will use it. Place the maximum number of vehicles you anticipate needing on hold during the first or second week of preproduction. The prop and art departments may need their vehicle a few weeks before production, depending on the quantity of equipment and materials that needs to be picked up; these departments may need to build, assemble, and transport items. Determine if one production truck can suffice early on for pickups for multiple departments. This will save you money.

Purchase key or combination locks for the back of each production truck so that the equipment and materials left on your trucks are safe. Arrange for secured overnight parking for your production vehicles.

Keep in mind when renting production trucks, vans, or cars that the rental company may give you a certain number of miles at no extra charge. If you exceed the given number of miles, you will be charged per mile at a prenegotiated rate. Negotiate in advance how many miles will be included at no charge and what the rate per mile thereafter will be. (Try to get unlimited free miles in exchange for a screen credit.) The rental house that you rent your production vehicles from will record the current mileage on the truck or van before you drive it off the lot. Get a copy of the paperwork on which the mileage is recorded for each vehicle, and also be sure that any damage previously done to the vehicle has been noted.

On *Swingers,* we rented one production truck a week and a half before production for small prop and art pickups, production expendables, and wardrobe. We stored materials and equipment either on the truck, which was locked and safely parked each night, or in the production office, where there was always a crew member around to ensure the safety of the equipment. We did not have a camera truck, so the camera equipment was taken to the set with wardrobe, production expendables, craft service, and catering items on the production truck. We always loaded all camera equipment onto the truck last so it could easily be taken off each night and stored in the production office.

Locks. You must make copies of keys to any locks used on production trucks and cube vans! Keys are often lost or damaged, and it will cost you money and time to have locks broken or new keys made. If a driver misplaces the key to the truck's lock, having copies on hand will ensure that the equipment can be readily accessed. Copies of keys should be left in the office in a file, and a duplicate set of all keys should be put in the AD kit.

Drivers. Determine how many drivers you will need for production vehicles and who they will be. On *Swingers,* we had department heads drive their department's vehicles, and a PA drove the production truck. Make sure that anyone who is asked to drive a production vehicle is comfortable with driving a truck and that he or she is able to do pickups; many trucks, depending on their size, require special driver's licenses. If not, you may need to hire extra crew members to drive vehicles and do pickups. If you are a union show, you will need to hire Teamsters to drive your vehicles and to handle all pickups and returns. Copies of drivers' licenses should be filed in the office and in the AD kit.

Mileage Sheets. If you will be paying mileage to crew members who use their personal vehicles for pickups, returns, or other errands, have mileage sheets available. (See the Office Setup Checklist.) It is also best to issue petty cash to those persons who will be running errands in case a last-minute purchase is needed or gas costs need to be covered.

On *Swingers,* Jon Favreau owned the Comet Caliente that served as Trent's car. We paid for some minor repairs on the car to be sure it was in proper working order for filming.

If you need some of your vehicles for only a few days and they are fairly common and readily available cars, try to borrow them from a friend or secure a flat rate deal on them from a neighbor or local auto shop. Picture vehicle rental houses can help you locate the vehicle you need, but they can be costly. Don't forget that insurance certs will be needed when you borrow or rent picture vehicles.

Craft and Catering Checklist

- Hire a craft service person and have him or her prepare food and expendables lists (week 3).
- Have craft service approach local cafes and restaurants regarding donations.
- Identify the eating areas at each location.
- Secure a caterer (a catering company, restaurants, and so on); sort out the menu so that there is a variety.
- Compile a list of local restaurants near each location that might be able to provide second meals or extra food on larger set days.
- Have petty cash available daily for second meals or extra meal needs.
- Arrange for special meal needs if necessary.
- Arrange for catering and craft service at distant locations.

About the Craft and Catering Checklist

Catering refers to the actual on-set meals, as opposed to *craft service,* which refers to the snacking and beverage station available throughout the shoot day. How you provide meals and snacks to the cast and crew will depend on your budget.

Craft Service. Make sure that your craft service person is committed and understands the importance of providing healthy snacks and sustenance for the cast and crew who will be working long hours. Have the craft service person prepare both a grocery list and an expendables list. Review the grocery and supply list, and make sure there are plenty of affordable options. As for rentals, craft service will need a table and chairs, at the very least, and may require coolers, thermoses, urns, a hot plate or microwave, a toaster oven, a cutting board, a first aid kit, and extension cords. If the craft service person has a lot of these items, rent them from him

or her as a kit rental. If not, add them to your production expendables list.

Soliciting Donations. It is almost always possible to get some food donated to your production. Have the craft service person, the production coordinator, or an intern speak to local cafés, restaurants, coffee shops, and so on. Manufacturers are sometimes interested in making a donation in exchange for product placement. On *Swingers,* we solicited donations of soft drinks, bottled water, coffee beans, cigars, and some second meals. On another film, we managed to get all of our coffee, daily bagels, and day-old pastries from a local bakery. If you're on a tight budget, these donations will help you keep costs down.

Identify the Eating Areas. The craft service person can help determine where food will be set up at each location and can assist, if necessary, with serving the catered meals. He or she should arrange to have adequate craft service each day, based on the number of cast and crew bodies on the shooting schedule. That is, you'll need more food for days when many extras are scheduled or visitors are expected.

Catering. The meals you feed people on a low-budget show can range from professionally catered meals to home-cooked meals. In addition to keeping your cast and crew energized, healthy, and ready to work, feeding them on the set keeps everyone together in one place and ensures that the workday proceeds without delays. Figure out how much money you can spend per person per meal. Call caterers and see if you can come to an arrangement that works for both of you. For example, tell them you have $10 per person and must feed 30 people for 15 days; what type of menu can they provide for that amount of money?

On *Swingers,* we had $5 per person per meal. In exchange for $5 per head and a production credit, we found six restaurants who were willing to provide meals. Some of the restaurants agreed to deliver the food to the set; others required that we pick it up. We signed contracts with each establishment that stipulated the terms of the agreement. The paperwork was turned over to the craft service person, who orchestrated pickup or delivery of the food and payment.

Restaurant List and Petty Cash. You will want to have a list of affordable and convenient restaurants handy when filming at each of your locations. Often a filming day will go into overtime and a second meal will need to be provided, or there will be visitors or extras on the set for whom you may want to make other meal arrangements. For extras, it is often cheaper to provide what is called a "box lunch" from local inexpensive restaurants than to have such meals catered. Your AD, if possible, should alert the craft service person and the production office about three hours in advance of needing a second or extra meals if overtime is anticipated on a particular day. Make sure that craft service has enough petty cash to purchase second or extra meals and has an accurate count of how many meals will need to be provided.

Special Meal Needs. There may be days when certain actors are working who may be on a special diet or make a particular request for a meal. Certain crew members may also need to abide by a particular diet. When you arrange set meals with your caterer, try to provide choices that will hopefully accommodate everyone's needs. For instance, both hot and cold foods should be available, as well as protein-rich foods (chicken, fish, meats, or tofu—some of your cast and crew members may be vegetarians). Arrange for any special meal requirements with your caterer and craft service person in advance. Accommodate any special meals needed within reason, keeping in mind that it is best to be fair to everyone and to avoid setting lavish standards.

Distant Location Craft Service and Catering. Prior to filming at any distant location, arrange for your set craft service needs and catered meals. Call the locations at which you will be filming or the local film commission and ask for recommendations for craft service companies or persons and caterers if you will be filming at a distant location for some time. If you will only be filming at a distant location for a few days, it may be cheaper to take the crew to lunch at a local restaurant determined in advance, or to have preordered meals picked up by your craft service person or a production assistant or delivered by the restaurant. You may want to hire a local craft service so that they are able to have a day to prepare items and rent expendables before production arrives. Investigate your options carefully to determine what is most convenient, affordable, and best for your cast and crew.

Still Photography Checklist

- Hire a still photographer; secure film and processing deals, and issue petty cash if necessary.
- Select specific filming days for the still photographer to shoot.

About the Still Photography Checklist

Lack of decent action production stills is an oversight of many indie productions. These photos are indispensable in press kits, fliers, posters, festival programs, industry magazines, and more. Don't forget that production stills are shots of the action occurring in front of the camera, not you and a

grip standing at the craft service table. Some behind-the-scenes photos can be useful for recording the making of your movie but aren't mandatory the way production stills are.

Still Photographer. Once your schedule is set, secure a still photographer. Take a look at the photographer's portfolio and get references to make sure that you won't end up with poor-quality pictures that will prove useless.

Most professional photographers process their work and purchase their supplies through a particular lab and supply house, usually at a reduced rate. If your still photographer is amenable, have him or her purchase expendables and arrange for processing. Reimburse any of his or her purchases or dole out petty cash and have receipts returned. Otherwise, call around to various labs and get quotes. Have the photographer shoot both black-and-white and color slide film.

Key Shoot Days. If your funds are limited, select several key production days for the photographer to shoot on set. Select these days according to which scenes and which actors will make the most useful publicity shots. Discuss this briefly with the director and possibly with the cinematographer. If you have any name actors in your film, have the photographer present when those actors are working.

AD Kit Checklist

The AD kit should include the following items:

- Call sheets
- Production reports
- Exhibit G forms
- Taft-Hartley forms
- Meal allowance sheets
- Location permits
- Location insurance certificates and blanks
- Location contracts and blanks
- Security guard and parking lot information
- Extras vouchers
- Copies of signed cast contracts
- Blank SAG contracts (weekly and daily)
- Cast, crew, and vendor packs
- Beeper/cell phone numbers
- Maps
- Extra keys to locations and vehicles
- Walkie-talkie sign-out sheets
- Still releases, personal releases, filming notices, extended hours releases, and neighbor releases
- Schedules, day-out-of-days sheets, and strip board
- W4 forms, Start/I-9 forms, and time cards

- Check request forms
- Petty cash envelopes
- Purchase orders
- Petty cash
- Accident reports
- SAG rule book
- Current shooting copy of the script

About the AD Kit Checklist

The AD kit is a portable file box that the AD brings to the set each day. In it, forms, schedules, contracts, reports, lists, and other paperwork are kept. It is important that the AD have the necessary paperwork on the set at all times. Production assistants and office staff should not have to drive back and forth between the set and the office to deliver and retrieve paperwork all day long. In addition, SAG, the film commission, permit officers, fire fighters, and police officers may come to your set and ask to see your paperwork, permits, and so on.

The set is the AD's office during production, and the AD kit functions as a mini filing cabinet with paperwork that the AD may need to refer to, fill out, or provide while on the set. Here are a few examples:

The AD may need to refer to a cast member's contract when filling out Exhibit G forms, call sheets, or the production report. Copies of cast contracts, blank Exhibit G forms, and call sheets should be kept in the AD kit.

If yours is a SAG show, Taft-Hartley forms must also be on the set so that any nonunion actors can fill them out when they begin work.

The AD or second AD will need to refer to a copy of the shooting schedule when filling out the next day's call sheet.

The AD or second AD must have cast members fill out W4 forms and start forms on the first day they report to work. Any extra crew members who are hired must also fill out these forms.

If yours is a SAG show, the AD should have a copy of the SAG handbook on the set so he or she can refer to SAG's rules and guidelines.

Copies of filming notices and releases should be kept in the AD kit so the AD can post them as necessary.

Crew members may have to fill out petty cash envelopes. Having them on the set in the AD box saves crew members time.

Vendor lists should be on hand so that crew members can quickly locate the phone numbers of equipment houses and vendors in case additional equipment is needed during filming. Equipment may be broken or damaged and have to be replaced immediately.

Cast and crew lists are important in case someone must be contacted.

A shooting copy of the script is handy in case the AD has to refer to a scene.

Additional equipment, materials, or expendables are often needed during filming, and having purchase orders on the set makes it easy to account for items and rent them immediately.

The AD may have to issue certificates of insurance for any last-minute equipment ordered.

Finally, it is essential that the AD have immediate access to extra keys to locations and vehicles in case keys are lost or damaged.

Purchase orders, insurance certificates, start forms, Exhibit G forms, releases, Taft-Hartley forms, or other paperwork that is filled out on the set by the AD department should be turned in to the office each day for copying, filing, and distribution.

Send to Set Checklist

The following items should be prepared during last week of preproduction and sent to the set on the first day of production:

- Extra office supplies
- First aid kit
- Flashlights
- Extra instant film and camera
- Street atlas or local maps and guides
- Three-ring binder
- Local film guide (like *LA 411* or *NYPG*)
- Batteries
- Extension cords
- Rope

About the Send to Set Checklist

The set should function like a mini office. Crew members will be spending most of their time on the set while in production, and supplies, books, forms, and other items should be on hand. (See also the Office Setup Checklist.)

Postproduction Checklist

The following tasks must be taken care of during the third and fourth weeks of preproduction.

- Interview postproduction supervisors.
- Arrange for an editing facility and equipment; discuss needs with the editor (week 2 or 3).
- Arrange for lab needs: dailies, transfers, developing, and processing (week 2 or 3).
- Purchase videotape for transfers, mag stock, and so on.
- Purchase stock footage if necessary.
- Purchase supplies for the editing facility.
- Compile a calendar or timeline of screenings, picture lock dates, mix dates, ADR recording, titles, music meetings, festival deadlines, and so on.

About the Postproduction Checklist

Editing Facility. Arrange during preproduction to rent editing space and equipment so that they are available when the editor comes on board, most likely during the first or second week of production. Call several facilities for quotes and a list of their equipment. Determine the medium on which the film will be cut (Avid, flatbed, or D-Vision), and discuss equipment needs with the editor. Find out if the editor prefers to work at a particular facility.

Try to make a combined flat deal on equipment and the editing suite if possible. Editing equipment and suites are usually priced on a weekly basis, and additional equipment is often priced separately. Find a facility that is conveniently located to the production office or the lab where the film will be processed for easy delivery and pickup. Ask for a few parking spaces if they are designated, and try to include that cost in the overall cost of the facility.

On *Swingers*, we were able to strike a deal at our editing facility. We made a flat deal paid in two installments; one upon striking the deal during preproduction, and the second toward the end of our rental period. This was in lieu of a weekly rate. The deal included the Avid system, hard drives, a VCR, a television, two parking spaces, and any additional equipment or accessories needed during the editing process that the facility could provide. The only additional expenses were for phone calls, food, and supplies for the editor and assistant editor. We anticipated needing the edit system and suite for 12 weeks, and we cut our deal accordingly. Ultimately, though, we needed an additional 8 weeks of editing time, and we were given a reduced rate for the subsequent rental.

Determine the number of editing weeks you will need carefully. If you need additional weeks, you may find that the facility has committed your room to another production and you are unable to continue using the space or the equipment.

Lab. Arrange and determine your lab needs in week 2 or 3 of preproduction. Your footage will need to be developed and processed in order for it to be viewed and assembled. Determine if you will have dailies made for each day of filming and when transfers of footage videotape (1/2-inch and a Betacam) will need to be made. Lab costs are expensive; secure quotes from several facilities before deciding on one. Finding the best price will take time. Ideally, your film will be developed and processed after the first day or two of shooting. Your director, DP, or editor, may have a relationship at a particular lab with which a deal could be negotiated. Make sure to establish a contact person at the lab who will be responsible for your dailies, paperwork, and scheduling all of your film's needs. You will want to discuss your film's needs with your editor and the director to properly communicate them to the lab. In some instances you may want the editor to speak directly with the lab.

Videotape. If you will be transferring your footage to video, it is cheaper to purchase 1/2-inch or Betacam tapes from a videotape supply house than to have the lab provide them to you at their cost. You will also need 1/2-inch or 3/4-inch tapes during the editing process if you will be using an Avid editor to output transfers of rough cuts to the music crew, festival committees, dialogue and sound editors, producers, director, and others. Purchasing videotapes by the case is usually cheapest, and if any are unused, you can sell them back to the store where you purchased them (usually at a reduced rate).

Stock Footage. On low-budget independent films, there are often scenes that are expensive to shoot but important to the look and feel of the film. For instance, if a movie requires a car chase, a car accident, a building being blown up, or a fire, it may be most cost-effective in such instances to purchase stock footage (footage that has already been shot). There are stock-footage houses at which you can purchase such footage; call around for the best quotes.

Supplies. Have either a production assistant or the assistant editor purchase supplies so that the editing room is equipped when the editors begin work. Pens, markers, tape, notebooks, paper, disks, videotapes, DATs, and so on, will be needed. The editing staff will also need petty cash (dispensed weekly) for food purchases.

Calendar. It is important to compile a calendar of deadlines and dates so that you can properly determine and schedule your postproduction needs (or if you have a postproduction supervisor, he or she will know how to schedule the film's needs). Determining the schedule of events during postproduction will keep you on track and on budget. The producer(s), director, and editor should determine when the editor's version of the film will need to be locked, when the director's cut will need to be locked, and when the ADR, foley, and mix should be scheduled. Determine when trial prints or answer prints will ideally be struck. The timing of these elements is often determined (and may need to change during postproduction) based on festival deadlines and the amount of money budgeted for postproduction.

Miscellaneous Needs Checklist

Depending on your script, you may have to secure and organize the following:

- Licensed weaponry person/weapons
- Welfare worker/children's tutor
- Animals and an animal trainer/wrangler (see discussion in Budget section)
- Stunts and a stunt coordinator
- Special effects, computer-generated images (CGI)

Weapons
If your script calls for guns, swords, knives, or other kinds of weapons, you may need to have a licensed weaponry person on the set depending on how the scene will be shot and if you will be using real weapons. You may be able to hire a prop master who has a weapons license, which will save you money. It may be a wise idea to contact stunt coordinators for some advice as to how to best deal with any weapons called for in your script.

Welfare Worker
If you will be employing minors, you must first contact the Child Labor Laws division of the State Labor Commissioner's office to be sure that you comply with the laws governing the employment of minors. A welfare worker and/or teacher will be required depending on the time of year (if school is in session) to ensure the safety and treatment of minors.

Stunts
Hopefully, on a low-budget show, you will have few, if any, elaborate stunts that will require the cost of a stunt coordinator, but it is best to hire one for safety purposes if you do. You may have a gun scene, a fight, or someone jumping out of a window. This may require a stunt person who is familiar with how to fall out of a window, throw a punch or take one, and what type of materials will be needed for certain

stunts, such as break-away glass or body pads. If you are a SAG show, you will need to pay your stunt coordinator SAG rates, so be sure to properly budget this expense.

Special Effects
Arrange early on for any special effects that may be required in your film. Depending on the effect, it may be done in postproduction by computer-generated images (CGI). An on-set special effect may be fireworks, a fuse box explosion, or spark, smoke, or rain. Call around to special effects houses to help determine your needs and costs. Discuss your special effects needs with your production and art departments, DP, gaffer, director, and prop master. They may be helpful in figuring out the most cost-efficient and safest way to perform an effect, or they may know someone who can be helpful. Special effects can be costly, so be sure that they are imperative to the film and that you approach them creatively in order to keep costs down.

THE LAST WEEK OF PREPRODUCTION

The final week of preproduction is extremely important. Equipment, vehicles, materials, and so on, will be picked up; all crew members will come on board; last-minute arrangements, deals, and adjustments will be made. Stop! Go back to the preproduction checklists and review every item on every list to see what must still be done. Make sure that nothing has been overlooked. Double-check all arrangements, contracts, paperwork, and deals. Make calls to cast, crew, caterers, locations, permit offices, rental houses, and so on to confirm arrangements. Are all of your locations (or at least the locations needed for the first two weeks of production) locked and secured by contract, and have all permits been obtained? Is everyone on schedule? Check the weather forecast for the first week of filming. Should you adjust the schedule based on weather or other production concerns? You don't want to begin principal photography on the wrong foot. Reviewing the checklist and confirming deals and arrangements will ensure that you account for everything.

Review your contracts and paperwork to be sure that everything has been sent to the appropriate organizations and individuals and that copies have been filed in the production office and included in the AD kit. Double-check that all of your vendors and locations have received certificates of insurance. Prepare the AD kit and send it to the set or with the AD so that it is ready for the first day of filming. Actualize the budget for those costs you are certain about to ensure that you have ample funds for filming and postproduction (and some padding for unanticipated costs that arise). Contact cast members working on the first day of principal photography with their call times, or verify that the AD or second AD has taken care of this.

The all-crew check-in meeting, which should already be scheduled, will take place during the last week of preproduction. Make sure that you have found a space large enough to accommodate the entire crew. The meeting will allow you to determine what is left to do, to troubleshoot any problems that a crew member or department is having, to determine whether the shooting schedule must be changed because a location has not been locked, the art department isn't ready, or equipment has not been secured, and to ensure that everyone is prepared and on schedule.

Go through the preproduction checklists during the meeting to verify that each department has taken care of its responsibilities. Hand out the most current shooting schedule, and review each location and scene with the crew. The crew should be familiar with the shooting schedule and the order in which scenes will be shot. Address any questions or concerns. Discuss the events planned for the first day of filming and distribute and review the first day's call sheet. Make sure that everyone has a ride to the set and knows how to get there. Thank the crew for their continuing hard work and dedication.

8 PRODUCTION

Production—it's like going to war. You're dealing with a group of people that's like the size of a platoon. Everybody knows what they have to do. You get in, you get out, you make home wherever it is. You have to deal with what the situation throws you, and it's very stressful, and you can't sleep at night. And the more involved you are with the outcome of it, the more twisted up you are inside.

—Jon Favreau, Swingers

During production, the line producer monitors both the set and the office, staying on top of all details and operations. It is the line producer's responsibility to ensure constant communication between the office and the set; he or she instructs the office about the set's needs. This is vital to a smooth show.

If you've done your job thoroughly during preproduction, the actual shooting period should be a bit calmer for you. Your job will be to ensure that every item on every checklist is taken care of and to troubleshoot as necessary. Refer daily to the production checklists in this chapter (see also CD-ROM).

TROUBLESHOOTING

Inevitably, something will go wrong during production, regardless of how well you did your job during preproduction. Lenses get dropped, people get hurt, things happen that are beyond your control. Perhaps you need a piece of equipment that was overlooked, or maybe something has been damaged and the entire shoot is waiting for a replacement, or perhaps a location has fallen through at the last minute.

If something unexpected comes up, remain calm. Have the coordinator or a production assistant begin to make phone calls immediately to price out your needs while you determine how best to deal with the circumstances. Refer to your budget to determine from which line item you can draw money. Perhaps you spent too much in certain departments but saved money in other areas that will allow you to pay for unexpected expenses. Don't forget to keep the cast and crew apprised of your progress in resolving any problems or delays. Gather as much information as you can, and consider all of the options before making a decision. It is important

for the show to remain on schedule, but making hasty or rash decisions will be more time-consuming and expensive in the long run.

MONITORING THE SET

You may want to work on the set while remaining in communication with the office. You must be available in the event that questions, problems, or concerns arise or decisions must be made, and you will have to oversee the set to ensure that the production is on schedule.

Set Checklist

You should tend to the following items when reporting to the set:

- Check in with the director and the assistant director. Get the set update, check that the day is on schedule, and resolve any problems that have come up.
- Check in with department heads: ask if they need anything, ensure that they are on schedule, and collect petty cash envelopes or issue petty cash as necessary.
- Check that meals are served on time.
- Check in with the cast to see if anyone needs anything.
- Decide about going into overtime, renting special equipment, scheduling changes, providing second meals, and other issues.
- Bring supplies to the set, and replenish the AD kit.
- See that all SAG forms, Exhibit G forms, Start/I-9 forms, and so on, are properly filled out and collected.
- See that call sheets are distributed.
- Deliver and sign checks and paperwork.

- Make sure that the department heads are compiling continuity notebooks as necessary (makeup, wardrobe, art department).

OFFICE RESPONSIBILITIES AND FUNCTION

The office is the life-line and the communication center of the shoot during production. For the set to function smoothly and efficiently, the office must be organized and stay one day ahead of the set. Ideally, the office should be open *at least* an hour before call time and an hour or so after wrap each day. If you are filming nights, keep in mind that businesses are generally open only during the day; therefore, the office may have to be open at least part of the day, and phone calls may have to be made then. Throughout the shoot, the office and the set should be in communication so that the office is prepared to fulfill any requests or directives that come from the set.

Office Checklist

The office may have to organize, arrange, and facilitate the following items during production:

- Acquire any additional equipment needed during filming; immediately replace equipment that has been damaged.
- Gather and send to the set paperwork, materials, equipment, and anything else needed during the day.
- Notify the lab if there will be a delay in delivering film; make sure that the lab's phone and fax numbers and hours of operation are posted in the office.
- Be sure that it is clear who will deliver and pick up film from the lab each day.
- Organize and pick up equipment and materials needed for the next filming day. Organize equipment pickup and return lists; notify those who are responsible for pickups and returns and review lists.
- Check the weather forecast for the next filming day; have the AD note the forecast on the call sheet.
- Make sure that the next day's call sheet is distributed either at lunch or at the end of the day; file copies in the production notebooks and office files.
- Coordinate the transportation of actors who must be brought to the set.
- Collect and file any paperwork regarding vendor pickups and returns at end of each day.
- Collect sound and camera reports and the script supervisor's notes for the editor at the end of each day.

- Collect completed petty cash envelopes from the crew, and actualize the budget in whichever line item this may be possible.
- Check the status of dailies with the lab each day; arrange a pickup.
- Schedule the screening of dailies with the director and the producers.
- Record the total amount of footage shot each day in the film log; purchase film stock as needed.
- Schedule and coordinate prelight/prerig days.
- Organize and plan any company move days.
- Replenish petty cash; prepare per diems if necessary.
- Confirm with the still photographer which days he or she is needed on the set; fax the still photographer a call sheet with directions to the location the day before.
- Replenish forms and have them available when crew members come into the office (stationery, fax sheets, check requests, petty cash envelopes and requests, and so on).
- Update the calendar or whiteboard with important dates, pickups, and returns; distribute updated schedules, day-out-of-days sheets, memos, and strip board.
- Update and distribute script changes (colored pages).
- Update and continue to compile the thank-you list.
- Compile the credit list showing how the credits will run; add new vendors, crew members, and so on.
- Send Exhibit G forms, Taft-Hartley forms, production reports, time cards, contracts, and other paperwork to SAG at the end of each filming week.
- Fill out SAG time cards at the end of each filming week; send them to SAG and the payroll company with appropriate on-set reports (production reports, Exhibit G forms, and so on).
- Make or finalize arrangements for out-of-town filming (travel, accommodations, food, and so on).
- Check in with the editor daily: Are the script notes clear and accurate? Has the editor received dailies? Are there any questions or messages regarding footage shot or additional footage needed that the editor wants communicated to the director?

WRAPPING OUT A SHOOT DAY

Because wrapping out of a location takes time, remember to allow enough time so that you avoid having to pay overtime. Check in with the AD toward the end of the day to see if the set is on schedule and to ascertain when he or she anticipates beginning to wrap.

End-of-Day Checklist

The following checklist for wrapping out a shoot day ensures that you are prepared and organized for the next filming day. Note that the items that follow are not all performed by the line producer. However, you should make sure everything on this list is executed by the appropriate crew.

- Review shooting schedule for the next shoot day; make sure all arrangements have been made.
- Confirm arrangements for the next day's location with the location manager.
- Confirm catering arrangements with the craft service person or the caterer. Total the number of people to be fed the next day.
- Check with the AD to make sure that the cast and additional crew needed for the next day's shoot have been notified of their call times and have a map or directions.
- Distribute the next day's call sheet if it wasn't done at lunch.
- Check in with department heads.
- Purchase more raw stock if needed; dole out raw stock for the next day to be sent to the set.
- Return or pick up equipment or materials as necessary.
- Properly store perishable craft service and catering items.
- Load vehicles with equipment, bearing in mind the order required for unloading.
- Clear out and clean up the location; have the trash removed.
- Collect copies of the camera and sound reports.
- Take the film and sound rolls directly to the lab after the shoot day wraps.
- Lock production vehicles after the equipment has been loaded; park all vehicles safely overnight. Collect and copy script notes.
- File script notes, sound reports, and camera reports in the production notebooks and the office files, along with call sheets, Exhibit G forms, production reports, Taft-Hartley forms, and other paperwork.
- Collect any completed petty cash envelopes from the crew.
- Screen the dailies if not screened during the lunch break.
- Replenish forms needed in the office or the AD kit.
- Review the to-do list with the office staff.

Daily/Weekly Cost Overview

A daily cost overview is a one-page sheet that allows you to compare what you anticipated spending and what you actu-

ally spent (see Figure 8–1). The cost overview usually includes information about how many scenes were shot in a given day, how much you anticipated paying actors and crew (here you account for any overtime or meal penalties), catering, raw stock, and miscellaneous unanticipated expenses. If you're not reporting to anyone else, such as a production company or investors, these daily cost overviews are for your own information so that you know where you stand in terms of the budget. If another entity is involved with the show, such as a mini-major, an executive producer, or a bond company, you may be required to turn in a cost overview sheet each day or weekly. Figure 8–1 will help you to actualize your budget. If you are working with a bond company, they will tell you exactly what is required.

Actualizing the Budget

Throughout the show you will accumulate final receipts and paperwork for all equipment and services rendered. At the end of the show, after all returns have been made and final invoices have been received, you will have to actualize your budget, comparing how much money you've actually spent and how much you anticipated spending for each line item.

If you created your budget with Movie Magic Budgeting, select Compare under the Tools menu in the control bar at the top of your screen. This will add two new columns to your budget, one labeled "Original" and the other labeled "Variance." When you insert an actual cost to the budget column labeled "Current," you will see your original projected cost, the actual cost, and the variance between them.

Because you will have to actualize your budget, it is essential that you collect paperwork from vendors and keep it organized. Once you've entered an invoice or receipt into the budget, mark it so you don't lose track of what you've done. If your daily cost overviews are for your own purposes only, you may want to actualize your budget as current numbers come in and leave the more formal cost overview sheet aside. You will determine which approach best serves your needs. The point is to be aware of how much you're spending so that you feel confident about making decisions. On low-budget shows this is particularly important because you have such limited funds.

It is also essential that you are able to discuss confidently where the film stands financially with other key members of your team. If your film is bonded, the bond company will require that you submit weekly cost reports. The accountant usually prepares this document with the line producer's assistance.

DAILY COST OVERVIEW

SHOW _____ PROD # _____

DATE _____ DAY # _____

START DATE _____

SCHEDULED FINISH DATE _____

REVISED FINISH DATE _____

	PER CALL SHEET	SHOT	AHEAD/BEHIND
# OF SCENES			
# OF PAGES			

	AS BUDGETED AND/OR SCHEDULED	ACTUAL	COST (OVER)/UNDER
CAST OVERTIME			
COMPANY SHOOTING HOURS			
MEAL PENALTY			
EXTRAS & STAND-INS			
CATERING			
RAW STOCK			
UNANTICIPATED EXPENSES:			

TOTAL FOR TODAY _____

PREVIOUS TOTAL _____

GRAND TOTAL _____

PREPARED BY _____ APPROVED BY _____

Figure 8–1   Daily cost overview

COMPANY MOVE DAYS

Company move days are notoriously difficult because they require that the production pick itself up, move to an entirely different location, and set up for filming again the same day. Whenever possible, organize company moves so that the new location is near the current one. Company moves are not altogether different from personal moves—they're a pain in the butt, and they're exhausting. That said, the better organized the company move is, the less painful and time-consuming it will be. If company move days are well organized, they can save your production time and money.

Company Move Checklist

Company moves need to be carefully planned. Refer to the following list to ensure that you properly organize any company move days:

- Load the equipment into the production trucks bearing in mind what will have to be unloaded off the truck first at the new location; this should be coordinated in advance.
- Make sure that all cast and crew members have directions, a map, and transportation to the new location.
- If possible, send a production assistant ahead of the rest of the production to post parking and bathroom signs, to familiarize him- or herself with the space, and to determine where to unload equipment and set up tables, chairs, and other items.
- If possible, have the craft service person leave a small cooler at the old location with drinks and snacks, and send him or her to set up at the new locale before the rest of the company arrives so that there are coffee, cold drinks, and snacks awaiting them.
- Have the AD ensure that every last bit of equipment, paperwork, and supplies has been loaded into the trucks. The AD and the location manager should be the last ones off the set; send the second AD to the new location or vice versa.
- Make sure that the location is left in proper order; refer to the End-of-Day Checklist.
- Whenever possible, have the company move to a location where you will do more than one day of shooting to avoid having to wrap out the second location that same day (too tiring).
- If you have equipment that the vendor must deliver and pick up, inform the vendor in advance that you will need the equipment moved. (This is often the case with cranes, generators, and other heavy equipment.)

- Provide any cast and crew members who were not needed at the previous location with a call sheet for the new location.
- Determine in advance to which location the caterer will report on the company move day.
- Indicate clearly on the call sheet that there are two locations for that day; include maps and directions to both locations.
- Call the office to check in when the crew arrives at the new location.

DISTANT LOCATIONS

As discussed in Chapters 6 and 7, you must make the necessary arrangements well in advance for filming at distant locations. You will need all of the same elements when shooting at a distant location as you do when you're shooting locally, but you usually won't have the same support infrastructure of contacts or the same easy access to equipment. Depending on the scale of the shoot, you may want to hire a local coordinator or production manager to assist you and to ensure that all goes smoothly. If this extra expense is unrealistic for the size and budget of your film, make sure that you've taken all of the elements of the shoot into consideration and determined how best to deal with them.

Distant Locations Checklist

You will need to deal with the following items if you will be filming at a distant location:

- Travel arrangements and living accommodations for cast and crew
- Parking arrangements for crew vehicles and production trucks
- Catering and craft service
- Transportation of crew, materials, and equipment to the location
- Equipment storage
- Office space and setup
- Insurance if you are filming in a different state
- Film stock purchase if needed; a proper place to store film
- Equipment rental if additional equipment is needed
- Local unions
- Shipment of film to the lab if necessary
- Screening of dailies

About the Distant Locations Checklist
Travel and Living Accommodations. Confirm the lodging arrangements made for the cast and crew. Let the hotel or motel know when you anticipate arriving, ask for directions,

and get the name of a contact person. Prepare maps for the crew. Make sure there is secure, ample space in which to park crew vehicles, picture cars, and production trucks, and find out where you will be able to store equipment, materials, and film safely. Ask the hotel or motel to fax you a list of local restaurants and hospitals near your shooting location.

If you will be flying to the location, call the airline to confirm your reservations. Make sure that the airline tickets are in hand and that you coordinate with the cast and crew how each person will get to the airport and at what time and where the crew will meet. Arrange cast and crew transportation from the airport to the location or lodging facility. When traveling, have petty cash on hand for tips. If any cast or crew members will be reporting to the distant location at a different time or day than the rest of the production, arrange to pick them up from the airport.

Per Diems. As discussed in Chapter 7, you will have to provide per diems to all nonlocal cast and crew members. Be prepared to distribute per diems the day you arrive at the location. Because per diems are usually distributed in cash, you will have to withdraw cash beforehand from your local bank.

SECOND-UNIT FILMING AND PICKUPS

Basically, a second unit is a scaled-down crew that usually includes the director, the director of photography, the AD, the assistant camera operator, the second AC, the camera operator, and a production assistant. You may need prop or art department personnel; special effects people; wardrobe, make-up, and hair; and a gaffer as well. It depends on the nature of the shoot. On larger-budget productions, a second unit sometimes has its own director, and the camera operator becomes the second-unit DP; on occasion, an entirely different crew is hired.

A second-unit crew is most appropriate on low-budget shows for shooting exteriors, inserts, and other scenes that don't require principal cast members or a great deal of lighting. An example of when a second-unit crew might be used is if you are shooting in LA interiors that are scripted as Las Vegas locations and the exteriors of Las Vegas are needed. In this case, it makes most sense for a second-unit crew to travel to Las Vegas to shoot the necessary exterior shots. Second-unit shooting can save you time and money and is quite efficient when carefully planned. Depending on how the editing process evolves, you may find that you need pickup days to shoot more coverage of a given scene or that you need different footage than you have.

Second-unit filming on a low-budget shoot should be scheduled for the final days of production if possible. This enables you to wrap the majority of the crew while a small handful of people stay on board for several days of second-unit filming.

THE LAST WEEK OF PRODUCTION

Wrapping out the show must be carefully planned and organized. A week before completing principal photography begin to compile return lists, and be sure that you have budgeted for a PA or two to remain on for a week of wrap to return equipment, vehicles, materials, and expendables that department heads don't need to return themselves. The production manager or coordinator should also remain on for a week or so of wrap to close out vendor accounts, finalize vendor and SAG paperwork, facilitate getting deposits back, coordinate returns, organize and store paperwork and materials for the production company, and secure final numbers from vendors so that you can actualize the budget through the production period and know how much money is available for postproduction. A few department heads may need several days to wrap out their respective departments; paperwork, equipment returns, petty cash envelopes, continuity notebooks, and so on must be completed and turned in to the office.

Checklist for the Last Week of Production

The following items must be dealt with in the last week of production with an eye toward wrapping:

- Make sure that the postproduction supervisor is on board.
- Compile return lists for equipment, vehicles, and expendables.
- Coordinate and organize pickup days and second-unit filming.
- Organize vendor and SAG paperwork.
- Complete the crew credit list; make sure all crew members have signed off on it.
- Close out vendor accounts; collect final paperwork and numbers from vendors.
- Collect outstanding petty cash envelopes from the crew as appropriate.
- Organize the wrap party.
- Send thank-you notes and gifts.

Postproduction Supervision. During the last week of production, start scheduling the film's postproduction needs. The producer (or line producer) may have already secured some initial bids on items needed to complete the film, such as ADR, foley, mixing, festival deadlines, and so on.

As discussed in Chapter 6, if you can afford a postproduction supervisor, it is advisable that you hire one, even if just for the initial few weeks of postproduction. During the first few weeks of postproduction, you will have to continue handling the final wrap of production. The timing of events during the editing process is very important. Deadlines must be met, and it is important that the elements be properly planned and carefully organized. The supervisor's familiarity with the requirements of postproduction will save you time and money. It is possible, however, to navigate through postproduction on your own if the budget does not allow for a postproduction supervisor. (See Chapter 9.)

Wrap Party. If the budget can't sustain a blowout wrap party for the cast and crew, come up with a creative way to celebrate finishing the show and to thank the cast and crew for their hard work and dedication. Whether it is a dinner at someone's house, a party, or a gathering at a local bar (a no-host bar, if necessary), it is important to show the cast and crew how much you appreciate them. You may want to invite the cast and crew to screen dailies to see how all of their hard work has paid off.

On *Swingers,* we couldn't afford a wrap party, but we did invite the cast and crew for cocktails and dailies. When we sold the film, we had a "deferral" party and handed out deferral checks.

WRAPPING OUT PRODUCTION

Officially, the line producer's job ends when all of the production's loose ends are wrapped up. With your low-budget film, the division of labor may not be as clearly delineated as it is here; you may be the postproduction supervisor or the producer as well as the line producer.

As the line producer, you will oversee the return of equipment, close out paperwork, finalize cast and crew payroll, complete and file SAG paperwork, close vendor accounts and secure final numbers, collect production and continuity notebooks, and actualize the budget. Wrapping out the show should take no more than two weeks, but you may not receive final numbers, paperwork, and deposits back from vendors for a few weeks after you have wrapped. The budget must be actualized as the final numbers and deposits come in. This is the time to be sure that all paperwork, contracts, and forms are in order and properly filed. They may have to be delivered to a distributor later.

Final Wrap-out Checklist

You will have to handle the following items when wrapping out the show:

- Shoot inserts and pickups if necessary.
- Return equipment, expendables, and materials.
- Return all production trucks, rental cars, and picture vehicles.
- Store any purchased equipment, props, and materials in a storage facility.
- Close out vendor accounts and secure final numbers.
- Close out and code petty cash envelopes; actualize the budget.
- Finalize cast and crew payroll.
- Complete and file vendor paperwork.
- Check the festival deadlines; make VHS dubs of the film for festival prescreenings and use.
- Give the script supervisor's notes and continuity notebook to the editor.
- Select still photos to be printed from the still photographer's contact sheets for festival usage and publicity.
- Give the editor petty cash for supplies and food.
- Collect the continuity notebooks from the various departments; give them to the production company.
- Complete the production notebooks with production forms and SAG forms; give them to the production company.
- Finalize SAG paperwork that must be completed at the end of the show and send it to SAG; get the bond back once the cast payroll has been completed.
- Get deposits back from vendors.
- Pick up from the lab any leftover film stock or videotape; sell back excess film stock and videotape to vendors.
- Make sure that the editor has everything from the lab and all of the necessary equipment.
- Return cores, bags, and cans to the lab.
- Cancel phone and fax lines that are no longer needed.
- Return rented or borrowed office equipment and furniture.
- Actualize the budget through the production period.
- Send final thank-you notes.

About the Wrap-out Checklist

Returns to Vendors. Returning rentals to vendors on time is essential to keeping your costs down because, most likely, you will be charged for every day beyond the expected return date. If you have your pickup and return lists in order, the process should be fairly painless. Check in with all department heads and make sure that they are conducting their own returns; ask if they need assistance. It may be less expensive to have a production assistant return art department materials, for example, than to have art department personnel do the returns themselves. On the other hand, it may be more efficient for each department to do its own returns because department members know which equipment is from which vendor.

Make sure that when the production truck is loaded, consideration is given to the order in which the equipment will be unloaded. That is, the first item to be returned should be the last item loaded on the truck. Otherwise, whoever is returning the equipment is going to have a horrible time when he or she arrives at a vendor and must find equipment buried toward the front of the truck.

Whenever a return is made, the vendor must provide paperwork confirming receipt of the returned items, a list of any items that are damaged or missing, a deposit check if one was issued, and a final invoice. If necessary, the person making the return should ask that the final invoice be faxed to the production office as soon as possible and that a hard copy be sent through the mail. Always attach a hard copy of the final invoice to the purchase order to which it belongs, and file it.

Closing Out Production Accounts. If you have the funds in your production account to pay bills directly, issue checks to close out production accounts as soon as possible after receiving the final invoices. Most vendors expect payment on a net-30 cycle (within 30 days), so it is not essential that bills be paid right away. However, if you're trying to wrap out a production, the sooner bills are paid, the sooner you will be officially wrapped and able to actualize your budget. Vendors sometimes issue the deposit upon return of the equipment, but more often they keep the deposit until the final payment has been made. If you're working with a large company that has an accounting department, hand over all of your purchase orders with the final invoices attached, and the accounting department will facilitate payment to the necessary parties.

9 POSTPRODUCTION

Postproduction is more expensive than most filmmakers realize. I would say that if somebody had a choice of having enough money to get the movie in the can, but they're going to have to spend a lot more time trying to raise the rest of the money, so should I wait, or should I go? . . . I think most people are going to say, "Let's go." And whether that's right or wrong, I think that's an impulse to not wait until all the moons are perfectly aligned because they could get into a situation where they could never [be].

—Peter Broderick, Next Wave Films

ORGANIZING THE FILM'S POSTPRODUCTION NEEDS

Often, if a postproduction supervisor has not been hired, the line producer remains on board throughout postproduction. Depending on your relationship with the show, you may be involved in organizing the film's postproduction needs. If you have remained on board as the line producer, begin determining the postproduction needs of the show during the initial weeks of postproduction, if not sooner. If you have a postproduction supervisor, he or she will be able to help you arrange the scheduling of all elements at the appropriate time during the editing process.

Postproduction Checklist

The following items must be handled during postproduction:

- Create a tentative postproduction schedule with preliminary deadlines (editor's assembly, director's cut, sound mix, music meetings, color timing, festival deadlines, ADR, foley, titles and opticals, final answer print, screenings, and so on).
- Hire the music supervisor and composers.
- Map out festival deadlines.
- Meet with publicists.
- Schedule ADR.
- Schedule foley.
- Arrange for titles and opticals.
- Schedule sound mix.
- Assemble press kits (should include still photos, synopsis, bios, and so on).

- Arrange for the MPAA rating, a title/research clearance report, and E&O insurance.

EDITING

As the line producer, your role during postproduction is as the postproduction supervisor, which essentially means pulling together and organizing all of the necessary elements of post in a timely and affordable way. The producers, the director, and the editor will confer during the first week of post and discuss the film's postproduction schedule. A calendar of important dates, such as festival deadlines, director's cut, screenings, ADR, foley, and mix dates, will be compiled. Most likely, there will be deadlines to meet, and being organized and meeting those deadlines will help you remain on budget.

TIPS FOR POSTPRODUCTION

The trick during postproduction is to be as organized, efficient, and thorough as possible without rushing or compromising the film. It is costly and time-consuming to have to reschedule any of the postproduction events. Here are some creative ideas and tips on dealing with a few postproduction needs.

Automated Dialogue Replacement (ADR—Looping)

If possible, schedule just one session of ADR if the actors are available. Only ask actors to come in and record ADR if it is absolutely necessary for a scene. Recording ADR on a stage is expensive, but it may be the best option if there are several days of ADR and several actors to record. Investigate your options carefully.

On *Swingers,* we spent two days recording ADR in the producer's living room. Our ADR needs were few because our production tracks were relatively clean. Because our resources were limited, this was the most viable option. We compiled a list of all of the lines we needed to rerecord and all of the additional lines we needed from each actor, and we scheduled ADR within a two-day period. We cued the dailies to the relevant scene so that the actors could sync their lines while viewing the scene. Our sound mixer was equipped with the necessary sound equipment and microphones, and he cued the actors with their lines at the beginning of each take.

Sound Mix

On *Swingers,* because we cut on an Avid system, we were able to do a temp mix, which not only saved us time and money required for a temp mix in a studio, but also saved us time and money on our final mix because we were as ready as we could have been. All the elements—dialogue, music, and effects—were premixed; the levels just needed to be adjusted in the final mix.

Titles and Opticals

Titles can be expensive; it depends on how long the end credit crawl is on the film, how many single cards will be run in both the main and the end titles, and how elaborate the credit sequence is. On *Swingers,* we compiled our main and end title credits exactly as we wanted them to run on the film, printed them from a computer (we installed the fonts we wanted onto our computer), and then photographed them. This saved us a tremendous amount of money compared with having a title house create, photograph, and then print the credits, and then have them processed at a lab for an additional cost.

Music

While assembling the film, the director and the editor will set various songs and pieces of music to the film to establish which choices best suit the story and set the mood. If you are cutting on an Avid system, sync the music to the picture—at least temporarily.

A music supervisor is an extremely worthwhile investment if you plan to use licensed music rather than an original score; he or she can assist you with music licensing, publishing rights and fees, and festival licenses if needed. If your budget is too limited, seek help from people who have some expertise in this field, and refer to guidebooks to help you navigate through the film's music needs.

The music supervisor's job is multifaceted. He or she suggests songs, score, source cues, and a composer, and arranges for recording facilities for any score that is composed for the film. If the film will be playing at festivals, festival master use and synchronization licenses must be secured for any music used in the film. Unless it is an original score, festival licenses are generally inexpensive and negotiable (sometimes free) and far more affordable than broad distribution master use licenses and sync fees. While the music supervisor is negotiating and securing the festival rights to songs, he or she will also be securing quotes on broad distribution rights. If the film secures distribution, the distributor will want to know how much it will cost to purchase the rights to the music in the film. Often, songs that you may want to use are not affordable. A music supervisor who is familiar with securing rights and licenses and negotiating fees will help you find songs that are within the film's price range and still work for the film.

A music supervisor can also assist in attracting the interest of music labels that might want to package the film's sound track. Having a label involved or interested can be advantageous because the label can help pay for some of the music in the film and may want to put some of its songs or artists on the sound track and in the film at no cost to you. Having a label interested in packaging and releasing the sound track can be an attractive selling point with a distributor.

BEFORE YOU LOCK THE PICTURE

What we provide to a filmmaker, beyond the actual cash we can give them for finishing funds, is in many cases more important than the money. We'll give a filmmaker feedback; in fact, we'll give filmmakers feedback even if we aren't able to invest. And since the movie isn't done, they might be able to utilize some of that information or perspective. We're not involved in the project, we're not involved with the friends and family, we look at it and tell them what we think. We can tell them what the strengths are and what are some of the reservations that we have.

—*Peter Broderick, Next Wave Films*

If the line producer is still involved just before the picture is locked, it is most likely as postproduction supervisor or because he or she is the producer of the film. For the director, there is a distinct line between maintaining auteurship of the film while considering the opinions of others and relinquishing creative control to accommodate the whims of audiences and other people who may not know what's best. The time just before your picture is locked is crucial because the director's decisions during this period ultimately shape the movie. When you have been through the editing process multiple times, it becomes evident that the director and the editor could cut the footage together three or four ways, resulting in three or four different films. Certainly, not all of these options will work, but it is hoped that one of them does.

For example, in an early cut of *Swingers,* there was very little of Vince Vaughn's performance. This would not have been a favorable version of the film. In fact, almost all of us involved in the film at that point were disappointed when we viewed that cut of the film. Fortunately, the team knew that there was a film to be unearthed in the coverage they'd seen in the dailies. Further input came several times, closer to locking the picture, when several of the team members' agents viewed the film. Had the film not been working, we would have cast our net slightly wider and solicited advice from elsewhere.

There are professionals who consider themselves independent film specialists and who have watched hundreds of cuts of independent films and given advice at this crucial point. In many instances, this advice enabled the films to become movies that could really play to an audience, as opposed to a film that only plays to you, your friends, the cast, and the crew (see the Peter Broderick interview on the enclosed CD-ROM).

The period just before the picture is locked is your final chance to make changes. You may be too myopic at this point in the project to be able to tell how the film is playing and what could and should be changed. Don't assume that to ask the advice of others is to give up your creative control or

vision. Filmmaking is a collaborative process, and this an important time to listen to the advice and opinions of others. Seek the opinion of trusted outsiders before you lock the picture and cut your negative.

MOVING TOWARD A COMPLETED FILM: LOCKING THE PICTURE

The final weeks of postproduction will be spent locking the picture. Final changes will be made, the final sound mix will be completed, the color-corrected prints of the film will be struck, and video copies of the locked picture will be made. If you are no longer the line producer but are now the post supervisor, this is the time to make sure that everything is in order and accounted for. Following are the tasks that may need to be accomplished.

Once the picture is locked, arrange for the negative to be sent from the lab to a film vault. Both the A- and B-roll negatives must be safely and properly stored in a climate-controlled film vault, along with the sound rolls. If you can't afford a film vault, make space in a cool, dark, dry closet. Make sure the dailies, the continuity notebook, and the editor's notes are in a safe place (you'll need to refer to them if you find a distributor and have to go back and make changes to the picture), along with any other equipment and materials that belong to the production.

During the final weeks of postproduction, the producers and the post supervisor will begin to wrap out the show completely. If you haven't had time to complete and file paperwork, now is the time to do so. Clearly label files and organize them so that paperwork can be easily found later. If the production office will be shut down after postproduction, arrange for a safe place to store all of the files and any office equipment that belongs to the production. Usually, all of the show's paperwork belongs to the entity that made the film. As the producer or the line producer, you may want to keep copies of some files or paperwork for your own records.

Once all accounts have been closed, all equipment and materials have been stored, and all bills have been paid, actualize the budget. There may be a few outstanding final numbers, but you will most likely be able to actualize the budget in its entirety. If you have remained on the show through postproduction, part of your job is to provide the production with the final accounting of the show. (See "Actualizing the Budget" in Chapter 8.)

FESTIVALS

Get the submission dates for festivals to which the film may be submitted. Most festivals provide information on their web sites about the festival and application deadlines, and some have applications that can either be downloaded off the Web or requested via e-mail. Compile a list of festival deadline dates, and identify the festivals to apply to based on the estimated date for completing postproduction.

When thinking about festivals, be realistic about the film and its audience. The film may not be a festival film or appropriate for certain festivals. Although some films don't belong on the festival circuit, for others, festivals may be the only appropriate venue. It can be difficult to maintain your perspective on something you are close to, so seeking the advice of others can be invaluable. There is a great deal to be learned about filmmaking, distribution, publicity, and so on, at festivals. They can be supportive and exciting, and the connections made there often can further careers. There are, however, other ways to promote a film and attract distributors. Give some careful thought to how your film will best be served.

Depending on which festivals the film is being submitted to and what the requirements are, prints may need to be struck or 1/2-inch video copies of the film made. Check deadlines and read applications and the submission requirements carefully. Be prepared to send a check so that the application can be processed. When submitting an application you may also be required to provide still photos of the actors, bios of the filmmakers and key cast, and a synopsis of the film—most of the elements included in a press kit. Distributors see many films when traveling the festival circuit, and an attractive, informative, and organized press kit may help distributors distinguish your film from the rest.

The producer and the director should prepare a strategy in the event the film is accepted to a festival. Here are a few important questions to address when planning the film's festival strategy:

- What is the goal for the film?
- Which distributors should see the film?
- Does anyone in the core filmmaking team know any of those distributors personally, or does anyone know someone who does? In other words, who can make a call on the film's behalf and ask that a distributor see the film?
- Should a publicist be hired to help promote the film at the festival before securing distribution?
- What type of deal do the filmmakers want?
- Who in the core filmmaking team is savvy enough to discuss and negotiate a deal, or should a producer's rep be engaged?

SCREENINGS

Regardless of whether the film will be submitted to any festivals, a screening for agents, filmmakers, or publicists can be helpful in generating some positive word-of-mouth about the film in the filmmaking community. A positive "buzz" about the film will work to its advantage. It is one of the best ways to attract the interest of distributors and to make sure that they attend screenings of the film, whether at festivals or at a distribution screening.

A well-thought-out strategy is essential, and as the line producer, you may be asked to help organize any special screenings. Here are a few things to keep in mind. Does anyone from the key team of filmmakers know any agents or other filmmakers who have useful contacts? Might these contacts be willing to attend a screening of the film? Compile a list of distributors to invite to the screening. Choose distributors who you think would respond favorably to the film and would best market and promote it.

The scheduling of the distribution screening is also important. Do not schedule a screening on a night when there are other screenings or premieres that distributors may be attending. Don't organize a distribution screening during any major festivals. Most distributors will be attending the festivals and won't be able to attend your screening. Unless you want to organize individual screenings for distributors (which can be costly and time-consuming) or make video copies of the film to send to distributors, the distribution screening will most likely be a one-shot deal, so do it right.

When organizing a distribution screening, have invitations, postcards, or fliers sent to distributors either via mail or fax. Mail or fax invitations at least two weeks before the scheduled screening. Include pertinent information on the invitation, including an RSVP phone number. Compile a list of people who plan to attend the screening as they respond.

Have press kits made up to give to distributors at the screening. Have a poster created for the film to hang at the theater. Even with limited means, there are a fair number of affordable options for creating a poster (you might make your own) and other graphically appealing support materials for the film. Make sure that the venue for the screening is accessible and affordable, that it can accommodate the number of people invited, and that ample parking is available.

Designate someone to stand by the door and check the names of attendees as they arrive. This is important; it will tell the producer(s) who saw the film so they can follow up. Someone should be available to speak with the distributors after the screening; if necessary, hire a representative to speak on the film's behalf.

If there is too little money left for two separate screenings, you may want to invite the cast and crew to attend the distribution screening. By combining the screenings, both needs are satisfied; distributors will see the film, and so will the cast and crew. Mixing these two audiences has a further advantage: The cast and crew will be an extremely "friendly" audience and will provide a beneficial atmosphere for the agents, distributors, and others at the screening.

IF YOU DON'T GET A DISTRIBUTOR

If you don't get a distributor, you have a couple of options. Self-distribution is a tough row to hoe, but it may be worth the effort to get your film out to the world. Most likely, self-distribution will mean semi- or nontheatrical bookings, as opposed to real theatrical bookings. In today's market, it may be close to impossible to self-distribute a theatrical release. (We don't like to say that anything is *impossible,* but this may well be pretty close to it.) Because the marketplace is so glutted with films, it can even be difficult for the smaller distributors to get their slate of films booked in theaters. The mini-majors have more money to spend on their print-and-advertising budgets and can provide the exhibitor with a steadier flow of material. The larger distributors have the most bargaining power with the theaters. However, if your film has had a successful run on the festival circuit, it is possible to book it at universities, colleges, museums, and organizations that have a particular interest in your film.

Another option is to self-distribute your film on video. This is probably easier than self-distributing screened viewings; you can access underground video rental stores all over the United States. Further, depending on the film, you may be able to make some sales to television, both domestic and foreign. If you have no contacts in this area, it is worth your while to commission a foreign sales agent or producer's representative to assist you with such sales. Although sales of independent films to foreign television are not as lucrative or widespread as they were in the early 1990s, this is still a feasible option, and it is a way for your film to be seen and possibly to recoup its costs, if only just a little. Often, the fees for television sales are negotiated on a per-minute basis. (See the resource guide at the back of this book for more on this subject.)

10 A FINAL WORD

If you want to make a movie and you have a dream, you do whatever you can to get it made. And if you have that kind of perseverance, the films will ring true because they are such an honest effort. It becomes a part of your life. If you follow through, usually those kind of films are the ones that surprise people out of left field. And you can look at Slacker *or* Crumb, In the Company of Men, *as just a few. Movies like* Safe, Welcome to the Dollhouse, *all of these people put these movies together on shoestrings and had tremendous success and launched careers. But it was probably the worst nightmare of their lives getting the money for the movies. It seemed to make the filmmaking even better because they had to be more creative.*

—*Tom Bernard, president, Sony Pictures Classics*

BREATHE—IT'S OVER

If you've completed your film, that is a huge feat. Don't underestimate what you have done. Now, grow thick skin, and do it quickly. No matter what your film is, there will be those who like it and those who do not. It is important to try to have some perspective on what you've done and to maintain an inner sense of accomplishment despite what may become of the project and despite what others' opinions about it may be. Opinions are just that.

It is hoped that your goals for the film, whatever they may be, will be realized. But if they aren't, assess what is realistic for the project (Lock a video deal? Make a cable television sale?), and move on to your next film. There is never any guarantee as to how a film will turn out. It is essential that we learn from the process and enjoy the journey. Focusing too much on results can lead to disappointment. Ideally, we continue to grow and learn as filmmakers and as people with each film we make, and from each film we gain perspective, insight, experience, and a sense of accomplishment.

RELIEVE SOME STRESS

All you can talk about is the movie. The movie, the movie, the movie . . .

—*Jon Favreau,* Swingers

Need a break? If you're feeling stressed out and in need of a break from whatever chaos you're in the midst of, you may enjoy reading a couple letters that came through the *Swingers* production office.

Both letters are from Joan Favreau, Jon's grandmother, who played the Blue-Haired Lady at the $5 table in Las Vegas. Her participation in the film warmed all of our hearts. The first letter is one she sent to us right after production (Figure 10–1), and the other letter followed the *Swingers* premiere, which she traveled from Queens, New York, to Los Angeles to attend (Figure 10–2).

September 23, 1995

I was indeed surprised and actually thrilled to be asked to do a small part in Jonathan's movie. My son Charles, hearing this, immediately obtained a round-trip ticket to Las Vegas. On Tuesday, Charles drove me to the airport, but before we arrived he made a stop at an old-fashioned ice cream parlor. He ordered my favorite ice cream, topped with nuts and whipped cream. I enjoyed the surprise treat, and off we went to the airport. We arrived in plenty of time. Charles chatted with me and then wished me a pleasant trip.

The air trip was pleasant. I ordered a gin and tonic, making the flying trip a lark. Upon my arrival in Las Vegas, a handsome young man with windblown hair called out, "Joan Favreau!" as he was walking down the ramp towards me. I, with such relief, waved back at him and smiled. He introduced himself as Wally, and he tenderly took my hand and walked me through the terminal.

Outside the terminal was a cute red car with a stunning young lady called Nicole, who greeted me with a warm embrace. I knew right then and there this was going to be a great stint. They drove me through the Vegas strip, describing the large hotels and huge display of lights.

Upon arriving at the casino, the crew was having their evening meal. At my entrance, they all greeted me simultaneously, "Hi, Grandma Favreau!" I felt a warm and friendly feeling. Standing there was my grandson Jonathan, handsome and full of enthusiasm. He walked over to me after the crew gave me that warm welcome, and he hugged me tenderly. They immediately fed me and told me I was to do my scene in about an hour.

Being well fed, I was turned over to the makeup man. I told him to make me beautiful. He tried. The wardrobe person dressed me in a lovely lavender-color suit. She then tied a white chiffon scarf around my neck, giving the entire outfit a smart look.

Not knowing much about the movie, Jon had a young man coach me. He coached me well. The scene was well done. The crew stood up clapping loudly and reassured me again and again. The cast continued shooting other scenes through the night.

What a delightful crew. All young, good looking, and willing to work hard. What amazed me most was the support and loyalty they have for Jon. I noticed just the reason: communication.

The next day was my big scene. We rehearsed over and over again at the blackjack table. At last, it was cast and done well. It truly was a joy doing that scene. The participants were a jolly group. We laughed and joked about Jon and Vince's part in the scene. It got so that each one had a story or an incident to tell. I pitched in, too.

Thursday was my free day. Jon made sure he left time from his busy schedule to take me to the famous strip. He called a cab, and we left for the sights on the strip. We arrived and walked along, looking in amazement at the bright lights, brilliant marquees, and signboards. To make the tour complete, we entered Caesar's Palace. It was magnificent. I thought I was back in Italy. The statues, the fountains, the boutiques, the blue-clouded moving ceiling—I was in awe of the grandeur of this superstructure. To complete this lovely visit to the strip, Jon ordered dinner. We sat under the lovely blue sky and in full view of the magnificent sights. Jon ordered an Italian meal for us, which was the typical order for the day. We ate and enjoyed. We now had to return to the hotel, where the crew was waiting for Jon for a scheduled scene. His crew reminds me of the Energizer Bunny. It keeps going, and going, and going . . .

I was now on my own. I gambled a bit, then remembered that I had a 6:30 A.M. plane flight. It was now 11:30 P.M., and a knock came at the door. I slipped on my robe and opened the door. It was one of the crewmen inviting me to join them in the room opposite my room. I went in and was served cake and a Coke. I watched them work. It was 3:30 A.M. when I realized I had to get to bed, but it was too late.

The wake-up call came through, so I dressed in a hurry. I met Wally and Nicole at the main desk. Nicole handed me a large container of orange juice, which I drank on my way to the airport. I said my good-bye to Nicole. Wally affectionately took my hand and again walked me through the terminal. He sat me down at my proper spot and kissed me good-bye.

It was a delightful trip back. At the end of the Kennedy terminal was my son Charles. He embraced me tenderly and was anxious to sit me down in the car and turn me on. I spoke the entire trip home, never stopping to take a breath, and my son Charles loved every moment of it.

Later the next day, I missed Jonathan's telephone call, but the tape said it all. He was pleased with my performance, concerned about the long and tiring trip home, and told me he loves me. I really was touched by his affection for me.

Love,

Grandma Favs

Figure 10–1   First letter from Joan Favreau

Swingers (The Premier)

March 21, 1996

Hi!!

When Charles and I stepped out of the car we noticed long lines of young and old people waiting to get into the theater. Never for one moment did we think they were waiting to see "SWINGERS". The theater was large. It soon was filled to capacity. Seated at least 1,000 and soon standing room only. We were escorted to our reserved seats. I felt a bit important. We met Nicole, she looked stunning with her new hairdo and her leather outfit. We also met with Cary Woods, the Producer and many others.

Soon the lights dimmed and all went silent. On the huge screen appeared MIRAMAX. It was very impressive. Then the opening credits. When JON FAVREAU'S name flashed alone on the big screen, his name seemed larger than life itself. My son Charles squeezed my hand which he was holding at the time. I was so moved for I knew I was surely blessed.

As the movie opened, the music was perfect. It was loud and a catching tune setting the audience up for a fun show. MIKE, who was Jonathan, did a remarkable performance. He was a down-hearted young man raking the audience feel his pain. MIKE was a jilted lover. His friends tried very hard thruout the movie to change his moody attitude to a "Happy go lucky guy". They were so overly concerned that it made MIKE irritable thruout the picture.

Trent, a handsome young man did a superb job of acting, specially his torrid love scene. At the height of one of the love scenes, MIKE was so desperate he wanted to make a phone call to see if his loved one had a kind word. He knocked at the very door that a heated love making was going on. TRENT opened the door, partly naked and threw a condom out to MIKE thinking he too was in a heated situation. The audience went wild. It was also a good laugh when the four cars followed one another after an unsuccessful evening with dames at the bars. We did laugh when MIKE went to the answering message machine to get repeated responses that continued to drive him mad. The audience loved him in that scene. No news for MIKE was not easy to live with. That gun scene was a bit frightening but it was done well.

As for my small part in the movie, I sure was no raving beauty but I can assure you my lavender suit looked great.

When MIKE finally made out with some dame and did some fast stepping on the dance floor, his friends and the audience cheered. Finally they saw a bright spark in the life of their friend. They now knew their job was well done. MIKE was back in the fold and ready to start living it up again.

I enjoyed,

Grandma

Figure 10–2   Second letter from Joan Favreau

RESOURCE GUIDE

REFERENCE BOOKS

Handbooks and Manuals

Carroll, Bonnie. *The Reel Directory: Northern California Guide to Film, Video, Multimedia.* Catati, CA.

Honthaner, Eve Light. *The Complete Film Production Handbook.* Boston: Focal Press, 1997.

Mackaman, Julie. *Filmmaker's Resource.* Watson-Guptill, 1997.

A guide to workshops, conferences, artist's colonies, and academic programs.

LA 411 Resource Guide. Professional reference guide by LA411.

MPE Hand Guide. Semi-Annual.

A semi-annual motion picture, TV, and theater directory.

NYPG Handbook. New York: NYPG, Ltd.

Production Support Manuals

Litwak, Mark. *Contracts for the Film and Television Industry.* Beverly Hills, CA: Silman-James Press, 1994.

Contains 40 useful contracts for producers that cover all areas of film and television production.

Litwak, Mark. *Dealmaking in the Film and Television Industry.* Beverly Hills, CA:, Silman-James Press, 1994.

Covers everything from negotiations to final contracts.

Singleton, Ralph S. *Film Budgeting.* Los Angeles: Lone Eagle Publishing, 1996.

Levison, Louise. *Filmmakers and Financing: Business Plans for Independents.* Boston: Focal Press, 1998.

Singleton, Ralph S. *Film Scheduling.* Los Angeles: Lone Eagle Publishing, 1984.

Singleton, Ralph S. *Film Scheduling/Film Budgeting Workbook.* Los Angeles: Lone Eagle Publishing, 1984.

Singleton, Ralph S. *Movie Production and Budget Forms . . . Instantly!* Los Angeles: Lone Eagle Publishing, 1985.

Screenplay Systems: Movie Magic Budgeting and Scheduling Reference Guides. Burbank, CA: Screenplay Systems, Inc., 1993.

Festivals

Langer, Adam. *The Film Festival Guide.* Chicago: Chicago Review Press, 1998.

A guidebook for filmmakers, film buffs, and industry professionals. Includes the background of each festival and what premiered there, how to submit films, interviews with festival directors, and top ten festivals.

Gaydos, Steven. *The Variety Guide to Film Festivals.* New York: Pengee Books, 1998.

The ultimate insider's guide to film festivals around the world. Tells where to go, how to enter, and whom to call and discusses the stars, the screenings, the parties, the filmmakers, the star makers, and the deal brokers.

Bowser, Kathryn. *AVIF Guide to International Film and Video Festivals.* Published through the support of the National Endowment for the Arts Challenge Grant Program, Canada, 1996.

Distribution

AFMA Member Profile. Annual.

Yearly report on member acquisition, production, and development.

Hollywood Creative Directory. Santa Monica, CA: American Film Marketing Association, Annual.

Hollywood Distributors Directory. Annual.

Covers more than 575 companies, including domestic distribution companies and foreign sales agents; includes more than 2,400 names and titles; and discusses cable channels, marketing, publicity, merchandising, and acquisitions.

Mookis, Ioannis. *Self-Distribution Handbook.* New York: AIVS, 1999.

Legal

Donaldson, Michael. *Clearance and Copyright.* Beverly Hills, CA: Silman-James Press, 1996.

Litwak, Mark. *Contacts for the Film and Television Industry.* Los Angeles: Silman-James Press, 1994.

SUPPORT ORGANIZATIONS

Academy of Motion Picture Arts and Sciences
8949 Wilshire Blvd.
Beverly Hills, CA 90211
Phone: 310/247-3000
Fax: 310/859-9619

American Cinemathéque
1800 N. Highland Ave., #717
Los Angeles, CA 90028
Phone: 323/466-3456, ext. 117
Fax: 323/461-9737
E-mail: amcin@msn.com
Website: www.americancinematheque.com

American Film Marketing Association (AFMA)
10850 Wilshire Blvd., 9th Floor
Los Angeles, CA 90024
Phone: 310/446-1000
Fax: 310/446-1600
E-mail: info@afma.com
Website: www.afma.com

Anthology Film Archives
32 Second Ave.
New York, NY 10003
Phone: 212/505-5181
Fax: 212/477-2714

Association of Independent Video and Filmmakers (AIVF)/
Foundation of Independent Video and Filmmakers (FIVF)
304 Hudson St., 6th Floor
New York, NY 10013
Phone: 212/807-1400
Fax: 212/463- 8519
E-mail: info@aivf.org
Website: www.aivf.org

California Lawyers for the Arts
1641 18th St.
Santa Monica, CA 90404
Phone: 310/998-5590
Fax: 310/998-5594

Film Forum
209 W. Houston St.
New York, NY 10014
Phone: 212/627-2035
Fax: 212/627-2471
E-mail: filmforum@aol.com
Website: www.filmforum.com

Film/Video Arts
817 Broadway, 2nd Floor
New York, NY 10003
Phone: 212/673-9361
Fax: 212/475-3467

Hudson Valley Film and Video Office
40 Garden St., 2nd Floor
Poughkeepsie, NY 12601
Phone: 914/473-0318
Fax: 914/473-0082

Image Film/Video
Bennett St. NW, #N1
Atlanta, GA 30309
Phone: 404/352-4225
Fax: 404/352-0173

Independent Documentary Association
1551 S. Robertson Blvd., #201
Los Angeles, CA 90035-4257
Phone: 310/284-8422
Fax: 310/785-9334
E-mail: ida@artnet.net
Website: www.documentary.org

Independent Feature Project
104 W. 29th St., 12th Floor
New York, NY 10001
Phone: 212/465-8200
Fax: 212/465-8525
E-mail: IFPNY@ifp.org
Website: www.ifp.org

Independent Feature Project (IFP)/Midwest
1803 W. Byron, #1E
Chicago, IL 60613
Phone: 773/281-5177
Fax: 773/281-5178

Independent Feature Project (IFP)/North
401 N. Third St., #490
Minneapolis, MN 55401
Phone: 612/338-0817
Fax: 612/338-4747

Independent Feature Project (IFP)/South
PO Box 145246
Coral Gables, FL 33114
Phone: 305/461-3544
Fax: 305/446-5168

Independent Feature Project (IFP)/West
1964 Westwood Blvd., #205
Los Angeles, CA 90025
Phone: 310/475-4379
Fax: 310/441-5676

Independent Television Service (ITVS)
51 Federal St., #401
San Francisco, CA 94107
Phone: 415/356-8383
Fax: 415/356-8391
E-mail: itvs@itvs.org
Website: www.itvs.org

Jerome Foundation
400 Sibley St., #125
Saint Paul, MN 55101
Phone: 612/224-9431
Fax: 612/224-3439
E-mail: rbyrd@jerometdn.org
Website: jerometdn.org

Montage Entertainment, Inc.
60 W. 57th St.
New York, NY 10019
Phone: 212/245-9477
Fax: 212/245-9477
E-mail: jstone@montage.org
Website: www.montage.org

National Association of Musicians and Composers
    (NAMAC)
346 Ninth St.
San Francisco, CA 94103
Phone: 415/431-1391
Fax: 415/431-1392
E-mail: namac@namac.org
Website: www.namac.org

National Video Resources, Inc.
73 Spring St., #606
New York, NY 10012
Phone: 212/274-8080
Fax: 212/274-8081
E-mail: NVRInfo@nvr.org
Website: www.nvr.org

New York Foundation for the Arts
155 Ave. of the Americas, 14th Floor
New York, NY 10013
Phone: 212/366-6900
Fax: 212/366-1778
E-mail: sponsor@artswire.org
Website: www.nyfa.org

Public Broadcasting Service
1320 Braddock Pl.
Alexandria, VA 22314
Phone: 703/739-5000
Fax: 703/739-0775
Website: www.pbs.org

The Reel School
29 Greene St.
New York, NY 10013
Phone: 212/965-9444, ext. 240
Fax: 212/965-9520
E-mail: reelschool@filmmakers.org
Website: filmmakers.org/school.htm

Sundance Institute
225 Santa Monica Blvd., 8th Floor
Santa Monica, CA 90401
Phone: 310/394-4662
Fax: 310/394-8353

Guilds and Unions

American Federation of Television and Radio Artists
5757 Wilshire Blvd., 9th Floor
Hollywood, CA 90036
Phone: 323/634-8100

American Film Institute (AFI)
2021 N. Western Ave.
Los Angeles, CA 90027
Phone: 323/856-7600
Fax: 323/856-7778
Website: www.afionline.org

Directors Guild of America, Inc.
7920 Sunset Blvd.
Los Angeles, CA 90046
Phone: 310/289-2000
Fax: 310/289-2029
Website: www.dga.org

Screen Actors Guild (Los Angeles)
5757 Wilshire Blvd.
Los Angeles, CA 90036
Phone: 323/954-1600
Fax: 323/549-6656
Website: www.sag.com

Screen Actors Guild (New York)
1515 Broadway, 44th Floor
New York, NY 10036
Phone: 212/944-1030
Fax: 212/944-6774

Writers Guild of America East, Inc.
555 W. 57th St.
New York, NY 10019
Phone: 212/767-7800
Fax: 212/582-1909

Writers Guild of America West, Inc.
7000 W. Third Street
Los Angeles, CA 90048
Phone: 323/951-4000
Fax: 323/782-4800
Website: www.wga.org

U.S. DISTRIBUTORS

Angelika Entertainment Corp.
1261 Madison Ave.
New York, NY 10128
Phone: 212/996-8215
Fax: 212/876-4365
Website: www.angelikafilm.com

Anthology Film Archives
32 Second Ave.
New York, NY 10003
Phone: 212/505-5181
Fax: 212/477-2714

Arrow Entertainment, Inc.
135 W. 50th St., #1925
New York, NY 10020
Phone: 212/258-2200
Fax: 212/245-1252
E-mail: arrow@arrowfilms.com
Website: www.arrowfilms.com

Artisan Entertainment
157 Chambers St., 12th Floor
New York, NY 10007
Phone: 212/577-2400
Fax: 212/577-2890

Artistic License Films
250 W. 57th St., #606
New York, NY 10107
Phone: 212/265-9119
Fax: 212/262-9299
E-mail: ArtLic@aol.com

The Cinema Guild, Inc.
1697 Broadway, #506
New York, NY 10019
Phone: 212/246-5522
Fax: 212/246-5525
E-mail: TheCinemaG@aol.com
Website: www.cinemaguild.com

Fine Line Features
888 Seventh Ave., 20th Floor
New York, NY 10106
Phone: 212/649-4800
Fax: 212/956-1942
Website: www.FLF.com

Fox Lorber Associates
419 Park Ave. S., 20th Floor
New York, NY 10016
Phone: 212/686-6777
Fax: 212/685-2625

Fox Searchlight Pictures (Los Angeles)
10201 W. Pico Blvd., Bldg. 38
Los Angeles, CA 90035
Phone: 310/369-4402
Fax: 310/369-2359

Fox Searchlight Pictures (New York)
1211 Ave. of the Americas, 16th Floor
New York, NY 10036
Phone: 212/556-8258
Fax: 212/556-8248

Gibbs Smith Publisher/Beecher Films
PO Box 667
Layton, VT 84041
Phone: 801/544-9800
Fax: 801/544-5582

Good Machine
417 Canal St., 4th Floor
New York, NY 10013
Phone: 212/343-9230
Fax: 212/343-9645

Gramercy Pictures (Los Angeles)
9333 Wilshire Blvd.
Beverly Hills, CA 90210
Phone: 310/385-4400
Fax: 310/385-4405
Website: www.polygram.com

Gramercy Pictures (New York)
825 Eighth Ave., 25th Floor
New York, NY 10019
Phone: 212/333-1431
Fax: 212/333-1420

IFM Film Associates, Inc.
1541 N. Gardner St.
Los Angeles, CA 90046
Phone: 323/874-4249
Fax: 323/874-2654
E-mail: ifmfilm@aol.com

Independent Pictures
42 Bond St.
New York, NY 10012
Phone: 212/226-2444
Fax: 212/625-1348

In Pictures
1024 12th St., #1
Santa Monica, CA 90403
Phone: 310/451-8722
Fax: 310/451-9722

Jacobs Entertainment, Inc.
48 E. 43rd St., 7th Floor
New York, NY 10017
Phone: 212/986-7488
Fax: 212/986-2524

LEO Films
6249 Langdon Ave.
Van Nuys, CA 91411
Phone: 213/666-7140
Fax: 213/666-7414
E-mail: lustgar@idt.net
Website: movies-online.com

Lions Gate Films, Inc.
561 Broadway, #12B
New York, NY 10012
Phone: 212/966-4670
Fax: 212/966-2544
Website: lionsgate-ent.com

Miramax Films (Los Angeles)
7966 Beverly Blvd.
Los Angeles, CA 90048
Phone: 323/951-4200
Fax: 323/845-4211

Miramax Films (New York)
375 Greenwich St.
New York, NY 10013
Phone: 212/941-3800
Fax: 212/941-3928

New Line Cinema (Los Angeles)
116 N. Robertson Blvd., #200
Los Angeles, CA 90048
Phone: 310/854-5811
Fax: 310/854-1824

New Line Cinema (New York)
888 Seventh Ave., 19th Floor
New York, NY 10106
Phone: 212/649-4900
Fax: 212/649-4966
Website: www.newline.com

October Films (Los Angeles)
9229 Sunset Blvd., #615
Los Angeles, CA 90069
Phone: 310/248-6222
Fax: 310/248-6226

October Films (New York)
65 Bleecker St., 2nd Floor
New York, NY 10012
Phone: 212/539-4000
Fax: 212/539-4099
Website: www.octoberfilms.com

Palm Pictures/Manga Entertainment
727 N. Hudson St., #100
Chicago, IL 60610
Phone: 312/751-0020
Fax: 312/751-2483
Website: www.islandlife.com

Panorama Entertainment Corp.
125 N. Main St.
Port Chester, NY 10573
Phone: 914/937-1603
Fax: 914/937-8496

Paramount Classics
5555 Melrose Ave.
Chevalier Bldg., #212
Hollywood, CA 90038
Phone: 323/956-2000
Fax: 323/862-1212

Phaedra Cinema
5455 Wilshire Blvd.
Los Angeles, CA 90036
Phone: 323/938-9610
Fax: 323/938-9731
Website: phaedracinema.com

Picture This! Entertainment
7471 Melrose Ave., #7
Los Angeles, CA 90046
Phone: 323/852-1398
Fax: 323/658-7265
E-mail: Gaypicture@aol.com
Website: www.PictureThisEnt.com

Raven Pictures International
1771 Post Rd. E., #134
Westport, CT 06880
Phone: 203/876-7630
Fax: 203/876-7631
E-mail: ravenpics@earthlink.net
Website: raven-pictures.com

Samuel Goldwyn Films, LLC (Los Angeles)
10203 Santa Monica Blvd.
Los Angeles, CA 90067
Phone: 310/284-9282
Fax: 310/284-8493

Samuel Goldwyn Films, LLC (New York)
560 W. 43rd St., #32E
New York, NY 10036
Phone: 212/594-3334
Fax: 212/268-9289
E-mail: bijou@ix.netcom.com

Seventh Art Releasing
7551 Sunset Blvd., #104
Los Angeles, CA 90046
Phone: 323/845-1455
Fax: 323/845-4717
E-mail: seventhart@earthlink.net
Website: www.seventhart.net

SoHo Entertainment, Inc.
105 Greene St.
New York, NY 10012
Phone: 212/431-3737
Fax: 212/431-3733
E-mail: HKsoho@aol.com
Website: www.sohoent.com

Sony Pictures Classics
550 Madison Ave., 8th Floor
New York, NY 10022
Phone: 212/833-8833
Fax: 212/833-8844
Website: www.spe.sony.com/classics

Strand Releasing
1460 Fourth St., #302
Santa Monica, CA 90401
Phone: 310/395-5002
Fax: 310/395-2502
E-mail: strand@strandrel.com
Website: www.strandrel.com

Stratosphere Entertainment
767 Fifth Ave., #4700
New York, NY 10153
Phone: 212/605-1010
Fax: 212/813-0300

Su-City Pictures East
262 Elizabeth St., #GF
New York, NY 10012
Phone: 212/219-9224
Fax: 212/219-9224
E-mail: sk@su-city-pictures.com
Website: www.su-city-pictures.com

Trimark Pictures
2644 30th St., 2nd Floor
Santa Monica, CA 90405
Phone: 310/314-2000
Fax: 310/452-8934
Website: trimarkpictures.com

Troma Entertainment, Inc.
733 Ninth Ave.
New York, NY 10019
Phone: 212/757-4555
Fax: 212/399-9885
E-mail: troma.com
Website: www.troma.com

Turbulent Arts
673 Oak St., #1
San Francisco, CA 94117
Phone: 415/552-1952
Fax: 415/552-3620
Website: www.slowburn.com/turbarts.html

Unapix Films
200 Madison Ave., 24th Floor
New York, NY 10016
Phone: 212/252-7711
Fax: 212/252-7626

WinStar TV and Video
419 Park Ave. S.
New York, NY 10016
Phone: 212/686-6777
Fax: 212/545-9931
Website: www.winstarnewmedia.com

Xenon Entertainment Group
1440 Ninth St.
Santa Monica, CA 90401
Phone: 310/451-5510
Fax: 310/395-4058
E-mail: sthous@gte.net

Zeitgeist Films, Ltd.
247 Centre St., 2nd Floor
New York, NY 10013
Phone: 212/274-1989
Fax: 212/274-1644
E-mail: mail@zeitgeistfilm.com
Website: www.zeitgeistfilm.com

LEGAL INFORMATION

Barab, Vaughan, and Kline
Production counsel: acquiring rights, incorporation, dealing with unions, hiring actors, music, distribution, and so on. Serves as production counsel for about 25 movies per year but does no securities work. 20% discount to IFP members.
Contact: Mark A. Pittman at 310/859-6644.

Fredricks and Vonderhorst, Law Offices
Full-service law firm for production companies, including financing, production, and distribution. Specializes in finding European cofinancing for projects that already have small deals with American companies or have stars or recognizable names attached. Offers representation of writers and directors but not actors or musicians. 20% discount on all fees to IFP members.
Contact: Dennis F. Fredricks at 310/472-1122.

Harris Tulchin
Full-service entertainment attorney. Offers representation of writers, directors, and actors. Financing and distribution agreements. Acts as producer's rep. Flexible rates. 10% discount to IFP members.
Contact: Harris Tulchin at 310/914-7979.

Mark Litwak Law Offices
20% discount on all fees to IFP members.
Contact: Mark Litwak at 310/859-9595.

Michael Donaldson, Esq.
Flexible rates.
Contact: Michael Donaldson at 310/271-5123. Fax: 310/271-4760.

Pierce Gorman
New open-door policy.
Contact: 310/788-3939. Fax: 310/778-3950.

Surpin, Mayersohn, and Edelstone
Entertainment law. Flexible rates.
Contact: Shelley H. Surpin or Paul Mayersohn at 310/552-1808.

Other Resources

Beverly Hills Bar Association
Attorney Referral Center: 310/553-6644
California Lawyers for the Arts
1641 18th St.
Santa Monica, CA 90404
Phone: 310/998-5590
Fax: 310/998-5594

Additional branches in San Francisco, Oakland, and Sacramento
Los Angeles County Bar Association
Attorney Referral Center: 818/880-0120

FILM FESTIVAL AND MARKETS CALENDAR*

January

Brussels International Film Festival
Chaussée de Louvain 30
1210 Brussels, Belgium
Phone: (32) 2 22739 80
Fax: (32) 2 21818 60
Contact: Christian Thomas, director
E-mail: infoffb@netcity.be
Website: http://ffb.cinebel.com

Gothenburg Film Festival
Box 7079
S-40232 Göteborg, Sweden
Phone: (46) 31 410 546
Fax: (46) 31 410 063
Contact: Gunnar Bergdahl
E-mail: goteborg.filmfestival@mailbox.swipnet.se
Website: http://www.goteborg.se/kultur/filmfestival/

*The information provided in this section is provided by Mark Litwak, attorney-at-law.

National Association of TV Program Executives (NATPE)
  Conference
2425 Olympic Blvd., Suite 550E
Santa Monica, CA 90404
Phone: 310/453-4440
Fax: 310/453-5258
Contact: Kate Chester

Nortel Palm Springs International Film Festival
1700 E. Tahquitz Canyon Way, #3
Palm Springs, CA 92262
Phone: 619/322-2930
Fax: 619/322-4087
Contact: Craig Prater
Website: http://www.psfilmfest.org

Rotterdam International Film Festival
PO Box 21696
3001 AR Rotterdam, The Netherlands
Phone: (31) 10 411 8080
Fax: (31) 10 413 5132
Contact: Simon Field
E-mail: iffr@luna.nl
Website: http://www.iffroterdam.nl

Slamdance Film Festival
6381 Hollywood Blvd., #520
Los Angeles, CA 90028
Phone: 213/466-1786
Contact: Peter Baxter

Sundance Film Festival
PO Box 16450
Salt Lake City, UT 84116
Phone: 801/328-3456
Fax: 801/575-5175
Contact: Geoff Gilmore
E-mail: sundance@xmission.com
Website: http://www.sundance.org

February

American Film Market
10850 Wilshire Blvd., 9th Floor
Los Angeles, CA 90024
Phone: 310/446-1000
Fax: 310/446-1600
Contact: Brady Craine
E-mail: info@afma.com
Website: http://www.afma.com

Berlin International Film Festival
Budapester Strasse 50
10787 Berlin, Germany
Phone: (49) 30 254 890
Fax: (49) 30 254 89 249
Contact: Moritz de Hadeln, festival director

CineMart
PO Box 21696
3001 AR Rotterdam, The Netherlands
Phone: (31) 10 4118080
Fax: (31) 10 4135132
Contact: Sandra Den Hamer

Monte Carlo Television Festival and Market
4, Blvd. du Jardin Exotique
MC98000 Monaco
Phone: (377) 9310 4060
Fax: (377) 9350 7014
Contact: Wilfred Groote
Website: http://www.tvfestival.monaco.mc/

Portland International Film Festival
Northwest Film Centre
1219 S.W. Park Ave.
Portland, OR 97205
Phone: 503/221-1156
Fax: 503/226-4842
Contact: Bill Foster
Website: http://www.nwfilm.org

March

New Directors/New Films
Film Society of Lincoln Center
70 Lincoln Center Plaza, 4th Floor
New York, NY 10023
Phone: 212/875-5610
Fax: 212/875-5636
Contact: Richard Pena
Website: http://www.filmlinc.com

Santa Barbara International Film Festival
1216 State St., #710
Santa Barbara, CA 93101
Phone: 805/963-0023
Fax: 805/962-2524
Contact: Diane M. Durst
E-mail: sbiff@west.net
Website: http://www.west.net/-sbiff

South by Southwest (SXSW) Film Festival
PO Box 4999
Austin, Texas 78765
Phone: 512/467-7979
Fax: 512/451-0754
Contact: Nancy Schafer
E-mail: sxsw@sxsw.com
Website: http://www.sxsw.com

April

Gen Art Film Festival
145 W. 28th St., Suite 11C
New York, NY 10001
Phone: 212/290-0312
Fax: 212/290-0254
Contact: Ian A. Gerard
Website: http://www.genart.org

Los Angeles Independent Film Festival
5455 Wilshire Blvd., #1500
Beverly Hills, CA 90036
Phone: 213/937-9155
Fax: 213/937-7770
Contact: Robert Faust
Website: http://www.laiff.com

Mip TV International Television Program Market
Reed Midem Organization
PO Box 572
11 rue du Colonel Pierre Avia
75726 Paris Cedex 15, France
Phone: (33) 1 4190 4580
Fax: (33) 1 4190 4570
Contact: Andre Vaillant
Website: http://www.miptv.com

The New York Women's Film Festival
225 Lafayette St., Suite 200
New York, NY 10012
Phone: 212/465-3435
Fax 212/586-7282
Contact: Sara Goodman
Website: http://www.nywfilmfest.com

San Francisco International Film Festival
1521 Eddy St.
San Francisco, CA 94115
Phone: 415/929-5000, ext. 110
Fax: 415/921-5032
Contact: Cathy Fischer
Website: http://www.sfiff.org

Taos Talking Picture Festival
216M N. Pueblo Rd., #216
Taos, NM 87571
Phone: 505/751-0637
Fax: 505/751-7385
Contact: Kelly Clement
E-mail: ttpix@taosnet.com
Website: http://www.taosnet.com/ttpix/

May

Cannes International Film Festival
99 Blvd. Malesherbes
75008 Paris, France
Phone: (33) 1 4561 6600
Fax: (33) 1 4561 9760
Contact: Gilles Jacob
E-mail: festival@festival-cannes.fr
Website: http://www.festival.cannes.com

Seattle International Film Festival
801 E. Pine St.
Seattle, WA 98122
Phone: 206/324-9996
Fax: 206/324-9998
Contact: Darryl Macdonald
E-mail: mail@seattlefilm.com
Website: http://www.seattlefilm.com

Troia International Film Festival
Forum Luisa Todi
Av. Luisa Todi, 65
2902 Setubal Codex, Troia, Portugal
Phone: (351) 65 525 908
Fax: (351) 65 525 681
Contact: Mario Ventura Henriques
Website: http://www.inis.pt/inis/festroia

June

Banff Television Festival
1516 Railway Ave.
Canmore, Alberta T1W 1P6, Canada
Phone: 403/678-9260
Fax: 403/678-9269
Contact: Pat Ferns
E-mail: info@banfftvfest.com
Website: http://www.banfftvfest.com

Florida Film Festival
1300 S. Orlando Ave.
Maitland, FL 32751
Phone: 407/629-1088
Fax: 407/629-6870
Contact: Matthew Curtis
E-mail: filmfest@gate.net
Website: http://www.enzian.org

Nantucket Film Festival
PO Box 688
Prince St. Station
New York, NY 10012
Phone: 212/642-6339
Contact: Joy Huang
Website: http://www.nantucketfilmfestival.org

Sydney Film Festival
PO Box 950
Glebe, NSW 2037, Australia
Phone: (61) 29 660 3844
Fax: (61) 29 692 8793
Contact: Paul Byrnes
E-mail: sydfilm@ozonline.com.au
Website: http://www.sydfilm-fest.com.au

July

Galway Film Fleadh
Cluain Mhuire
Monivea Rd.
Galway, Ireland
Phone: (353) 91 751 655
Fax: (353) 91 770 746
Contact: Anthony Sellers
E-mail: gafleadh@iol.ie

Karlovy Vary International Film Festival
Panska 1
Prague 1, 110 00 Czech Republic
Phone: (420) 2 2423 5413
Fax: (420) 2 2423 3408
Contact: Eva Zaoralova
E-mail: iffkv@tlp.cz
Website: http://www.tip.cz/internet/iffkarlovy_vary

Melbourne International Film Fest
207 Johnston St., 1st Floor
Fitzroy, Victoria 3065, Australia
Phone: (61) 3 9417 2011
Fax: (61) 3 9417 3804
Contact: Sandra Sdraulig
E-mail: miff@netspace.net.au
Website: http://www.cinemedia.net/miff

Wine Country Film Fest
Box 303
Glen Ellen, CA 95442
Phone: 707/996-2536
Fax: 707/996-6964
Contact: Stephen Ashton
E-mail: wcfilmfest@aol.com
Website: http://www.winezone.com

August

Edinburgh International Film Festival
Filmhouse
88 Lothian Rd.
Edinburgh EH3BZ, Scotland
Phone: (44) 131 228 4051
Fax: (44) 131 229 5501
Contact: Lizzie Francke
E-mail: info@edfilmfest.org.uk
Website: http://www.edfilmfest.org.uk

Hollywood Film Festival
433 N. Camden Dr., Suite 600
Beverly Hills, CA 90210
Phone: 310/288-1882
Fax: 310/475-0193
Contact: Carlos de Abreu
Website: http://hollywoodfestival.com/

Locarno International Film Festival
Via della Posta 6
6600 Locarno, Switzerland
Phone: (41) 91 751 0232
Fax: (41) 91 751 7465
Contact: Marco Muller
E-mail: pardo@tinet.ch
Website: http://www.pardo.ch

Montreal World Film Festival
1432 de Bleury St.
Montreal, Canada H3A 2J1
Phone: 514/848-3883
Fax: 514/848-3886
Contact: Serge Losique
E-mail: ffm@interlink.net
Website: http://www.ffm-montreal.org

Venice Film Festival
La Biennale di Venezia
Settore Cinema E Spetta Colo Televisivo
Ca'Giustinian, 1364/A
San Marco, 30124 Venice, Italy
Phone: (39) 41 521 8711
Fax: (39) 41 523 6374
Contact: Felice Laudadio

September

Boston Film Festival
PO Box 516
Hull, MA 02045
Phone: 617/925-1373
Fax: 617/925-3132
Contact: Mark Diamond

Breckenridge Festival of Film
PO Box 718
Breckenridge, CO 80424
Phone: 970/453-6200
Fax: 970/453-2692
Contact: Julie Bullock
E-mail: filmfest@brecknet.com
Website: http://www.brecknet.com/BFF/home.html

Deauville Festival of American Films
c/o Promo-2000
36 rue Pierret
92200 Neuilly-sur-Seine, France
Phone: (33) 1 46 40 55 00
Fax: (33) 1 46 40 55 39
Contact: Lionel Chouchan
E-mail: publics@imaginet.fr

Independent Feature Film Market (IFFM)
104 W. 29th St., 12th Floor
New York, NY 10001
Phone: 212/465-8200
Fax: 212/465-8525
Contact: Valerie Sheppard
Website: http://www.ifp.org

Mipcom, Reed Midem Organization
PO Box 572
11 rue du Colonel Pierre Avia
75726 Paris Cedex 15, France
Phone: (33) 1 4190 4580
Fax: (33) 1 4190 4570
Contact: Andre Vaillant
Website: http://www.mipcom.com

New York Film Festival
70 Lincoln Center Plaza
New York, NY 10023
Phone: 212/875-5638
Fax: 212/875-5636
Contact: Richard Pena
E-mail: filmlinc@dti.net
Website: http://www.filmlinc.com

San Sebastian International Film Festival (The International
   Film Festival of Donostia)
Plaza de Oquendo, s/n
20004 San Sebastian, Spain
Phone: (34) 43 481 212
Fax: (34) 43 481 218
Contact: Diego Galan
E-mail: ssiff@mail.ddnet.es
Website: http://www.ddnet.es/san_sebastian_film_festival/

Temecula Valley International Film Festival
27945 Jefferson Ave., Suite 104A
Temecula, CA 92590
Phone: 909/699-6267
Fax: 909/301-1414
Contact: Jo Moulton

Telluride Film Festival
53 S. Main St., #212
Hanover, NH 03755
Phone: 603/643-1255
Fax: 603/643-5938
Contact: Bill Pence
E-mail: tellufil@aol.com
Website: http://www.teluridemm.com/filmfest.html

Toronto International Film Festival
2 Carlton St., Suite 1600
Toronto, Ontario, Canada M5B 1J3
Phone: 416/967-7371
Fax: 416/967-9477
Contact: Piers Handling
E-mail: tiffg@torfilmfest.ca
Website: http://www.bell.ca/filmfest

Vancouver International Film Festival/Film and TV Trade
   Show
1008 Homer St., #410
Vancouver, British Columbia V6B 2X1, Canada
Phone: 604/685-0260
Fax: 604/688-8221
Contact: Alan Franey
E-mail: viff@viff.org
Website: http://www.viff.org/viff/

October

American Film Institute (AFI) Los Angeles International
   Film Festival
2021 N. Western Ave.
Los Angeles, CA 90027
Phone: 213/856-7707
Fax: 213/462-4049

Fort Lauderdale International Film Festival
2625 E. Sunrise Blvd.,
Fort Lauderdale, FL 33304
Phone: 954/563-0500
Fax: 954/564-1206
Contact: Gregory von Hausch
E-mail: Brofilm@aol.com
Website: http://www.Filmmag.com.FLIFF

Hamptons International Film Festival
3 Newtown Mews
East Hampton, NY 11937
Phone: 516/324-4600
Fax: 516/324-5116
Contact: Bruce Feinberg

International Filmfestival Mannheim-Heidelberg
Collini-Center
Galerie, 68161 Mannheim, Germany
Phone: (49) 0 621 102 943
Fax: (49) 0 621 291 564
Contact: Daniela Koetz, program coordinator
E-mail: ifmh@mannheim-filmfestival.com

Mifed
Fiera Milano Largo Domodossola 1
20145 Milan, Italy
Phone: (39) 2 480 12912
Fax: (39) 2 499 77020
Contact: Elena Lloyd
E-mail: mifed@fmd.it
Website: http://www.fmd.it/mifed/

Mill Valley Film Festival
38 Miller Ave., Suite #6
Mill Valley, CA 94941
Phone: 415/383-5256
Fax: 415/383-8606
Contact: Mark Fishkin

Mipcom, Reed Midem Organisation
PO Box 572
11 rue du Colonel Pierre
75726 Paris Cedex 15, France
Phone: (33) 1 4190 4580
Fax: (33) 1 4190 4570
Contact: Andre Vaillant

Sao Paulo International Film Festival
Al. Lorena 937, CJ. 303
01424-001 Sao Paulo, Brazil
Phone: (55) 11 883 5137
Fax: (55) 11 853 7936
Contact: Leon Cakoff
E-mail: info@mostra.org
Website: http://www.mostra.org

Vancouver International Film Festival
1008 Homer St., Suite 410
Vancouver, British Columbia V6B 2X1, Canada
Phone: 604/685-0260
Fax: 604/688-8221
Contact: PoChu AnYeung

November

French Film Festival
PO Box 908
Sarasota, FL 34243-0908
Phone: 941/351-9010/4300
Fax: 941/351-5796
Contact: Tom Loken
E-mail: fffn2zasm@aol.com

Gijon International Film Festival
PO Begona, 24, Entlo. PO Box 33205
Gijon, Asturias, Spain
Phone: (34) 8 534 3739
Fax: (34) 8 535 4152
Contact: Jose Luis Cienfuegos, festival director; Jose Luis
    Rebollos, festival programmer
E-mail: festcine@airastur.es
Website: http://www.airastur.es/gijonfilmfestival/

Hawaii International Film Festival in Honolulu on
    Hawaii, Kauai, Maui, Molokai, Lanai
700 Bishop St., Suite 400
Honolulu, Hawaii 96813
Phone: 800/752-8193
Fax: 800/528-1410
International phone; 808/528-3456
International fax: 808/528-1410
Contact: Christian Gaines
E-mail: hiffinfo@hiff.org
Website: http://www.hiff.org.

Heartland Film Festival
613 N. East St.
Indianapolis, IN 46202
Phone: 317/464-9405
Fax: 317/635-4201
Contact: Jeffrey Sparks

International Documentary Filmfestival Amsterdam
  (IDFA)
Kleine-Gartmanplantsoen 10
1017 RR Amsterdam, The Netherlands
Phone: (31) 20 627 3329
Fax: (31) 20 630 5300
Contact: Ally Derks
E-mail: idfa@xs4all.nl
Website: http://www.dds.nl/-damocles/idfa

London Film Festival
South Bank, Waterloo, London SE1 8XT, United
  Kingdom
Phone: (44) 171 815 1323/4
Fax: (44) 171 633 0786
Contact: Adrain Wootton
E-mail: jane.ivey@bfi.org.uk

Northwest Film and Video Festival
1219 S.W. Park Ave.
Portland, OR 97205
Phone: 503/221-1156
Fax: 503/226-4842
Contact: Bill Foster
Website: http://www.nwfilm.com

Southern African International Film and Television Market
PO Box 3832
Johannesburg 2000, South Africa
Phone: (27) 11 714 3229
Fax: (27) 11 714 3275
Contact: Dezi Roeich

Tokyo International Film Festival
4F, Landic Ginza Bldg. II
1-6-5 Ginza, Chuo-ku, Tokyo 104, Japan
Phone: (81) 3 3563 6305
Fax: (81) 3 3563 6310
Contact: Yasuyoshi Tokuma
Website: http://www.tokyo-filmfest.or.jp/

December

Mip Asia
Reed Midem Organization
PO Box 572
11 rue du Colonel Pierre
75726 Paris Cedex 15, France
Phone: (33) 1 4190 4400
Fax: (33) 1 4190 4409
Contact: Andre Vaillant
Website: http://www.mipasia.com

GLOSSARY

Above-the-Line Costs. In a budget, the expenses that relate specifically to the creative components of the film. The story rights, writer, director, producer(s), and cast are all considered to be above-the-line costs. (Compare *below-the-line costs.*)

Actualize. To compare actual costs against original anticipated costs. At the end of the show, after all returns have been made and final invoices have been received, you must actualize the budget to determine how much money you've actually spent compared to how much you anticipated spending for each line item. This is how you will account for any overages or shortages.

AD Kit. A portable file box that the assistant director brings to the set each day that contains forms, schedules, contracts, reports, paperwork, lists, and so on. The AD kit functions as a mini filing cabinet with paperwork that the AD may need to refer to, fill out, or provide while on the set.

ADR. See *automated dialogue replacement.*

Agency Fee. The 10% fee that each cast member pays his or her agent. It is common practice within the industry for the production to pay the agency fee in addition to the actor's salary.

Allow. Money allocated for a given expense within a budget line item, the exact cost of which has not yet been determined. (Compare *flat fee.*)

Assistant Director (AD). The AD assists the director on the set and is commander of the set. The assistant director designs the final shooting schedule and works closely with the director. He or she communicates directly with the actors and the crew, organizes the set, and keeps the production on schedule. The AD is also responsible for call sheets, Exhibit G forms, production reports, schedule changes, meal breaks, overtime, accident reports, and so on.

Automated Dialogue Replacement (ADR). ADR substitutes or adds dialogue to your film after it has been shot. After you've been in the editing room, you can determine which lines of dialogue need to be rerecorded because they are unclear and which additional lines of dialogue are needed in the film. ADR sessions take place after the shoot has wrapped. You will need to determine which actors are needed for ADR after you determine your needs. (Also called *additional dialogue recording, advanced dialogue replacement,* and *looping.*)

Bag. A lightproof sack used to store the film as a precaution to keep it from being exposed to light.

Below-the-Line Costs. In a budget, the expenses that refer to the manual labor or technical aspects of the film. Crew, equipment, locations, props, wardrobe, sound, and transportation are all below-the-line costs. (Compare *above-the-line costs.*)

Blanket Permit. A single permit that is secured for filming at several locations within the city's filming zone and within close proximity to one another. A blanket permit can save you money because you won't need a separate permit for each of your locations. Contact the permit office of the city in which you are filming to determine if you can obtain a blanket permit for your locations.

Box Rental. See *kit rental.*

Breakdown. Identifying all of your characters, locations, extras, vehicles, props, and so on, for a given scene; put this information on a breakdown sheet. You will break down each page of your script to account for and properly schedule and budget your film. Once you have a breakdown sheet for each scene in your script, you will be ready to begin creating your shooting schedule.

Call Sheet. A form used to log the daily call times issued to the cast and crew during production. The front of the call sheet lists the director, producer(s), location, weather, interior/exterior location, scene, cast, and special equipment needed for a particular day. The back of the call sheet lists each cast and crew member and the time he or she is needed on the set.

Can. A container for storing film. You will need extra film cans on the set for downloading shot film, short ends, recanning, and so on. Make sure that you have the right size cans for your film loads.

Catering. The meals provided to cast and crew members on the set during production. (Compare *craft service.*)

Chain of Title. Documents that show proof of ownership of a script or story from its beginnings. Among the documents that might be included in a chain of title are the certificate of copyright, the option/purchase agreement, and the writer's agreement, if there is one.

Chart of Accounts.   A list of the account codes that correspond to each line item in the budget. Use these codes when actualizing the budget, writing checks, and coding petty cash envelopes.

Company Move Day.   A day on which the production moves from one location to another. Company moves must be carefully factored into your schedule and well planned because they can require a fair amount of time.

Completion Bond.   A bond that is often required when a film's financing is secured through an independent film company or a bank. This insurance policy serves as a guarantee to the financing entity that the film will be completed. A completion bond is usually computed at 3% of the budget total.

Contingency.   Money, usually budgeted at 10% of the below-the-line costs, that the completion bond company requires that you have. Contingency serves as a cushion should there be cost overruns on your film. It also works as an insurance policy for the completion bond company. A higher contingency may be required for larger-budget films.

Continuity.   Tracking and accounting for all of the details and elements within each scene shot, assuring the continuity of the film. Because films are not shot in proper order from the first scene to the last, special care must be paid to the continuity of the film. It is essential to have a record of the look of each actor and the design of each set for reference to maintain continuity.

Continuity Notebook.   A notebook used to help maintain a film's continuity. It includes photos of actors and sets, the script supervisor's notes, and lined pages of the script, all of which are essential to the editor. A continuity notebook will allow you to recreate how an actor was dressed and made up so if you have reshoots, the script days will match.

Contractual Charges.   The costs that are applied to the budget as percentages of the overall budget, such as the completion bond, contingency, overhead, and insurance.

Core.   A hard piece of plastic found in the center of the film roll that keeps the film rolled properly.

Craft Service.   The snacking and beverage station available on the set throughout production. (Compare *catering*.)

Dailies.   Either the work print or the digital version (depending on how the film will be edited) of all of the film shot in a given day. Typically, the director, the director of photography, the producer, and others may view the dailies each day.

Day-Out-of-Days Sheet.   A form that indicates for which days each element of a production will be needed. You can prepare a day-out-of-days sheet for your props, extras, vehicles, locations, actors, and special effects, for example.

Day Player.   Any actor who works three or fewer consecutive days. (Compare *weekly player*.)

Deferral Agreement.   An agreement between the producer and a crew or cast member in which money is deferred until a later date. A deferral agreement is a good way to signify to crew or cast members that *if* a low-budget film makes money down the line, they will be compensated. Arriving at an appropriate deferral amount for each crew member is somewhat arbitrary. We take the difference between what the crew member is actually paid and what we would have liked to have paid him or her had the budget been higher, and attach a small premium to compensate the crew member for contributing his or her time at a cut rate.

Delivery.   The process of transferring a film over to a distribution company after it has been completed. In addition to the film itself, delivery requirements may include proof of errors-and-omissions insurance, paperwork and contracts, proof of chain of title, and documentation of music clearance.

Domestic Production-Distribution Deal (P-D deal).   Financing given to a firm by a production company that can guarantee a theatrical release prior to production. If you can make a domestic distribution deal with a company, anticipate that the money they give you for the domestic rights to your film should cover between 40% and 60% of your negative cost.

Dubbing.   The process of combining all of the various sound elements (dialogue, music, and effects) on a dubbing stage while watching the film. Most films are mixed into four analog channels (left, center, right, and surround). This is referred to as *matrix stereo*. (Also called *mix*.)

Equity Financing.   Hard cash invested in a film by a company or an individual—be it a family member, friend, or professional investor—in exchange for either rights or profit points.

Errors-and-Omissions (E&O) Insurance.   Insurance that protects the distributor against assuming any legal liabilities by purchasing the film. E&O insurance protects the production company or distributor from liability lawsuits for slander, unauthorized use of the film's title, using living people's names, and copyright infringement. If you secure a distributor, E&O insurance will be a delivery requirement.

Expendables.   Smaller items, other than equipment, that can be rented cheaply, usually from the same vendor. You may need to purchase or rent certain items to shoot at a given location. Examples include items such as wardrobe steamers, wardrobe racks, cones, bullhorns, tables, chairs, desks, director's chairs, rope, bungee cords, coffee urns, coolers, craft service equipment, tablecloths, handcarts for carrying equipment, hangers, and makeup tables.

Extra.   An actor who is required in a shot but has no speaking role. Extras are important to the look and feel of a film and create the atmosphere.

Favored Nations.   A term used to indicate that a cast or crew member will receive treatment on par with the best that the producer is offering anyone else on the set, but not better. It refers in particular to pay and to perks (dressing rooms, travel, accommodations, and so on).

Fine Cut. The cut of the film before the final cut and after the rough cut.

First Composite Answer Print. A print that results from the first color timing pass and marries, or combines, the picture with any opticals and the soundtrack.

Flat Fee. When the cost remains the same regardless of how many weeks it ultimately takes to complete filming or of how much overtime is worked. Crew compensation and equipment rental can be arranged on the basis of a weekly fee or a flat fee. (Compare *allow*.)

Foley. The sounds effects added to a film to help communicate the full effect of each scene, consisting of either sounds that were not clean off the production track and must be replaced, or sounds that must be added to the film. A foley artist uses props to create sounds such as kissing, rain, and footsteps on a sound stage while matching it to the picture.

Foreign Presales. The sale of the rights to a picture on a territory-by-territory basis before the film is actually shot.

Fringe. Any cost that is above and beyond a central cost. For example, sales taxes, employee taxes (.80% Federal Unemployment Insurance [FUI], 5.4% State Unemployment Insurance [SUI], and 6.20% Social Disability Insurance [SDI]), and agency fees are all considered fringes.

Gaffer. One of the cinematographer's key people, along with the key grip, in creating the lighting effects on the set.

Gap. The shortfall between the money you have and the money you need to cover the full cost of a picture. To obtain gap financing from a bank, you will need to present any presale contracts and guaranteed equity investment contracts, along with other items such as a budget and script.

Headboard. The top portion of a strip board. It contains key information about the production such as the picture title, director, producer, assistant director, etc. as well as character names and identification numbers and other information pertinent to the production. (See also *strip board*.)

Hold Days. Days when a principal player is not working but is being "held" by the production and is not free to take other work. You must generally pay actors for hold days. If you are working with one of the Screen Actors Guild low-budget agreements, this consecutive employment requirement may be waived.

Key Grip. One of the cinematographer's key people, along with the gaffer, in creating shadow and lighting effects.

Kit Rental. A fee paid for equipment or supplies that a crew member provides to the production. For example, you may need to budget a kit rental fee for a makeup artist who has her own makeup supplies. The fee depends on the department and the budget of the show. Fees paid for kit rentals are not subject to payroll taxes. (Also called *box rental*.)

L&D. See *loss and damage*.

Loan-Out Company. A corporation that "loans" the services of its employees. Certain members of the above- and below-the-line staff may want to be paid as "loan-outs." When hiring a loan-out, the producer (or the producer's payroll company) does not deduct employee payroll taxes or add fringes to the loan-out's rate. Instead, the loan-out company is responsible for absorbing the tax liability on the income. Any employee whom you pay as a loan-out must provide you with papers of incorporation and a federal identification number or employee identification number (EIN).

Loss and Damage (L&D). Money that is budgeted to ensure that the production will be covered in the event that equipment or materials are lost or damaged during the course of the show. The most conservative way to handle budgeting for L&D is to set aside an amount in each department's budget equal to the amount of the deductible on the production insurance policy. For example, if your deductible is $1,200, you would budget $1,200 for L&D in each department category. (Insurance deductibles must usually be met on a per-occurrence basis.)

Magazine. The mechanism that attaches to the camera body that holds the film stock.

Mix. See *dubbing*.

MOS. A term used to describe scenes shot without sound. According to legend, this acronym is derived from a German director's order, "Mit out sound."

Motion Picture Association of America (MPAA) Certificate. The MPAA certificate certifies that the film has been rated by the MPAA and that its production meets the association's regulations and standards. The MPAA views the finished film and assigns it a rating, which is required if the film is to be released. The cost of the certificate is based on the budget of the film. The MPAA certificate is a delivery requirement for all distribution companies.

Negative Cutting. The process of conforming the negative to match the edited work print or digital "fine cut." Conform your negative only when you have locked your picture.

One-Line Schedule. A shortened version of the shooting schedule. The one-line schedule doesn't list props, set dressing, vehicles, and similar items, and characters are identified by number only.

On Location. Filming at a distant location where either cast and crew members are working as nonlocals and will need to be traveled around and paid pier diem. The production is required to pay for the traveling and living expenses of cast and crew members who must travel from their homes in Los Angeles, for example, to Park City, Utah, to work. If you hire your cast and crew in Park City, on the other hand, they are local hires, and you do not have to pay for their traveling and living expenses. On location is also used to distinguish a preexisting location where you are filming from a set that has been built on a stage or is on a lot.

Optical. A type of effect that is shot optically and placed into the film during postproduction. You may need to correct shots in your film that need to be repositioned or made clearer, or you may need to place elements into the film that are not actually there, such as a creature, volcano, windstorm, laser beam, or falling star.

Overhead. Overhead can cover certain preproduction costs, office rental, utility costs, nominal development costs, and out-of-pocket expenses of those who are involved with the project for some time before the film is financed. On an independent film, overhead, if it is applied at all, is applied as a percentage of the overall budget; it might be anything between 1% and 10%.

P&A. See *prints and advertising.*

PC. See *petty cash.*

P-D Deal. See *domestic production-distribution deal.*

Per Diem. Money allocated to cover food and other out-of-pocket expenses of the cast and crew members while on location. Unions have minimum per diem (per day) rates. For nonunion cast and crew, set the per diem rate at a reasonable amount given the cost of living where you are shooting.

Permit. A certificate issued by the city in which you are filming that entitles you to shoot at a particular location. To obtain a filming permit, you will be required to pay a fee that will be determined by the city, your location or locations, and the zone in which you plan to film.

Petty Cash (PC). Money set aside for small purchases, such as gas, tolls, tips, parking, office supplies, inexpensive props, and food.

Pitch. To pique someone's interest in your film so that will want to know more or read the script. A brief description of what your film is about.

Preference Claim. A penalty for having hired a nonguild actor. Preference claims cost $400 in 1998.

Prelight/Prerig. Any day or portion of a day spent preparing a set, stages, or location for filming. Depending on the lighting needs of the show and the rental arrangements for the location, you might be able to have your lighting and grip departments prelight/prerig a location before filming. This day of setup allows the shoot day at the location to get off to a quicker start.

Principal Player. An actor needed for more than three days in a row. Also referred to as a weekly player to SAG.

Prints and Advertising (P&A). The costs of striking prints of a film and the advertising costs for promoting the film in the marketplace. These costs are typically absorbed by the distribution company and are prenegotiated in your contract with a distributor.

Production Insurance. All independent productions must be insured to secure equipment, locations, transportation, props, wardrobe, cast, crew, and so on, and the policy must be purchased before the production period officially begins. Typically, production insurance is calculated at 1.5% to 3% of the budget depending on the budget and the life of the film.

Production Report. The production report accounts for the on-set events of a given shoot day. During production the assistant director fills out a production report daily. Crew times, crew meal times, camera call times, first shot, the quantity of footage shot, which scenes were shot that day, and which shots were retakes are all recorded on the production report. Production reports also list such information as faulty equipment, meal penalties, and on-set injuries.

Product Placement. Placing products referred to or called for in a script into the film, serving as advertising and promotion for the product as well as a source of revenue or in-kind donation to the production, depending on the arrangement with the manufacturer.

Raw Stock. Film stock that has not yet been shot and will be loaded into camera magazines when ready to be used.

Recan. Film stock that was loaded into a magazine but was never shot and then was literally recanned.

Rough Cut. An early cut of a film. Assembling a film and determining which footage best tells the story is what the editing process entails. After making extensive notes, incorporating new ideas and changes, and assembling several rough cuts, you will eventually be ready for the fine cut.

Scale. The minimum crew and cast payment established by a union (or, for a nonunion set, the minimum amount paid to a crew member in any given category).

Schedule. To determine how many days it will take to shoot a film and then within each shoot day which scenes will be shot and in what order.

Scout. To explore a potential location to determine its ability to meet the film's needs. The director will want to scout potential locations to find the best possible one. Once the majority of your locations have been locked, the location manager and the line producer will schedule scouts of each location to determine setups, equipment needs, power availability, lighting needs, and so on.

Second-Unit Filming. Scaled-down crew that usually includes the director, assistant camera operator (AC), second AC, operator, and production assistant. (You may need a prop or art department person as well.) On bigger-budget productions, a second unit might have its own director. Sometimes, the camera operator becomes the second unit's director of photography, or an entirely different crew is hired.

Skeleton Crew. A scaled-down crew, most appropriate when shooting under conditions in which space or time is limited and a smaller crew would facilitate getting the shot.

Special Shooting Unit. A second-unit crew that is assembled to shoot scenes that don't require actors, such as exterior setups or interior or exterior establishing shots. The smaller crew of a special shooting unit is less costly than a full crew. A special shooting unit may be scheduled during actual filming, at the end of a shoot, or throughout the editing process. (Sometimes called a *pickup*.)

Stand-in. An actor who takes the place of another actor and resembles him or her. A stand-in is most appropriate when you have name talent and are shooting scenes without sound or background shots. It may be less expensive to use a stand-in, and an actor sometimes requests one. The rate for stand-ins is usually the same as the rate for extras.

Station 12. To determine if an actor is in good standing with SAG, call the station-12 desk at the guild, prior to allowing him or her to work on your set. If the actor has not paid SAG dues, he or she must do so before beginning work. The production company will pay a fine for any actor working on a set whose status has not been cleared with the guild.

Strip Board. Individual strips, each representing one scene, are arranged on a board creating the shooting schedule. (See also *headboard*.)

Synopsis. A brief written description of what a script is about. It should grab the reader. It's not a scene-by-scene breakdown. A synopsis is often required for investors or financing companies in order to pique their interest, hopefully resulting in their wanting to read the script.

Titles. Main titles typically run at the beginning of the film and indicate the film's title as well as key credits. End titles run at the end of the film (also called credit crawl) and list all cast and crew, music, and often vendors who have participated in the film's making.

Top Sheet. The first page of a budget, which reflects the categories and their totals but doesn't show line-item detail.

Turnaround. The amount of time the cast and crew are given from the time they are released from work on a given day before they must return to work the next day. Guild and union guidelines require a 12-hour minimum turnaround for cast and crew members.

Vendor Account. An account that allows a production to rent equipment and be billed for it, rather than having to pay up front. A vendor account is established by filling out a credit application. It is favorable to establish a vendor account with any business from which you will be renting equipment or garnering services (e.g., lab or editing facility, wardrobe and prop houses, camera house, etc.).

Weekly Player. An actor who works under a weekly contract. If an actor is needed for more than three days in a row, he or she should be paid as a weekly player based on weekly rates set by SAG. (Compare *day player*.)

White Copy. The draft of a script when preproduction begins. White is the first color in the color-coding system used to identify different drafts of a script.

INDEX

About the CD-ROM...

All of the files on this CDR run through an **Adobe Acrobat PDF** interface. To access the files, you must have either **Adobe Acrobat** [Exchange] **3.1** or higher or **Acrobat Reader 3.1** or higher installed on your computer. **Acrobat 4.0 is recommended**.

To install Acrobat Reader 4.0 directly from the CD, follow the appropriate instructions found within the **Readme** file. You can also run Acrobat Reader 4.0 directly from the CD by launching the application within the Software\CD\ folder.

All of the files on the CDR are linked directly to **WELCOME.pdf**. Open this file within Acrobat and point and click to the file you'd like to access. You can return to this **Welcome Screen** from the opening screen of each subsequent section by pressing the **RETURN TO WELOME SCREEN** button found at the top of each page.

To access the MP3/MPEG-1 audio and video interviews, you'll need to have a media player installed on your computer. There are many players available for free or as shareware. For Windows, we recommend **Windows Media Player**. Macintosh users can use **MacAmp** in combination with **QuickTime**. For information regarding mp3 files and the appropriate media players for your system, check out www.mp3.com. Log on here for installation instructions and troubleshooting, or to learn more about playing MP3 files.

Don't forget to check out the **Focal Press Catalog** or the **Movie Magic Budgeting** demo software. For the complete CDR contents, turn to **page viii**.

For technical assistance with this CDR, email techsupport@bhusa.com. Be sure to reference **CD-03892-PC** or **CD-03892-MAC**.